"Job Seekers' Garden Club (JSGC) of St. Louis has been _____ for our St. Vincent de Paul Conference at Ascension Chu... in Chesterfield, MO. We receive numerous calls each month from people asking for assistance because of financial difficulties, many of which are caused by unemployment. JSCG has been a reliable and timely resource in helping people find worthwhile employment."

Gary Volk
President
Ascension Conference of the Society of St. Vincent de Paul

"I believe to be successful, you need to help lift others up in the good and bad times. It's the 'ripple effect'—one kind deed can have a profound impact and save thousands of lives. Bob and Lexie encompass this and so much more. They are both compassionate, selfless, and kind. Job Seekers' Garden Club is a true blessing to the St. Louis community."

Kara M. Casagrande, CSC
Professional Employment Consultant
Snelling Personnel Services in Brentwood

"Job Seekers' Garden Club has become an essential part of our business community. Through the dedicated efforts of Bob Kolf, Lexie Dendrinelis, and their team of volunteers, they have not only helped individuals find meaningful work that aligns with their talents but have also connected businesses with high-quality candidates to strengthen their workforce. Beyond job placement, the Job Seekers' Garden Club has fostered a supportive and educational environment—one that cultivates a culture of respect for individuals, employers, and the meaningful work that drives our community forward."

Tom Lancia
Executive Director
Creve Coeur-Olivette Chamber of Commerce

"Whenever my G.R.I.T. Community members are in a job-seeking mode, I always refer them to Job Seekers' Garden Club. I know they're not just getting access to opportunities—they're stepping into a supportive group that truly cares about helping people grow and succeed."

Jennifer Bardot, MA, MS
Chief Executive Officer
G.R.I.T. Community

DISCOVERING YOUR PURPOSE IN TODAY'S WORLD

Finding Hope While Navigating Career Disruption

COMPILED BY
Bob Kolf and Lexie Dendrinelis

Discovering Your Purpose in Today's World
Finding Hope While Navigating Career Disruption
Bob Kolf and Lexie Dendrinelis

Published by Job Seekers Garden Club, St. Louis, MO

Project Management and Book Design: DavisCreativePublishing.com
Editor: Jennifer Capler

Publisher's Cataloging-in-Publication
Names: Kolf, Bob, compiler. | Dendrinelis, Lexie, compiler.
Title: Discovering your purpose in today's world : finding hope while navigating career
    disruption / compiled by Bob Kolf and Lexie Dendrinelis.
Description: St. Louis, MO : Job Seekers' Garden Club, [2025]
Identifiers: LCCN: 2025909609 | ISBN: 9798998893308 (paperback)) | 9798998893315 (ebook)
Subjects: LCSH: Career changes. | Vocational guidance. | Self-actualization (Psychology)
    | Business networks. | Creative ability in business. | Job hunting. | BISAC: BUSINESS
    & ECONOMICS / Careers / General. | SELF-HELP / Motivational & Inspirational. |
    PSYCHOLOGY / Career Counseling.
Classification: LCC: HF5384 .D57 2025 | DDC: 650.14--dc23
    2025

Dedication

I dedicate this book to my mom, Agnes Kolf (nee Birkholz), and to my dad, Thomas Kolf. Without them, I would not be who I am today. I am grateful to them for bringing me into the world, blessing me with two brothers and six sisters, and providing me with a proper upbringing and a happy childhood full of wonderful memories.

Looking back, I'm grateful to my grandparents, aunts, uncles, cousins, as well as prior generations on both sides of the family who immigrated here from Germany. Looking forward, I am grateful to my wife, Vicki, and for the many blessings that God has bestowed on us, including three daughters, three sons-in-law, eight granddaughters, and one grandson.

I hope this book inspires them to find their God-given purpose in the world, to treat others in a way that they want to be treated, and to continue to make this community and world a better place.

BOB KOLF

"If not now, when?"
—Rabbi Hillel the Elder

This book is dedicated to those answering the question above—executing their calling, seizing opportunity, searching for purpose, and making life happen. A life goal of mine has been to publish a work that would have a positive impact on others' lives. I never dreamed it would be as special as achieving it with forty authors at the same time! Can you say, "The magic of a team?" Wow! Each of you inspires me, and this book is dedicated to you and your life stories.

To my dear friend, the late Kelly Mixer, a professional writer and journalist. I understand now why you loved the authorship process and final product. My first opportunity to publish is dedicated to you.

LEXIE DENDRINELIS

Acknowledgments

Since 2020, I have been on an inspirational journey. The global pandemic, which started in 2020, and the aftereffects, which are still with us today in 2025, awakened the world and my inner spirit. I have met so many incredible people through many amazing organizations in the past five years.

Here are a few of the places where I found inspiration:

- The Society of St. Vincent de Paul Conference and the Men's Bible Study Group at Ascension Catholic Church in Chesterfield, MO, keeping me grounded in my faith while serving the poor and supporting each other in our spiritual journey towards heaven.

- The St. Louis Mosaic Project and the International Institute of St. Louis, making our community amazing and diverse by supporting immigrants in our community.

- RISE Services, "Creating Opportunities for and with People," and other similar organizations serving and developing purposeful opportunities for those with intellectual and developmental disabilities.

- The "Networking with Purpose" luncheons, a collaboration of TIN, Job Seekers' Garden Club, and many other networking groups in Greater St. Louis, providing faith-based business connection opportunities.

- Military veterans, single moms, refugees (those who have served, those who have been through so much, and those who need our continual prayers and support).

–Bob Kolf

How did this goal happen? Ideation, discussion, long runs, reading, and patience, patience, patience. Timing is everything, and the timing was perfect in 2025! Thank you to my family, my friend Bob Kolf, and the Job Seekers' Garden Club community for the support to complete this book and get it out in the world.

–Lexie Dendrinelis

TABLE OF CONTENTS

The Time is Now

The time is now. We each have one precious life, and many of the hours that make our years are spent working. We believe this makes working with purpose crucial. Many generations have experienced defining shifts: the invention of the wheel, the building of the Pyramids, the Crusades, the discovery of electricity, the Industrial Revolution, World Wars, the Great Depression, and space exploration are all periods of time that changed the way of thinking and living for the next generation. The time from 2020 to 2025 was a tumultuous and consequential time in our history. It changed how we view life and our decisions going forward.

Born out of this period is the Job Seekers' Garden Club and a community effort to guide, nurture, and support individuals through the process of finding purpose in their career—true career wellbeing. We, Bob Kolf and Lexie Dendrinelis, have come together to tell the story of the human spirit as we know it and as it exists in our community. The goal of this anthology book is to leave a legacy, share reflections, and provide career and life inspiration to the reader. It is truly amazing the commonality of our experiences in life.

It is our belief that as humans, we have more in common than we have differences. We want to know the meaning of life and seek to discover our purpose, whether guided by religious beliefs or not. We strive to make our imprint and have an impact, large or small. We want to be loved and appreciated. We are curious about what happens when we die. Regardless of gender, ethnicity, economic status, or religious beliefs, we are way more alike than we are different.

The global pandemic, which began in March 2020, brought the idea of similarities and differences front stage. It still affects us five years later. Many people lost loved ones and jobs or knew someone close who did. Many people became solopreneurs or entrepreneurs. For some people, the pandemic deepened their religious faith, and others questioned even more. Other people became more fully committed to family life and personal self-care. Many people flourished, finding more time in their day and financial success. The added time at home led to more time spent together, sprucing up living spaces, and creativity to get the work done without being in the same room. No matter the individual experience, we were all profoundly affected.

We all have stories to tell. The authors in this anthology are a cross-section of our great community and are excited to share their stories with you. We represent men and women. We represent different cultures, different religions, different belief sets. We represent the most vulnerable. We represent single moms, veterans, disabled, corporate employees, and small business owners. We represent different levels of financial success but are equally rich in spirit and values. We represent immigrants and refugees. We represent those who have served time and are looking for second chances in life. We represent those who have recovered from addictions and have found new meaning and purpose in life. Mistakes aplenty, we are resilient and strong, and together, we are amazing! We are human. And we hope the stories and this book inspire you to live your BEST life!

—*Bob Kolf and Lexie Dendrinelis*

JOB
SEEKERS'
Garden Club™

About Job Seekers' Garden Club

Job Seekers' Garden Club was founded in 2020 in the Greater St. Louis area, a thriving community located on the banks of the Mississippi River in the state of Missouri, U.S.A. Bob Kolf is the Founder and current Executive Director of the 501(c)(3) nonprofit incorporated in the State of Missouri on October 30, 2020, as Job Seekers' Garden Club of St. Louis. Lexie Dendrinelis is the current President of the Board of Directors. We exist to assist individuals who have lost a job, want to change jobs, or want to find greater meaning in their current job. We provide a community to support them during a time that can be very lonely. Job Seekers' Garden Club was started as an organization to help job seekers discover their purpose in today's world and to find hope and community while navigating career disruption. For more about our nonprofit, please see the resource listing at the end of the book to learn more.

Bob Kolf

Every Life is Precious and Purposeful

My career and my purpose have always been related, but my life's purpose is so much more than my career. Being a disciple of Christ, a husband, a father, and a grandfather are all part of God's purpose in my life today.

Discovering my purpose in today's world has been a lifelong journey of experiences, prayer, and knowledge. My advice is to live in the present, which is where peace and happiness are found. Oftentimes, when my mind drifts to the past, I think about all the mistakes I have made. This is a sure way to slip into a deep, dark hole of depression. When this happens, I turn to God and prayer and think of the lessons I have learned. When my mind turns to thoughts of a future that is beyond my control, I become very anxious. Once again, I turn to God and prayer to help me live in the present. I attempt to live each day as if it were my last one.

Who I am today is a culmination of my early childhood experiences, my environment, and my choices. I naively thought that when I retired in 2017 from a 40-year career as a structural engineer, I would live out my life playing golf, watching sports, and travelling. Yes, I enjoy these things, but I have discovered that my true joy can be found when I am present to help others in need. I have rediscovered God's purpose in my life over the course of the past 5 years. Ever since the global pandemic began in 2020, I have been on a journey of discovery.

Growing up in Milwaukee in the 1950s and 1960s, I would often ask my mom and my dad, "Why am I here?" or "What is my reason for existing?" I would always get the same answer: "It's to get to heaven." I would get the very same answer from my aunts, uncles, grandparents, teachers, and clergy. Because of the consistency in their answers, I know this to be true. My parents set me on the right path. They introduced me to God, His only begotten son, Jesus, and to the Holy Spirit. My parents taught me the difference between right and wrong. They taught me to share and to treat others the way that I wanted to be treated. Most importantly, they taught me the power of faith, hope, and charity; to love God above all things and to love my neighbor as I love myself. To this day, I am grateful to God for the foundation upon which I was born.

My dad was a computer programmer, a perfectionist, and my role model. My mom was a social worker who taught me how to be respectful and caring. I owe all that I am to their example and guidance and to the 8 siblings that they blessed me with. I am a product of the love they showed me through their devout Catholic faith, their love of God, and their obedience to their wedding vows.

There is one memorable event in my life that I look back upon for the lasting impact that it had on me. It occurred on October 28, 1962. It was the day that I received my First Holy Communion. I was always fascinated by the holy act of consecration that takes place at Mass on the altar in the Catholic Church when a priest takes and blesses the bread, breaks the bread, says the sacred words and the bread is transformed into the body of Christ; similarly, when he takes and blesses the chalice of wine, says the sacred words and the wine is transformed into the blood of Christ. I truly believe that I was being called by God to become a priest and to replicate this miracle at daily Mass. It wasn't just about the miracle itself;

it was about serving others by making this eucharistic gift available to all who believe, along with the other six sacraments of the Catholic Church.

I explored this early calling by attending St. Francis de Sales Prep Seminary in Milwaukee during my Freshman year in high school. I discerned after a year of study that I was not quite ready to commit to the priesthood. I transferred to Marquette University High School, where I excelled in math and science. Upon graduation, I attended the University of Arkansas, where I obtained a Bachelor of Science degree in Civil Engineering. I had a 40-year career in civil/structural engineering. At the peak of my career, I was a department manager and a hiring manager with 35 direct reports.

I dedicate this chapter to my beautiful and loving wife, Vicki; to our 3 beautiful daughters and their loving husbands; and to our 9 extra special blessings from God, our beautiful grandchildren. They are our future hope in making this community and world stronger and more vibrant by growing close to God and learning what His purpose is for their lives.

When I retired from my career in 2017, I started helping others find new opportunities. I joined the Chesterfield Regional Chamber of Commerce, where I met Brian Young and Mitchell Mandel with RockIt Careers. I also started working as a 1099 employee for Aerotek, now known as Actalent. I would find talented engineering professionals who were open to new opportunities. I would have RockIt Careers enhance their resumes to bring out the best version of themselves. I would then pass these resumes on to Aerotek for job placement. If placed, I would receive a commission check. When I ran out of resources from my 40-year engineering career, I turned to networking groups and LinkedIn to find talent.

In March 2020, St. Louis County in Missouri went on lockdown due to the global pandemic. I was told that I was "non-essential" and had to go home. It was a very eerie sensation, and I began to experience feelings of depression. I turned to LinkedIn, where I formed a new group, with inspiration from the Holy Spirit, to help those in the Greater St. Louis region who had lost their jobs due to the pandemic, which is estimated to be over 200,000. Over the course of 5 years, from 2020 to 2025, the LinkedIn group I started, named *Job Seekers' Garden Club of St. Louis,* grew to over 6,000 members, consisting of job seekers, recruiters, and connectors.

On October 30, 2020, the networking group was turned into a 501(c)(3) nonprofit organization. I created a red, green, and yellow logo with a meaningful purpose. Red represents the job seekers who need to be passionate and purposeful in their job search. They need to put their heart and soul into finding their new opportunity. Green and yellow are the colors of hope. Green is for Mother Earth and represents the recruiters in our group. Yellow is for sunshine and represents the amazing connectors in our group. The nonprofit organization does for job seekers what gardeners do for plants—we care for them, nurture them, and help them grow in their careers by eliminating the weeds of negativity. The Job Seekers' organization has helped hundreds upon hundreds of people find new opportunities through networking.

The people I have met along the way have transformed me into a better person. I have met refugees from Ukraine and Afghanistan, many through my involvement with the St. Louis Mosaic Project. I have met people who have lost most of their life's savings through my involvement with The Society of St. Vincent de Paul at Ascension Catholic Church in Chesterfield. I have met single moms with nowhere to turn who have discovered a warm and caring community with Job Seekers' Garden Club. I have met veterans who have served our country and have looked for comfort, uplifting, and new career opportunities. Recently, through working with RISE Services of Missouri, I have grown to love and appreciate those with intellectual and developmental disabilities and those much less fortunate than myself who need help learning hard and soft skills so they can become competitively employed.

What have I learned from 2020 to 2025? When I meet for coffee with an individual for a 1-on-1 conversation, I am there to listen. I learned how to listen through my 8 years as a Stephen Minister at Holy Infant Parish in Ballwin. Using active listening skills, I learn what the individual needs. They not only need a better-paying job to pay their mounting past due bills, but they usually need help with much more. They may need help with their mental acuity. They may need someone to care about them as a human being—to be their advocate, their friend, someone to pray for them, and to let them know what a special gift from God they are. Their needs are no different than my needs. Their needs are no different than the needs of all humans.

Every human needs to feel loved and to have purpose in their lives. The more I get to know people I meet from China, Brazil, Ecuador, Turkey, Egypt, Japan, Russia, India, Germany, Australia, Israel, Iran, Finland (the happiest country in the world), Malawi (the warm heart of Africa), and other parts of the world who have made St. Louis, Missouri, their home, the more I learn that I have way more in common with them than I have differences. We all have the very same needs to be loved, to belong to the community, to have purpose in our lives, and to have hope for the future in this world and in the next. We are all equal in the eyes of God.

What are the mission and vision of Job Seekers' Garden Club? Where do we go from here? As Founder and Executive Director of Job Seekers' Garden Club of St. Louis, I am proud to share our mission/vision statement as follows:

To foster a warm and caring community in which job seekers, recruiters, and connectors come together to nurture and support one another, and to find both career and growth opportunities through networking to make St. Louis a stronger and more vibrant community.

If you live in the Greater St. Louis, Missouri, metropolitan area, here are my suggestions for job seekers, recruiters, connectors, and business entrepreneurs to find great connection opportunities:

- Attend multiple monthly events with **Job Seekers' Garden Club of St. Louis.** Check out our website and LinkedIn group by the same name.

- There are plentiful networking and connection opportunities with **The Inside Network (TIN)** to grow in faith through bible study, a charitable card writing ministry, and monthly "Networking with Purpose" Luncheons. Contact author Susan Neumann. She is very welcoming and caring.

- There are multiple weekly networking opportunities with businesspersons through **RAD Networking Group.** Contact author Amber Webb Maxfield. She will welcome you with open arms.

- There are many opportunities to form strong business relationships through **ACA Business Club of Greater St. Louis.** Contact Whitney Toates. She is the amazing leader of one of the best groups of professionals and entrepreneurs in the region. She will instantly make you feel at home in this private club.

Together, let's make the world a better place for our children, grand-children, and future generations. This is my re-found purpose in today's world—to make our community and world stronger, safer, and more vibrant, all while building God's Kingdom on earth. I close this chapter with the same prayer from St. Francis that I closed my chapter in *Notes from Dad,* compiled by Jason Meinershagen, 2024:

Lord, make me an instrument of your peace.
Where there is hatred, let me sow love.
Where there is injury, pardon.
Where there is doubt, faith.
Where there is despair, hope.
Where there is darkness, light.
And where there is sadness, joy.

O divine master,
     grant that I may not so much seek to be consoled
     as to console;
to be understood as to understand;
To be loved as to love.
For it is in giving that we receive—
     it is in pardoning that we are pardoned.
     And it's in dying that we are born to eternal life.
     Amen.

Bob Kolf is a disciple of Christ, a husband, a father of three, and a grand-father of nine. He is the founder and executive director of Job Seekers' Garden Club of St. Louis. He is a parishioner at Ascension Catholic Church in Chesterfield, MO, where he and his wife, Vicki, are active members.

Bob's journey through life has been filled with many challenges. He loves to travel, watch sports, and play an occasional round of golf. It has been his experience that the people you surround yourself with and how you respond to unforeseen circumstances define who you become. God and family first is how he has approached life. In times of need, they are available to turn to. He is very grateful for all the blessings in his life and for the opportunity to help and serve others.

Please scan the QR code to connect with this author.

Lexie Dendrinelis

28 Days

Opportunity Day

"We are making changes within the organization, and your role has been eliminated." Exhausted from a business trip where I spent much of it in a hotel with food poisoning, I was not sure I heard the words correctly. I repeated them back, asking for clarification. "Did I hear you say, my role has been eliminated?"

"Yes, you heard me correctly. There is nothing you need to do further. You will receive a month's severance and benefits. Everything will come to you shortly to your personal email."

"Umm…ok?" I answered. Totally shocked and yet surprisingly calm, I paused and remained quiet. If you know me, a lack of words is out of character.

"It is not due to performance, and that will be reflected in your documents. I am happy to be a reference if you wish," the person continued.

"Oh, ok, thanks. So, do you need to know anything about this past week and my work?" I said. "No, we will handle it from here," was the reply. Then the call ended.

I took a deep breath, and another deep breath, and then thought, "Stay present, stay in the moment." What does this mean? Of course, I knew what it meant, but I was short-term thinking. The kind like, right here, right now, what is my next move? Well, I could eat lunch, go for a walk, and take a nap before heading to school pick-up. I processed those actions in my head for a moment.

Eat lunch; this would be making my lunch *and* eating it in the kitchen, not at my desk with my camera off while on a call. Nice!

Go for walk; burn a few calories (I gained ten pounds in the prior year), breathe the crisp air into my lungs, and get energized.

Take a nap; I had very little sleep that week during my travels, and it felt like a luxurious treat to myself.

I have a phrase on my office whiteboard that states, "Make today so great that yesterday gets jealous." So, all I needed to do was execute on the remaining portion of that day and make it great! Game on, let's go!

When I woke from the nap, hard reality began to set in…this was real. This was not the vacation day I had been wishing for during the last year. Within seconds, the long-term thoughts began to set in: fear of finding work, what if I can't pay my bills, what about school tuition, how did I allow this to fail? I am the sole supporter of my family. Wait, I allowed this to fail?! As if I am the only party in the equation. The only one responsible. Whew!

The late Zig Ziglar, famous for positive thinking, tells a story about *stinkin' thinkin'*. I've listened to his speeches many times throughout my career, and I realized at that moment, I needed to check myself. I was letting *stinkin' thinkin'* creep into my mindset, and that is not what would serve me, my family, or anyone else around me well. I needed to double down on positivity!

The Ups and Downs

This was not my first job to end. I've had my job eliminated due to a reduction in force before, and even one ending due to company closure during the pandemic. I'm empathetic to job seekers because I know the havoc it can bring to your life. I also know the joy, excitement, and learning that can be found in the journey. It is why I am passionate about serving with the Job Seekers' Garden Club and commit to providing support, education, connections, and hope to anyone in the search.

My first job elimination experience was a thirteen-year career where the work was fun, never a day the same, had travel, and was innovative in my industry. It shaped me into a resourceful and confident professional. The company had 50,000 employees and a land of possibilities in my eyes. Essentially, any direction I thought my career interest would go, I could find at that company.

My role would often have me in the back of the room waiting for the trainers to take a break to send employees to meet with me. This allowed me to learn what they learned. While it was not directly applicable to my role, I took the safety tests, job-specific tests within the various departments, practiced with groups, and did everything I could to understand their work so I was relatable to them. The success of my role was dependent on the relationships and trust I had with the employees.

When that job ended due to a reduction in force, I was unsure of myself for the first time in my life. Would my Friday night friends still invite me to join? What about the retirement party in three weeks for a co-worker? Do I still go? Who am I, if I'm not "the health girl?" I should have never doubted still being included because, of course, the answer was yes; I was still included. I worked with wonderful people, many of whom I am still in touch with today. My co-workers valued me for the person I am, not the role I held in the company. The lesson to learn was to cultivate my work as something I did, but not as who I was. To have an identity outside of work. A trait that I learned did not come easily for me.

Luckily, I pivoted to a business development role three weeks later. For eighteen months, I leaned into sales pitches, requests for proposals (RFPs), online auctions, and attended trade shows. We were growing a company; it was fun, and I loved learning new skills! And over time, I could not ignore the pull of workplace wellbeing and directly helping other people. I chose to return to a role where I was delivering services, designing programs, and building caring relationships with employees. It was in this role that I learned more about the vendors we contracted with for services, and how the consulting team worked with us to craft a full suite of employee benefits. It was new, I loved it, and a seed was planted.

This seed led to my next career move, the vendor space. I engaged with many companies, understanding their demographic needs, population health, policies, and program designs. I learned client management and found tremendous satisfaction in applying my years as a client to shape our approach to serving a book of business, our client base. I continued to grow as a leader and found my purpose to now include mentoring and building a team.

During these years, my next role elimination was heartbreaking when our company closed during the pandemic. This was the most challenging period of my career, as I felt the responsibility to my team and had my own situation to navigate quickly. We connected one another to hiring companies in the industry and kept our virtual happy hours to cheer each other on in finding new work. I have a deep respect for each of my colleagues from the pandemic period, as it was a shock and a difficult time to be a leader.

A Return to Opportunity Day

The day after my last job elimination, I reflected on past career challenges and wins. I reminded myself of my belief developed back in my college days, I am the **CEO of Me**. This approach has led to great roles within a corporate career, being a small business owner twice, speaking on stages promoting health and leadership concepts, becoming a certified leadership trainer, and forming bonds of friendship throughout our country.

My spirits lifted, and I began to lean into positive self-talk. *I am resilient. I create positive momentum in my life and embrace this new challenge. Trust yourself and get started!*

Whew! I slept like a baby that following weekend and started off the next week with networking calls, in-person connections, and the excitement of a brand new world. A brand new me.

Each day started with a workout, either at home or at the gym. I signed up for webinars to keep me learning in my field, and a couple of courses not related to my field to expand my knowledge. Movement and learning are both areas I know feed my soul, so working out daily and learning were energizing.

I attended a Job Seekers' Garden Club (JSGC) networking and coffee event and boldly stated, "**28 days** everyone! That is the timeframe for the next great role to happen!" Why is **28 days** significant?

As I spent time connecting with family and friends, I had a conversation with a close cousin. I shared that in the **28 days** leading up to my job loss, I had a romantic relationship end abruptly and a best friend pass away suddenly. I was devastated emotionally. This "health girl" was maxed out. After listening intently, she offered her observation. "Lexie, you are trying to control too much. You are trying to be in charge of everything, and God is seeking your attention." Ouch! And double ouch! Not that God had made the previous **28 days** of heartbreak happen, but when was the last time I spent time in quiet prayer? A true moment of thanks? Why was I not turning each day over and placing my trust in Him? Ugh, she was right. I was out of balance, not practicing what I believe about total wellbeing.

A few days later, a book arrived in the mail, a daily devotional book from her. I began each morning with a reading of the day. Yep, even before my morning workout! I took a course on Finding Purpose, which led me back to a leadership class I took in college when I defined my purpose. It was simple; my work inspires others to live their *best* life! Yet in this, I lost sight of living *my* best life.

My career has been dedicated to teaching others the benefits of healthy living. I began as a group exercise instructor and, as I've shared, I have been fortunate to have grown into leadership roles designing programs, leading teams, driving business growth, and supporting company goals. I have traveled the country, met wonderful people, and am proud to call many of my co-workers friends. I am thankful for a life blessed with opportunity!

My challenge to you, the reader: I invite you to take charge of your life as a CEO. Regularly check in on the various departments: finance, physical, mental, career, social, and spiritual. There are many tools to help you assess between a current state and desired state. Pick one, complete it, and then set goals in each area. **We have one life to live, so keep leveling up and live in gratitude!**

For readers currently in a job search:

- It is not easy; sometimes it's downright *hard*. Stay positive!
- Surround yourself with people who encourage you, build you up, and want to see you succeed.
- Use social media platforms to find job leads. Then, go to the company website to apply. Not because it's a faster track to an interview, but because your positive mindset needs to be preserved for crushing interviews. Too much exposure happens on social media about how many months out of work, applications sent without response, and ghosting stories, allowing you to be influenced by the negativity.
- Pray for those who are searching and get back out of there. Protect your attitude!

- Consider roles that are not in your comfort zone. Explore new ideas and hobbies. Use this time, for however long, to grow yourself as a person and a professional.
- Attend job search workshops, such as the JSGC Career Conference, networking meetings, and virtual meetups, to become a skilled job seeker.
- Build a job search team. Have a resume writer, interview prep person, LinkedIn reviewer, recruiter, and, most importantly, a listener. Make sure to have someone willing to listen as your partner in the search.
- Create metrics so you can view progress and know when to adjust.
- Network, network, network! If it is not your next role, you may be the person who helps someone else find their role!

Driven to help others live their best life, Lexie has spent thirty years in the workplace wellbeing industry. She has held various positions, from leading a comprehensive wellness program start-up to strategic employer program design and evaluation. Throughout her career, she has served on awarding winning teams, built relationships with key partners to drive program success, and inspired individuals to live a healthy lifestyle. Lexie has worked for well-known companies in senior level roles, allowing her to understand the complexity and multiple needs of large organizations addressing population health and business outcomes. She has served on several workplace wellbeing industry committees, presented on wellbeing and leadership topics, and brings a drive for thought leadership to her work. In her relaxation time, Lexie enjoys cooking healthy meals, running, biking, reading, and spending time with her family and friends.

Please scan the QR code to connect with this author.

Nataliya Hado

The Purpose Inscribed in God's Plan

I never imagined that the phrase "radically changing a life" would ever apply to me. My life was anything but calm, but it was always filled with deep meaning and purpose. As a mother of four children—who attended school, participated in clubs, played instruments, got sick, and simply grew up—it would be an understatement to say that my life was carefully planned. Alongside our work commitments, my husband and I were both in the midst of defending our doctoral dissertations, actively involved in the Catholic community as founders of one of the first Catholic websites in Ukraine, and we had co-founded a Catholic publishing house.

Despite this whirlwind, we were deeply content with our lives and had no intention of moving. We traveled often throughout Europe, discovering our favorite cities and hidden gems. All our plans, however, were firmly rooted in our native country.

I was immensely satisfied with my career in European academic and corporate communications. After years of working as a journalist and editor, I received an invitation to teach at the journalism department of the second-highest-ranked national university in my country. I also taught at a branch of a Polish Catholic university and seminary. Additionally, I had experience in business communications, working as a corporate spokesperson for the largest grocery retailer in my region of Ukraine. I applied my background in journalism and business communication to an educational project for women in business with my own course. Finally, co-founding a Catholic publishing house, after gaining invaluable experience as an editor and translator in other Catholic publishing houses, solidified my belief that my life was truly mission-driven. Though it might sound crazy, everything in my life was so interconnected that it brought me profound fulfillment and joy.

The most meaningful part of it all was how my activities seemed to fit together like pieces of a puzzle. Each step and idea felt like it was part of God's greater plan for my life.

I truly believe that discovering your purpose in today's world is only possible through God, our Creator. Only He knows why He made us and what our true purpose is. His plan for our lives is the best way to guide us toward fulfilling that purpose. To help us, God provides us with intelligence, talents, desires, circumstances; He answers by Holy Scripture and continually sends His people into our lives to guide us toward discovering our purpose.

Finding the clarity for a particular solution isn't always simple—especially when you're forced to make quick decisions and radically change the course of your life.

However, we all have experiences to draw upon. And my experience was God's guidance in my life circumstances and my search for purpose.

I ended up in the United States. It was an unexpected and spontaneous decision. I had never even been to the United States as a tourist, let alone had experience teaching at an American university. Moreover, I wasn't even sure if I could succeed in this new chapter of my life.

At the same time, I was uncertain whether I would be able to continue teaching in my hometown. That morning, my peaceful world shattered—my hometown had suddenly woken up to the sound of sirens and news reports of an invasion by an unfriendly neighboring country. That morning, everything changed—and not just slightly. Our dream home, which we had only moved into three years ago, no longer felt like a safe place due to its location and the lack of a basement. The view I once enjoyed—planes taking off and landing, a reminder of the modern city we lived in—was replaced with the reality of war, with the noise of military planes and helicopters overhead.

The question that weighed most heavily on me was whether this decision fit into God's plan for each member of our family. The second question was how to navigate the uncertainty of embarking on something I had never done before. Of course, I was well acquainted with the works of American scholars, which helped me a lot, but the American education system and its means were new to me. English was my academic foreign language since I used mainly Polish and Italian in my work. I also had to give up a research project at a famous university in Poland, which was supposed to start at the same time as my arrival in the United States. However, above all, we were tormented by the question of whether we would be able to be useful to our country at such a great distance, as we were used to doing both before the war, through evangelization, and after the war, with humanitarian projects with our European friends.

In such moments, I remember times in my life when fear of the unknown took over. The uncertainty of those moments made me hold onto the hope that God would guide me down the right path because, above all else, I longed to live in alignment with His plan for my life. Every major decision I've made involved some degree of unknown outcome, but I always trusted that God would guide me.

Whenever I've faced moments of doubt—wondering if I was on the right path, praying for God's will—I recalled how He has already led me through previous uncertain times.

I remember very clearly the moments when I had to rediscover my purpose before. It gives me the strength to move forward. The experience of achieving a goal makes me believe that I can do it again!

One of the personal stories that has helped me stay grounded and reaffirm my purpose happened early in my academic career. I decided to pursue graduate school, and when the time came to choose my research topic, I knew without hesitation that I wanted to focus on Catholic communication. Having worked in Catholic online media for several years, I recognized an urgent need to develop a theory around Catholic journalism.

I proposed this idea to my senior colleagues; they were initially supportive of the concept. However, when it came to actually supervising my research, they flatly refused. They considered religious topics a "white spot" in the academic world, something too niche and difficult to tackle. Over the course of two years, they repeatedly suggested that I change my topic to something more conventional, something that could help me defend my dissertation more quickly. But I stood my ground, stubbornly determined that I would follow my passion and work toward developing Catholic communication as an academic field.

During those two years, I poured my energy into writing the first academic papers on the topic. I relied heavily on my own vision, researching foreign academic works. It was a difficult and lonely time, but my belief in the importance of my research kept me moving forward. I knew that this was not just for me; it was for the development of Catholic communication as a discipline and for future generations of students who would benefit from this research.

After two years of persistence, everything changed. My supervisor arrived at the faculty, someone with extensive knowledge of religion and a wealth of experience in the field. He was enthusiastic about my topic, and his support was exactly what I had been waiting for. Under his mentorship,

I successfully defended my dissertation, which went on to become the first comprehensive academic work on Catholic media. I even published a book based on my research, knowing that I had contributed something significant. It seemed to me then that I understood well what the Old Testament's Joseph felt, who sat in prison for two years, hoping for help from some human being, until God, in His own way, brought him out in His own time and much further than he had planned to go!

Another personal story that continues to fuel my hope comes from my early years when I was just beginning my journey into journalism. I was finishing high school with a goal of entering university to study journalism, but just as I prepared to apply, the rules for university entrance exams changed dramatically and unexpectedly.

At that moment, the teacher who was preparing students for university applications told me that I would never have enough time to properly prepare for the exams, especially given that I came from a rural school. Instead of accepting defeat, I decided to push myself harder. I threw myself into my studies with everything I had—more focused than ever before. It wasn't just about the hard work; I asked God to help me find a way. I was determined to follow my dream, but I knew I needed His guidance and strength. When the results were finally announced, I was overjoyed. I had taken first place in the entrance exam. The Department of Journalism opened its doors to me, and I was able to start my academic journey, free from the burden of tuition fees.

Looking back, I see how much that moment shaped me. However, before that, there was something else that taught me to listen to my heart's desire and not give up. I was in the ninth grade and was already thinking about journalism. Publications in the newspaper could significantly help me enter. I wrote an article and went with it to the nearest editorial office. The only one in a small town. After meeting with the editor, I became a regular contributor to the newspaper. To my amazement, money transfers started coming to my school in my name for the articles I had written. It was one of the first tangible rewards for my hard work and a huge validation that I was on the right path.

I know that experience was more than just about writing. It was about having the courage to take the first step, to put myself out there, and to trust that my passion and dedication would lead me to something meaningful. That small but significant moment taught me an invaluable lesson: if you have a desire in your heart, and you're willing to take risks and work for it, the opportunities will come.

I often tell this story to students and even at trainings. Most of them, when asked what the newspaper editor said to me about my proposal, are sure that he refused or advised me to study. If I had not considered the positive outcome of this conversation, I would never have become the first school student to write for this newspaper. Moreover, who knows whether I would have had such enthusiasm to enter the journalism department, work for famous newspapers during my studies, and ultimately endure two years of struggle for my research topic. I owe my progress and who I am today to situations like these. Every difficulty may appear threatening, but in reality, each one is an opportunity to rediscover our true purpose. I am sure God reveals His plan to us through the desire of our heart, and when we respond, He guides us on His path. I have realized how much remembering the finding of my purpose keeps me moving forward, even when I am not prepared for new challenges.

After arriving in the United States, God began to miraculously arrange everything I was worried about. My family was given the opportunity to be included in the project for Ukraine. With my colleague from university, we received an award for a scientific project that we worked on together. The publishing house's evangelistic project continued to work remotely. I have received enough encouragement from God's people to truly feel that He cares for me wherever I go. An especially meaningful part of that journey was meeting Bob, whose open-hearted invitation to join the Job Seekers' Garden Club became a true blessing. Through that warm and faith-filled community he founded, I experienced a deep renewal of hope and trust in God's guidance.

After moving to the United States, I understand more about God's plan for my life, even though I am still discovering and searching for answers. However, I know for sure that God is faithful, and since He sent me His people, circumstances, and desires, He will do it repeatedly.

I believe that no matter what part of the path you are on, He will guide you if you trust Him. With Him, you will go much further than you had planned before!

Nataliya Hado, PhD, came to the United States from Ukraine after a long career in European academia and corporate communications. She worked as a journalist, university professor, and spokesperson for the largest food retailer in her region. She currently teaches in the Department of Communication and Media at the University of Missouri–St. Louis (UMSL). She conducts research on propaganda and is currently writing a book.

Nataliya is a member of American professional organizations, including the Catholic Media Association (CMA), the National Communication Association (NCA)—where her co-project received an award—and the Association for Education in Journalism and Mass Communication (AEJMC).

With her husband, Ivan, who holds a PhD in Catholic theology, Nataliya co-founded a Catholic evangelization and publishing project. She is the mother of four daughters. The integration of her family life and Catholic mission is a constant source of inspiration and purpose for her.

Please scan the QR code to connect with this author.

Mitchell Mandel

Jobs Build Careers

If there was one thing that I did well when I entered the workforce, it was nailing the interview. I practically landed every position that invited me to apply. The old joke was, even though I interviewed well, it didn't always equate to me being the greatest of employees. Nonetheless, I knew how to get the job, and I felt I did well for the many companies that gave me a chance. I did hop from job to job as a young person and went through many professions until I found my purpose.

I was no stranger to hard work from a young age. My parents owned a lawn and hauling business, and I was the main weed-whacker kid at the ages of nine through fourteen. I worked in the fast-food industry for my first high school part-time job as a fry cook for a well-known national seafood chain, and then bounced from a burger drive-through to a chain inspired by Mexican cuisine, and finally, a sub shop. My first job was too greasy and did not agree with the acne of a fifteen-year-old teenager. In hindsight, I wish I would've stayed at the drive-through; it was the best of the fast-food experiences. I left my next job because the polyester staff uniform irritated my skin. I quit the sub shop after the owner became angry and threw a squeeze bottle of mayonnaise in my direction. I did not like working within the food industry, but I enjoyed the paychecks.

After my high school years and after leaving college, I worked in the multifamily apartment industry, starting as a groundskeeper, working my way up to clubhouse attendant, then leasing consultant, to finally becoming Assistant Manager/Bookkeeper. The leasing agent position was my favorite within this portion of my career. It was fun showing apartments, checking all the move-in-ready apartments, hosting events for the residents of the community, and working in the luxurious surroundings of the clubhouse. I was recruited away from the apartment industry and became a top-notch furniture salesman. Selling someone a new living room set or a dining room table was pretty easy for me. I liked the idea of making someone's home look better with nice new furnishings. Eventually, as I became somewhat bored with what furniture guys called "selling sticks," I always wanted to see if I would be successful "pushing tin." So, then, I tried my hand at selling vehicles right before the 9/11 tragedy. It was the worst time to jump ship and try something new. I was proud of my first four months selling automobiles, as I was able to reach quotas up until the planes hit the Twin Towers. Sales dried up quickly in the aftermath, and for financial reasons, I had to find the next thing rather quickly. It seemed as if I was geared to be in sales and service, as the occupation suited me and paid the bills.

Yet, it didn't bring me happiness or joy.

I felt like something was missing in this particular career path. Even though I hit my sales quotas, it wasn't fulfilling or exciting to me.

At one point in my life, my mom asked me why I switched jobs so frequently, and I said, "I wasn't happy" or "I didn't like the job." She said, "Nobody likes their job." I felt that that wasn't a good answer, and it couldn't be true. There has to be a job out there that would bring me happiness. My sister also teased me because she had learned that I had received five W-2s in one year. She wanted to know why I left Company A for Company B, and so on and so forth. My reply was, "I'm not happy there." My sister asked me if I had found the greener grass at the newest workplace, and I hadn't. She suggested that I stay with one company and tough it out. I usually listened to advice from my sister, yet I was still hunting for the "happy job."

As time passed on, I was hired to be a location sales manager for a telecommunications company. In the first day of training, I was pulled aside and offered a position to be a recruiter. There was a need for a second recruiter for the Saint Louis market, and they said I had the right personality and skillset to be successful in this role. Nothing is better than receiving a raise and a promotion on the first day! It was also the day I met my future business partner, Brian Young. He showed me the ropes and all the ins and outs of the recruiting trade, and we achieved success in building teams and meeting or beating goals for the market.

The recruiting profession carried me for the next fifteen years. I owe Brian Young a big thank you for preparing me to be successful in recruiting.

I believe I found my purpose and happiness within this role. It was rewarding in the sense that hiring the best people for the open job orders was a triple win.

The company benefited from hiring the new teammates. The new employees benefited in receiving new employment and opportunities to grow within the company, and I also benefited from the knowledge gained in interviewing and hiring sales associates, managers, data analysts, and registered nurses. One of the best parts of being a recruiter is when someone you hire becomes wildly successful in their new role. I had one gentleman start as a part-time sales associate who grew to become a location manager of two locations. He was going to college part-time when he first joined the company. Within two years, he had graduated school, gotten married, had a baby on the way, and purchased a new truck, replacing the old sedan that was on its last legs.

Another joy in recruiting is building a team. I once inherited a sales location that had only two employees. Those two employees were expected to fully operate that one location while meeting specific sales goals that two people were not able to reach. I was able to fully staff the location in a short amount of time, building the team from two people to eight, and within six months, the location went from fourteenth in the market, rising to number eight. Our team took sales from 20% to 103%, surpassing the 100% sales goal requirement. The District General Manager chuckled when he gave me the location and said, "Good luck with that…" In my mind, I thought, "Challenge accepted!" I was excited to see the location continue to be successful, the team get higher earnings with the commissions, and the pride the team showed knowing they were the ones to bring the Golden Triangle up from an unprofitable location that was last place in the market to a profitable spot.

Recruiting and helping job seekers is still my main focus today.

Brian and I launched our business, RockIt Careers, over eight years ago with the mission to help folks out of work or those who have expressed that they hate their job. We help people propel their talents forward with a professional resume and with job search guidance, marketing themselves effectively while also determining the career path that suits them best. We have been successful in helping people become employed once again. We also work with small and medium-sized businesses in finding new teammates to join their workforce families. I had always had dreams of becoming a business owner one day, but didn't take the leap of faith until Brian suggested we open our own business together. During our first four months, we did not have a single customer. We were networking and pounding the pavement until we had our first client. For a while, Brian and I were wondering if we had made the right move for ourselves in this business venture. Now, looking back and taking stock, it was the best move ever.

We also love to work closely with the Job Seekers' Garden Club, founded by Bob Kolf. When the whole country was on lockdown due to the pandemic of 2020, Bob created a force to be reckoned with. We were adamant in creating events and functions where job seekers, recruiters, and business owners could still meet and network to find new work and workers while everything else seemed to be at a standstill. Seeing the Job Seekers' Garden Club continue to grow and provide resources and insight to job seekers is truly amazing. I am happy to be a part of such a great charitable organization and have the honor of getting to hang out with the incredible Bob Kolf!

I appreciate all the jobs, mentors, bosses, and coworkers I had that led me to my current path as a career coach, a recruiter, and a business owner. I know I couldn't have found my way to this world of recruiting and coaching without the help of others, the training I received, the guidance imparted, and a little bit of luck along the journey. If there was one thing I knew how to do well, it was landing that offer and getting that job. Now, I get to help others do the same thing, and I love it!

I finally found happiness and joy within my profession.

I finally found my purpose.

Mitchell Mandel is the current Vice President of Job Seekers' Garden Club of St. Louis. In July of 2016, Mitchell co-created RockIt Career Consultation Services to help job seekers find their true life's purpose. Mitchell is currently living in Southeastern Mississippi, expanding RockIt Careers into new markets. He is a proud papa of two wonderful children: one son and one daughter. Mitchell also enjoys creating rap songs with the old high school hip hop trio, The Wanted Emcees! Old dreams die hard.

Please scan the QR code to connect with this author.

Susan Neumann

1,000,000 Cards Ministry

I will never forget the day I received the news that my husband and our son would both be deployed to Iraq at the same time to serve our country. It was March 3, 2003. The news seemed completely surreal and not possible that the Army would deploy them both for the next 14 months. I asked myself, "How did this happen?" and "Why would God allow this?"

Since our son joined the Army National Guard his junior year of high school in 2001, the year 9-11 happened, my husband felt compelled to serve. He was a Marine right after high school and served four years, so he always held a very patriotic spirit. He went to the Army National Guard office to inquire about signing up, and they had a one-year program that he could participate in without committing beyond that. Since he was forty-eight years old at that time, the Army National Guard did an age waiver, put him through all the tests, and he was placed into the same unit as our son, the 203rd Army National Guard Unit from St. Peters, Missouri. On May 16, 2003, I had to say goodbye.

After the initial deployment, our family's days were very difficult. We would hear on the news of bombings and wonder if they were still alive. The original deployment orders were for six months, but it wasn't too long after that the President of the United States of America enacted the US Boots on the Ground twelve-month deployment order. We were devastated, but we knew the only way we could help was to write letters and send packages. I decided to join the Family Readiness Group (FRG) and serve our soldiers that way. The wives and fiancés of the deployed soldiers would gather on Friday evenings to have dinner and support one another. Months passed, and we continued to write letters and send packages. We knew this was the best way to lift their spirits, by getting mail. Thankfully, they both returned home on July 23, 2004.

Since the time of my husband and son's deployment, I have always felt prompted to write cards to people who are sick or who have lost loved ones to lift their spirits. I have done this for many years now and knew deep down inside that one day I would be called to create a Card Ministry. I believe that in life, timing is everything. And that doesn't mean in "our time," but in "God's time." Obstacles would always appear to come into my world when I tried to get the card writing organization off the ground. I would ask myself if this was really my calling. Why is it so difficult to get started if it is?

I have always called myself in the workplace and even in school, the "overachiever." I always wanted the perfect performance review, and I had to get an A in every class. Was the overachievement personality trait preventing me from getting started? This was a constant struggle for me until I decided to attend a seminar in downtown St. Louis where the speaker asked: "Who has trouble reading books?" I raised my hand quickly. I never felt I could tackle a whole book because I needed a big time slot to do that. The speaker suggested reading two pages a day. I thought, "I can do that," and that year, I read three books. I realized then that sometimes you just need to let go of getting the perfect performance review or getting an A in every class and be willing to change your approach to things, like tackling them in smaller time blocks.

Regardless of my learning experiences and working to shift my mindset, the timing to start my Card Ministry never seemed right... until I got laid off from my corporate career on Feb. 12, 2020.

At the time, I was excited about the layoff. It could finally give me the opportunity to pursue my passion of being a travel agent and booking all-inclusive beach vacations for others. However, that year had different plans for me, and that was to take care of sick loved ones and be still and listen to God's calling. The people who know me well know that being still and listening have not always been my stronger traits. I love taking action because it makes me feel like I am accomplishing my task list.

Since I was raised in a household with five siblings, I learned that you had to speak up if you wanted to be heard, and the listening part only came into play later when we were disciplined. I am still learning that listening is a highly valued skill set and is a skill that requires continual work. God did give us two ears and one mouth, so he knew what he was doing.

In 2018, I started a faith-based networking group called The Inside Network (TIN). I had left a previous networking group when a dear friend lost her only child to cystic fibrosis, and the group I was in didn't seem to care about her struggles. It occurred to me in 2020 that I could leverage my networking group to get the Card Ministry started. I prayed about this quite a bit along the way. God kept telling me to teach the business owners within the TIN how to focus on gratitude, giving, and grace every day, and he will bring to them what they need. I followed very obediently what God was telling me to do, including sending care packages and cards to anyone we prayed for or who was brought into our path through TIN. The challenge was difficult at times because God would literally tell me on some days to drop everything I was doing to deliver a package on a doorstep, so I would drive to that person's home and do that.

It wasn't until October 27, 2023, while on the beach in Cancun, Mexico, that God told me, "I want you to send 1,000,000 cards to the world to share my love and light!" I returned home and told this to the TIN Bible Study ladies, and immediately the leader said to me, "I will introduce you to the Director of Voyce who serves seniors across the state of Missouri in long-term health care by being advocates for them." Voyce also does Project Holiday Cheer every year with a goal of sending out 40,000 Christmas cards to seniors. I immediately signed up to help and rally people in St. Louis to send Christmas cards. We obtained 3,445 cards by the deadline of November 30, 2023. This accomplishment gave me the idea to do the cards all year long and host card parties every month. My thought was this would bring people together to do something for the greater good.

Shortly after the idea, God opened other doors to partner with other non-profits that would benefit by having cards written for the people they serve. Two more partnerships were born. One partnership is with Alleluia Baskets, which puts together Easter Baskets every year for children and has added Senior bags. The second partnership, Little Patriots Embraced, serves our deployed soldiers and their families. God continues to open doors and provide the resources needed to make this happen. The Card Ministry closed out 2024 with a total running card count of 16,421 cards, and I believe the future will open the door for more people to do cards to contribute to God's goal of 1,000,000 cards to share his love and light.

In early 2025, God brought two more nonprofits into the path of the Card Ministry to help. One is called the Kaufmann Fund, whose mission is to help support veterans with all types of resources. I believe cards of gratitude should be something we do for veterans all year long, and our partnership with the Kaufman Fund will be centered around that. The Veterans Last Patrol is a nationwide organization that helps veterans in hospice, and we will do cards all year long to brighten their spirits before they are called home. Lastly, the vision this year will include a card writing program that can be done from home by anyone. This vision is geared to make card writing easy and to allow people the opportunity to write cards who can't participate in card parties in the St. Louis, Missouri, area. Anyone can participate in the at-home card writing, and one day, I envision that the Card Ministry will have card writers in every state of the USA, along with people in other countries across the world. I know that anything is possible when God is at the helm.

The mission for the Card Ministry has brought me so much joy and happiness because I am fulfilling God's purpose while giving others a way to serve. Until you find your purpose, true joy and happiness will be missing in your life. If you are interested in learning more about supporting the 1,000,000-card writing mission, please contact me through our website at: https://theinsidenetworkstl.com/card-ministry/.

Susan Neumann is a devout Christian with God's calling to serve the world through her Card Writing Ministry. She spent forty-two years in corporate America streamlining operations and managing teams while applying the Relationship Management approach and acquired a Bachelor of Science degree in Management and Communications. Susan has a passion to serve others, so she led Girl Scouts for six years, taught Sunday School and Confirmation Class for two years, serves currently as an Ambassador for the Job Seekers' Garden Club, and partners in co-leading weekly bible study. She loves traveling to beaches in the United States and internationally and has been on twenty beach vacations in five different countries with her husband. Going to the grandkids' sports activities and the movies are her other favorite pastimes, as well as crocheting blankets for them and sending care packages to those in need.

Please scan the QR code to connect with this author.

Amber Webb Maxfield

My 2020 Purpose

"You deserve to be happy, healthy, and whole—mind, body, and soul."

That's the heartbeat of my business and my mission today. I help people release emotional baggage, rewire subconscious beliefs, and reclaim their lives—without needing to relive their pain. But I didn't just wake up with this purpose. I discovered it the long way—through real life, deep struggles, and a series of wake-up calls that pushed me to find a better way, not only for myself but for my children and the people I'm now called to serve.

Let me take you back to where it all started.

Before the Breakthrough

For years, I drifted—without direction, without purpose. I wasn't chasing a dream or following a plan. I was just moving through life, trying things here and there, hoping *something* would click. College didn't feel right. The jobs I tried didn't feel like mine. Deep down, I knew I wasn't made for the 9-to-5 mold, but I had no idea what I *was* made for.

Things began to shift when I had my first son. Becoming a mom was a powerful experience, but it also brought all my unresolved wounds to the surface. I didn't realize how much I was carrying—how much of my own childhood, my own fears, and my own insecurities were still living inside of me.

Around the time my son was three, I hit a very dark place. I fell into a deep depression. I remember lying in bed in his room, barely able to lift my head, playing with him while lying down because I didn't have the energy to sit up. That's where I was: mentally, emotionally, and physically depleted.

But even in that state, there was something inside me, a quiet voice that said, *"This can't be it."*

I looked at my son, and I knew I wanted more for him. I didn't want him growing up thinking that a tired, emotionally drained version of me was all he would get. I didn't want to just survive—I wanted to be present. I wanted to thrive. And for that to happen, I had to start with me.

The First Spark

That moment was the first spark. It didn't ignite a wildfire right away, but it started something deep within me. Some seeds only sprout after the heat of a fire cracks them open, and looking back, that's exactly what was happening. My breakdown was becoming the beginning of my breakthrough. I started small, setting goals, writing them on the fridge with a dry erase marker. I made it visible because I wanted to see it every day. I wanted my son to see that I had dreams and plans.

I set the intention to go back to school before my son started kindergarten. It was my first big step toward reclaiming my identity beyond being "just mom." Don't get me wrong, I loved being his mom. But I knew there was more to me, and I wanted him to see that you can choose a new path, even when you're carrying the weight of motherhood, trauma, or burnout.

At that time, we were receiving support from Youth in Need, and one of their teachers came to our home to help us set and work on our goals. That season of support was life-changing. It reminded me that asking for help isn't weakness. It's the first step in getting where you want to go.

Another Catalyst: My NICU Baby

While I was still taking college classes, I became pregnant with my second son. And once again, life brought another challenge that became a catalyst for deeper growth.

During an ultrasound, we learned he had a congenital condition—CDH (Congenital Diaphragmatic Hernia). Babies like him are given a 40-60 percent mortality rate. It meant he'd need surgery just days after birth. He was born on his due date and spent five weeks in the NICU. We were lucky…that was considered short for babies with CDH. Still, it shook our world.

He came home on a feeding tube, and once again, I had to level up. I had already started questioning my parenting patterns with my first son, but this time, I knew I had to actively break the generational cycles. My default parenting style, what I inherited and absorbed, just wasn't going to cut it anymore.

This was around the time I got serious about personal development. I devoured books, podcasts, and YouTube videos. I followed mentors and motivational speakers online. I wanted to learn everything I could about growth, mindset, and healing—not just for myself, but for the people I loved.

One book, in particular, changed the game for me: *You Are a Badass at Making Money* by Jen Sincero. I listened to it on repeat in my car for months. That book didn't just inspire me—it lit a fire in me.

For the first time, I saw a path that made sense. Coaching. I could take my lived experience, pair it with new tools, and help others the way I wished someone had helped me. That's when I knew: I was meant to become a coach.

Taking the Leap

Even before my college semester ended, I signed up for my first coaching certification program. I jumped in. No turning back. I started networking, meeting people, building something from scratch while still caring for my young boys and managing all the normal chaos of life.

At first, I loved coaching, but I also ran into some walls. I noticed that I was helping my clients on the surface, but there were deeper blocks, both in them and in me, that weren't budging. I could feel the tension between what I *wanted* to help them with and what I was *able* to do with the tools I had at the time.

Then I heard about Neuro-Linguistic Programming (NLP).

I saw how it had transformed the lives and businesses of some of the people I respected most in my network. I researched it. I asked questions. I watched the transformation in others and thought, "I want that." About a year after first hearing about NLP, I enrolled.

It changed everything.

Healing the Root

Before my first NLP training, I broke out in painful, unexplained hives. At first, I thought it was something I ate or a product I used, but nothing seemed to help. I had to go through multiple rounds of medication, and still, the hives kept coming back.

Finally, I asked one of my instructors if it was possible that something emotional could be causing the reaction. She said, "Absolutely, yes."

That was a lightbulb moment. I remembered something I had buried for years: when I was a teenager, I was at the center of a huge family fight. I lost nearly half of my extended family and most of my close friends at the time. It was traumatic, and I had never really processed it. I just pushed it down. That pain had been sitting in my body for years.

In holistic health, skin conditions are often linked to issues around connection—either loss of connection or not wanting to be touched. My body was screaming at me to deal with it.

And with the tools of NLP and Timeline Therapy, I did.

I was able to let go of the trapped anger, grief, and sadness without having to relive the events. That's the magic of the work I do today: clients can heal without retraumatizing themselves. You don't have to tell your whole story. You just have to be willing to release it.

Since July 2020, I haven't had a single outbreak of hives.

My Life Changed—and So Did My Business

NLP gave me the tools to make real, lasting change, not just in myself, but in others. I went from chipping away at surface-level issues to getting underneath the surface and helping people uproot the subconscious patterns that were driving their problems.

I started helping clients with things like:

- Fear of success or failure

- Emotional patterns inherited from their parents

- Anxiety and procrastination rooted in old memories

- Deep grief and anger they couldn't name but always felt

And I was healing, too. My marriage improved. My communication deepened. I understood my kids more and had more compassion for my past. I realized I wasn't broken. I just hadn't been given the tools to process everything I had gone through.

Once I had the tools, it was like waking up inside the Matrix. I could finally see what had been running in the background of my life for decades, and more importantly, I could change it.

That's when my purpose became crystal clear.

What I Do Today

Today, I work with clients who are ready to release the pain, patterns, and programming they've carried for too long. I use the tools of NLP and Timeline Therapy to help them create powerful transformations from the inside out—without years of talk therapy or reliving trauma.

It's about freedom. Freedom from the story that's been running your life. Freedom from the baggage that was never yours to carry. Freedom to finally feel happy, healthy, and whole.

That's what I want for my clients. That's what I want for you.

Final Thoughts

My story isn't perfect. It's messy, human, and real. But it's mine. And through all the hard moments, I found purpose—not because I was looking for it, but because I was willing to grow through what I was going through.

If you've ever felt stuck, unseen, or weighed down by invisible baggage, I want you to know: there's a way out. You can heal. You can rise. And you don't have to do it alone.

Because healing isn't about who hurt you.

It's about who you get to become when you're finally free.

Amber Webb Maxfield is a transformational healing coach, speaker, and founder of **Amber Webb Coaching LLC** and **RAD Networking Group LLC**, a thriving community for entrepreneurs and professionals. With a focus on subconscious reprogramming, emotional release, and generational trauma healing, Amber empowers women and business owners to break free from limiting patterns, unlock their inner strength, and rise into their fullest potential. Her work combines practical mindset tools with deep emotional healing, using powerful modalities like NLP and Timeline Therapy. Amber's coaching journey began after her own profound transformation, and she's since dedicated her life to helping others experience that same shift. Based in St. Louis, Missouri, she lives with her husband and three children, balancing family life with her mission to create safe, supportive spaces for growth, connection, and lasting change. Amber believes true healing creates ripple effects—impacting families, communities, and the world.

Please scan the QR code to connect with this author.

Ken Eckert

Blessing Through the Pain

Hi. Thank you for taking the time to read this chapter. Being asked to participate in collaborating on a book, on its face, is an honor. Given some of my story, I have been encouraged to write a book for some years. Even well before the pandemic. More on that later.

What has been my number one reason that I have not done so previously? I continually asked myself, "What could possibly warrant me, an 'average' person, to think that I could, or even more, *should*, take part in writing a book?" There are so many great people worthy of writing a book, with very admirable stories of their own.

So, why write one now? Maybe *because* there are so many great, honorable, but average people, who should hear from *another* average person. In order that they appreciate their own story and know full well that they have plenty of company with similar difficult journeys to their own!

Being about halfway into my third quarter of life, "discovering one's purpose" is a major question that sets upon you. Perhaps *the* most major questions? Why was I put here; what is my future to be; what do I want to be when I grow up? How do I make up for lost opportunities, lost time, lost potential not fulfilled? What even makes me different than anyone else?

The answer to all those questions requires great introspection, consulting with others, and harsh experiences. Getting out into the world and taking action; being honest with yourself and others. And absolute significant emotional pain and vulnerability.

My personal "story" is much about adversity, illness, and disappointment, with perhaps equal portions of blessing, faith, joy, and happiness. Even a little bit of accomplishment. Alternatively, there is also plenty of abundance! Abundance of love for, and from, family, spouse, children, siblings, and friends. I received incredible support and amazing blessings from all of them.

Much of the pandemic period, for me, was active. As an essential worker, I had clearance to commute freely (traffic was fantastic). The pandemic followed shortly after a period in my life that took up much of my late middle-aged years, with significant, painful illness, disease, and disability. Along with extensive medical treatments, I also experienced personal, employment, and other adversities.

While I do not wish to be identified by—or thought of exclusively for—my medical history, that medical history has played an enormous part in how my last two decades have transpired. My medical history has also played a part in how I have been able to help and counsel others who have experienced very serious and very painful illnesses themselves. Very good people who did not know that there were others with experiences like their own and had not seen someone come out of it on the other side, in solid shape and relatively healthy.

There were many people who were strong for me, including some siblings, a spouse, three children, some fantastic friends, and coworkers, colleagues, and collaborators in multiple organizations. And finally, fellow church members in my Catholic Parish and former friends from college, old workplaces, etc.—that seemingly came from out of nowhere. Many people helped provide me strength, support, and *hope* through lengthy conversations, filling me with faith and spiritual growth, which later brought me to support numerous other people with hours of discussions and conversations.

In my future, I fully expect the possibility of more severe physical (and medical) pain. However, I believe that I am *now* genuinely at peace, were my life to cease and end today. I also believe I was instrumental in helping several other people to be at peace with their life today and over the last several years. I feel that I must make the best that I can with the time I have remaining. Whether that be thirty years down the road, which is quite a lot but may go by quickly. Or only five years, which will fly by like nothing. And that leads me to why I speak and what is next. What I hope and intend to do as *my* purpose.

In my past, there were multiple cancers, some life-saving chemotherapy sessions, and a few painful, unusual, lifesaving surgeries. I was at many doctors frequently (out of necessity). But I would not go at times when I should have. Primarily out of frustration, with so few answers, and out of financial and cost concerns. Plus, plain old common male stubbornness. Some people in my family thought me neglectful. They did not understand my frustration with doctors when it came to issues that were very difficult to diagnose (there is definitely a reason for the expression "practicing" medicine).

After a very long time of retreat from the medical system and pretending I was okay, my mid-life avalanche of illness and disease was discovered—coinciding with a medical crisis turned tragedy of a slightly older, very beloved sister, which ultimately resulted in her painful death. She previously had a serious lymphoma with chemotherapy, which helped her to become "cancer-free." But after seventeen years, it had returned and was complicated with *leukemia* on top of her lymphoma, resulting from the side effects of a newer pharmaceutical drug. The search for an urgent bone marrow match for leukemia began. And it began with the siblings.

From a Catholic family, we had a mother, a father, six older sisters, me, and one younger brother. Of the eight siblings, all living, I was the only six-out-of-six perfect match on critical markers. The rush to get me investigated medically was on. And only, perhaps, me and my wife knew at that time that there was a significant amount wrong to be found.

I have previously listed nearly all the conditions that were either found, or that I had, in a desire that another person experiencing or also suffering from any of these conditions might see hope or relief. Family and very close friends were aware of some of my medical conditions, but never have I been so open or public before this publication. I had three forms of cancer, any of which would make problematic my being a bone marrow donor to possibly save my sister's life. Most troubling was the Stage-4 lymphoma (the very same illness that my sister had originally).

Kidney cancer was second, resulting in the total removal of my right kidney. And number three was colon cancer with removal of the colon. Layered on to the above, I was born with several other "invisible" medical problems that included being born with no spleen, severe and frequent gout, ulcerative colitis (bordering on Crohn's disease), acute pancreatitis, and lupus.

At the moment of my sister's death, I had not been treated, only diagnosed and ruled out as a donor. In tears, I asked the Lord, "God, what more is there to be put upon me? How much more must I take?" My family's belief (with good cause) was that while I failed to save her life, it was her purpose to save mine. I agreed, but that only minimally reduces the unavoidable guilt.

A short time prior to my sister's death and my medical diagnosis, from 2013-2018, there was an employment group that was in its unfortunate twilight. The GO Network! in St. Louis, Missouri. The group met weekly and was there to help people who were unemployed and to improve their employment search. A great organization, it had been operating for several years at the St. Louis Archdiocese St. Patrick's Center. For various reasons, its time had come to end, and it needed to be dissolved.

A few of us participating in GO Network! were concerned that the need to help the unemployed still existed and decided to found a new leadership group and a replacement forum, or outlet, called Beyond Networking-StL. I was privileged to be one of those few co-founders. I was a leadership mentor, organizer, and coordinator through late 2022. There were times throughout that period of late 2013 and late 2022 in which I was incapacitated, and others carried out the mission of the organization. For part of those times, I had very limited duties, and for other parts, I had to completely bow out.

All three major cancers had numerous complications, including unscheduled emergency surgeries, severe sepsis infection, and a brief coma. In at least two cases, I was not expected to make it out alive. Whatever difficulties I personally had, I later observed other patients when I recovered and was semi-healthy. When at the St. Louis Barnes-Jewish Siteman Cancer Center, I observed other patients, witnessing their pain and injustice, appreciating my own recovery, and praying for their recovery.

I was in their place before, in the same physical conditions they were in. The times were harsh. But I am on the other side now and basically well. *Gratitude*, spiritual faith, and hope come very easily to me now! Since, and because of the hardships, I have been able to discuss my situation and experiences with many individuals in similar conditions. Many, at the request of their family members who knew me personally, knew how it turned out for me, who knew *their* loved ones were on the verge of giving up and had lost hope.

All the people I was able to share my experience and hope with received more years of life with their family. I have not been able to stay in touch with all the people I encouraged. There were many. I know of only one person who has since passed. I am happy, though, that he did improve for a couple of years, led a good, long life, and had some good time remaining with his family, including a newborn grandchild!

This mission of helping others find hope in their illness has been very similar to helping other people in seeking purpose and minimizing despair in their employment search.

Beyond Networking-StL survived a short time into the pandemic. The group paused briefly at the beginning of the pandemic. Then, the group went to virtual meetings and Zoom, like many other businesses and organizations. And while severely wounded, the group still existed. Then, a new, different group, Job Seekers' Garden Club (JSGC) of St. Louis, was founded by Bob Kolf during the pandemic. That group had some twists that we never had and some new energy that we no longer had.

We coaxed Bob into speaking and presenting to our membership, to support him and collaborate for the benefit of both groups. Bob presented twice while we remained active. A small number of the Beyond Networking-StL leadership decided that our efforts would be better served supporting JSGC, and we dissolved Beyond Networking-StL. We began volunteering with Job Seekers' Garden Club. I was sidelined from JSGC for nearly a year when, in 2023, I received an immediate emergency liver transplant, followed by an extensive recovery period.

The leadership of JSGC has counseled, consoled, and *congratulated* hundreds of people who have gone through their own difficult stories and challenges. But whether it is unemployment or ongoing illness, every individual should know they are not alone. There are people out there who have the same experiences on one level or another. And there are people who can help you, support you, and love you. God IS good. Sometimes he delivers "gratitude gifts" in very difficult packages.

Anyone suffering a serious illness, employment hardship, or other personal crisis, please feel free to contact me. Maybe I can help or get you help. I can listen, feel for you, and let you know that by no means are you the only one experiencing it; by no means are you on your own in battling it; and there may be serious, true hope for *you* to come out on the other side, in ways you might have never anticipated.

I hope you, or someone close to you, will find solace from my personal story.

And perhaps that you will find happiness in discovering *your* purpose!

Kenneth (Ken) Eckert is a business professional, helping individuals in the non-profit sector for twelve-plus years. Formerly, he was a store manager and worked in retail, sales, and customer service, and he was a non-profit volunteer.

Ken spends most of his volunteer time for the 501(c)3 Job Seekers' Garden Club, serving as Co-Chair of the Ambassador leadership group, helping individuals in their employment and job search. He was awarded the Job Seekers' Garden Club 2024 Volunteer of the Year.

Ken is a Catholic parish member and a member of the Knights of Columbus, though he is not as active as he would like.

Ken has many regrets and would do many things differently were he to have the wisdom when younger that he has today. Ken hopes that in "discovering his purpose," he will help other people to persevere during difficult times of their own journeys.

Please scan the QR code to connect with this author.

Amy Rannebarger

Showing Up—On Purpose

Purpose.

That elusive, slippery concept we're all supposed to "find," as if it's hiding in the clearance aisle of life. It's probably sitting next to last season's regrets and the expired dreams we forgot we had.

From the moment we're old enough to dream, we are handed a script. Go to school. Get a good job. Buy the house. Mow the lawn. Recycle. Rinse. Repeat.

Somewhere along the way, between family, jobs, kids, pets, and managing mortgage and car payments, we are supposed to find purpose. Like it's the golden ticket to fulfillment at the bottom of the cereal box.

But what happens when you check all the boxes and still feel... lost? Stuck?

People talk about "finding" or "discovering" purpose, as if it's some hidden treasure waiting to be found. But, what if, purpose isn't lost—what if you are? Purpose is woven into the fabric of who you are and shaped by the decisions you make, the struggles that you endure, and the truths you finally stop running from.

And it isn't something you pick up on aisle nine from the grocery store when life feels empty. It's not a scavenger hunt, and there's no map or GPS telling you when to recalibrate to get there faster. Purpose finds you—but only when you stop trying to be everything you're not and start showing up as everything you already are.

And that? That's the hard part, isn't it?

Being authentic? Being unapologetically yourself? Goodness, it's hard. It's messy. It's uncomfortable. It's terrifying. But it's also where life happens. And where you have to show up so purpose can find you.

Purpose found me in the most unlikely of places and when I was least prepared to receive it. It didn't show up during some grand milestone or after a big personal achievement. No confetti, no parade. It showed up at a time when I was stripped of everything I thought defined me—success, a title I thought meant something, my worth—dragging around the shoulda-coulda-woulda's like a self-imposed punishment, a constant reminder of all the ways I had fallen short.

After a long, high-achieving, and diverse career, I was unemployed, burnt out, completely lost, and questioning everything I thought I knew. About myself. About the people I trusted. And, in that space of exhaustion and complete disillusionment, the me that is me wasn't me anymore.

I felt so many things at that time of my life—anger, betrayal, sadness, guilt, shame. My mental health was fatigued and fragile. And the fire in my belly? It was gone. Replaced with fear, doubt, and this endless highlight reel of my past failures, whispering that I was never enough. Despite this weight that felt crushing, I still had to find a job. Being an adult doesn't leave much room for questioning your life choices.

I'd interview for roles in my industry, trying to find something—anything—to generate income. Every interview felt like shoving my feet into shoes that were two sizes too small. Didn't matter the role, nothing fit. That was when I actually had interviews—the employment market has been brutal since the pandemic. And with the saturation of candidates out there, your application is among a sea of other applicants. It's like some bizarre lottery, waiting for your number to get picked.

Beyond feeling lost, finances were a huge stressor that loomed overhead like this constant raincloud headed my way. Corporate life had assassinated the joy from a career I was proud of building, and I didn't have the energy or space any longer for corporate politics and drama or the expectation to "play the game," which is corporate-speak for: trust no one. So, there I was, completely uncertain of what was ahead, but absolutely sure that what was behind was better left there. And then...the universe did what it does best.

It nudged.

An amazing friend and colleague sent me some cryptic messages. "Meet here. Business casual." And a link to a networking event. Now, this wasn't just any friend. This was the kind of friend who would have physically dragged me out of my house if I didn't show up. (And don't we all need those kinds of friends?)

So...I went.

I had no idea that when I walked into the Friday Morning Coffee event, hosted by a nonprofit called the Job Seekers' Garden Club (JSGC), that this group of amazing people would have such an impact on my life. Or that here is where purpose would find me.

The first person to greet me was the founder, Bob Kolf.

His easy smile and kind eyes caught my attention first. Warm. Genuine. The kind of person who wears his heart on his sleeve without apology.

I introduced myself, feeling a bit uncertain. "I'm looking for the Job Seeker event—am I in the right place?"

Bob took my hand, locked eyes with me, and said, "You are exactly where you need to be."

I didn't know at the time how right he was. Those words didn't just plant a seed. They yanked me out of survival mode, flicked me on the ear, and whispered, "Pay attention. Something's about to change."

And over the next several months that followed, things began to shift.

At JSGC events, I was surrounded by people who had been through hell. Numerous job losses, financial wreckage, career pivots, identity crises, the list goes on. And yet, they still showed up. No pretending. No posturing. They all were seeking something more than just a job. They didn't know what, specifically, they just knew they didn't want to continue experiencing life as it was.

I didn't know exactly where I fit in or how I could help; I just knew that I had to try.

My background was in HR and People Operations, and I had the experience to offer something in the way of support. About two weeks after meeting Bob, I became an ambassador for the group. I was still trying to figure out my own career path and taking contract gigs where I could, but while I was navigating my next steps, helping others take theirs just felt like the right place for me to be.

Compassion is empathy in action. This is a leadership tenet that I have carried with me in every role and position that I have had in my 20+ year career. It's the foundation of every leadership coaching moment, every conversation advising decision makers, leaders, and business owners. And here again, that tenet was calling me, reminding me that leadership isn't about power or titles. It's about showing up and serving a need greater than your own.

So, I showed up. I helped where I could, and in doing so, this also helped me to heal. The transformations were happening in real time before me, and being part of that, being a witness to people regaining their confidence and taking control of their lives to move forward.

It was bucket-filling. Soul-restoring. Life-changing.

I found the parts of me that had been missing. The parts I thought were lost.

And this is when I realized purpose had been waiting for me all along. And it found me when I was finally myself.

Hope and opportunity. Themes that have been the undercurrent to so many aspects of my life—and long before I ever knew to call them my purpose. Hope for those who feel lost. And opportunity for those who are ready to take the next step. I've always been drawn to helping people move forward, whether they were navigating career changes, building teams, or scaling businesses.

I also never thought of myself as an entrepreneur.

If you had told me five years ago that I'd be building my own business—to help other businesses grow—I would have laughed. Loudly. The idea would have seemed completely out of reach and made no sense.

And yet...looking back? It makes perfect sense.

Every step of my career has led me here. And the amazing thing? These shoes fit. I don't feel squeezed too small. In fact, I feel free and ready to take on the world.

For the past two decades, I've built a career leveraging strategic HR, leadership, and people operations as growth accelerators. Not as an afterthought. Not as a compliance checkmark. But as the fuel that drives business success.

And when the opportunity to help the JSGC came my way? I didn't hesitate to use my experience to help this non-profit continue to do amazing things in our community where I could. Our community needs hope, opportunity, and the support to find it. Helping Bob and the JSGC fulfill their mission and get our community back to work—I saw the full circle moment staring me in the face. This is exactly where I was meant to be.

Maya Angelou once said, "I've learned that making a 'living' is not the same thing as making a 'life.'" So, yeah...hope and opportunity. Being part of helping those make a life, versus just make a living, that is purpose and compassion, collaborating for all the right reasons.

We all crave meaning. We're wired to seek purpose; it's probably tucked away somewhere in the same corner of our brains where we store old phone numbers and that random song lyric that hijacks your brain at 2 a.m.

Purpose is a part of us. It's the quiet whisper that nudges you forward, even when you don't know where you are going. It's not static. It's not linear. It breathes, it shifts, and it grows. What lit you up five years ago might not be what fuels you today. And to be clear, that's not failure. That's evolution.

Something else I have discovered? Purpose has layers. It's like peeling an onion—each layer strips away the expectations, the doubts, and the noise until you get to the core. For me, there's the "before" layer, when I was hustling to fit in, chasing some version of success that sounded amazing on paper but felt hollow in reality. Then, there's the "after" layer, when life shook the ground beneath me and forced me to see things differently.

And, you can have more than one purpose at a time. It isn't about having it all figured out either. It's about showing up anyway. Even when you are tired. Even when you are uncertain. Even when that nagging voice in the back of your mind whispers, "Who do you think you are?"

You show up.

Because purpose isn't waiting for perfect conditions; it's waiting for you to stop pretending to be something you aren't. And when you show up authentically? That's when things start to happen. You will feel it— that shift. The fire in your belly that comes alive. A fire that refuses to be ignored.

Authenticity fuels purpose. It's the match that lights the fire and sets ablaze your focus and intentions. And once that fire is lit? Purpose is no longer the thing you think is unthinkable. It's knocking on your door, asking if you are ready to stop hiding.

For me, it was some random day, doing some random everyday thing. This quiet moment happened when I realized I was no longer chasing purpose. It had been chasing me the whole time. It was just waiting for me to stop being someone I wasn't.

Here's another truth that gets overlooked in this thing we call life: Purpose is deeply personal and rooted within you. It's like snowflakes, no two are exactly alike.

But kindness? That's universal.

You can have all the ambition, drive, and purpose in the world, but if you forget to be kind along the way, you have missed the point.

Kindness isn't weakness. It's power. Power that you share with those who need it most. Kindness lifts others and creates space for them to be their authentic selves. And haven't we been talking about authenticity this entire chapter?

There's a moment, after all the confusion, the second-guessing, and the self-doubt...when everything clicks. And it's not because you finally have all the answers. It's because you stopped asking for permission to be who you already are.

You stop chasing.

You stop forcing.

And you just start being.

This is where purpose lives.

Not in the hustle. Not in the noise. But in the quiet, unshakable confidence that you don't have to be more to be enough. You have been enough all along.

And when you find that space, where authenticity and purpose are finally staring you in the face...give it away.

Yes, you read that right. Give it away. That's the not-so-secret, secret of purpose.

Purpose isn't something you keep; it's something you share. Your purpose is someone else's gift. Give it away, and watch the magic happen. So, if you are wondering where your purpose is hiding, stop looking and start showing up—on purpose.

Amy Rannebarger is the Founder and CEO of Sublimitas Consulting—equal parts HR maverick, people whisperer, and chaos-tamer for businesses trying to grow without losing their sanity (or their people). After 20+ years surviving corporate life, she walked away from the broken systems and burnout to build something better: a firm that helps founders and leaders build thriving, high-performing cultures without the red tape and corporate B.S.

But Amy's not just all business—she's a proud mom of two incredible humans, wrangler of five rescue dogs, and partner to an amazing, endlessly supportive spouse who keeps her grounded when life gets extra. Music gives her life, and on a beautiful day, you can find her on the road in her jeep, top down, jams cranked. She's a fierce advocate for women in leadership, an active community builder, and a relentless champion for a "life in pursuit of happy-ness."

Please scan the QR code to connect with this author.

Teresa Bishara

A Change of Purpose

Throughout my professional career, I was aware of many individuals who had to deal with external disruptions. A promotion that required a relocation, an aging parent, an accident, or an unexpected diagnosis—circumstances that people had to face that were difficult to manage. It is very typical for an external circumstance to foist change upon a person, but sometimes, the disruption comes from a change within the individual.

In addition to life events that are completely unplanned, sometimes changes are planned. Yet, when planned changes occur, the experience may transform us in unexpected ways. The most personal example I can think of is becoming a mother, whether for the first time or when a family is growing.

I saw many women become mothers and make the decision to go back to work, either full-time or part-time, or not go back to work at all. Of the women who continued to work, many struggled with feeling guilty.

While I sympathized with them, I could not truly understand how that felt until I became a mother myself, about two years after I started working in Human Resources for my company. I was often speaking to women about their maternity leave, and I was aware of the heavy emotional burden it could be for women deciding whether to return to work or not.

I had my second child in 2007 while working for the same company. I had some complications and a difficult post-partum recovery, so after I returned to work, I was physically and emotionally exhausted. I had a beautiful, healthy family, but even so, I felt overwhelmed and needed help.

I called the company-provided Employee Assistance Program and was referred to a wonderful therapist who informed me that I was experiencing post-partum depression. She gave me some practical ways to take care of myself in this newest season of life. I immediately took her advice, and it worked for me. As I continued to help employees at my company who were navigating life changes, I strongly encouraged them to reach out to the Employee Assistance Program for help.

In my neighborhood, I only knew one other woman who was a working mom; most of my socialization was through my work. I reflected on the numerous one-on-one discussions with other women through my work about navigating motherhood. I realized there were several of us at my company, specifically in the department I supported, who were juggling career demands with the needs of our young children and families, but most of the women didn't work directly with each other.

It dawned on me that it would be helpful to have a supportive network of women who were going through similar struggles due to their changing lives. I was hopeful that if we got together in a group, we would feel encouraged and reassured. I was sure that it would be an especially positive impact on the first-time moms, or those who had recently had another child. I wanted to give all the moms in the department the same opportunity I'd been blessed with, to hear directly from the seasoned moms who were willing to share their own experiences, and how they were overcoming the challenges of working and raising a family at the same time.

I reached out to the mothers that I knew personally, and everyone was enthusiastic about having a "mom's group." I initiated what is sometimes called an "affinity group" for mothers working for the sales department at the company I worked for. We were spread across the United States geographically, working remotely from home offices, in a male-dominated industry. There were not a lot of spaces in the workday to have personal discussions about home life beyond the typical surface-level pleasantries. We needed ideas and encouragement, and to feel that we were not alone. This was before Facebook or any other social media was available, and we only had phone calls and emails to connect with one another.

We scheduled our first conference call for one hour, and it was such a hit that we had one call a month to discuss what was working for us as we managed the priorities of work and home life. We had all started working before marriages and having children, and it necessitated working differently to meet the needs of our young families. We could no longer put in ten or twelve-plus-hour days without sacrificing time with our families. We would communicate after the call by sending emails and encouraging each other, or sometimes commiserating together. We gained a sense of community and sisterhood that we didn't have before. We realized that we were not alone in our struggles. Simply understanding that we were experiencing similar issues set our minds at ease and allowed us to give ourselves more grace and set more realistic expectations. Looking back, I am so proud of putting that group together during that season.

About five more years passed, and I found myself facing an internal disruption. I was in an ideal situation career-wise; I liked my work, my boss, my company, I was paid well, and I worked from home. However, my children were in elementary school and were becoming aware that after school, I was not available to them until dinnertime.

Simultaneously, I could not shake the unhappiness I felt; every day, I felt like I was not doing enough for either my company or for my own family. I could not stop feeling like a failure as a wife, mother, and employee. I felt as overwhelmed as if I were in a library with a thousand books to read, and they had to be read all at once. I was still laboring under the illusion that I could just work harder, and I'd find the elusive balance that would allow me to feel happier.

After struggling with this for quite some time, I realized that while I loved my job, I did not want to work while my kids were still at home. I was experiencing a misalignment of my values. A part of a bible verse kept coming to mind: *"No one can serve two masters. Either you will hate the one and love the other, or you will be devoted to the one and despise the other"* Matthew 6:24.

It felt impossible to give my all to either my home or my work, and I had been trying to accept that and change my expectations, but it continually gnawed at me. I never imagined myself as a stay-at-home mother when I was younger, I expected to work even if I had a family. I was experiencing a disruption that was my own change of heart about working. With the support of my husband, I left the job and company I loved so I could be with my family at home full-time.

Despite my fears about what I was leaving behind and possibly never having another career, I felt I had to trust God would bless me in the future as he always has in the past.

In the spring of 2021, I was blessed with an unexpected opportunity to find a renewed sense of purpose due to the local economic conditions brought about by the pandemic. This took place during an intentional pause of my professional working life.

From 2013 to 2020, I had been a busy wife and mom, actively involved as a volunteer for my children's school and our parish, attending games and school events. I was on the go every single day until suddenly, just like the rest of the world, everything stopped. At first, when our family was told that school was canceled and people would work remotely, it was nice taking a break from the flurry of activity.

The people in my circle of friends and family initially thought it would be a short time until we could resume our regular lives. My husband and I, along with our friends, were doing what we could to make the experience feel almost like a game for the kids, keeping our spirits high while praying for our friends and leaders. As the days, then months, wore on, it became harder to keep a positive attitude. Our kids, my husband, and I all missed seeing our friends and being able to gather and go about our daily lives. I worried about the impact this was having on my children, their friends, and the other children in our community and around the world.

One day, in the midst of this situation in early 2021, I read an article in the *St. Louis Review* about a local man who had started helping people who had lost their jobs due to the downsizing because of the ongoing pandemic. Bob Kolf had noticed people in his parish who needed help in their job searches. He soon realized that many people had spent decades with their companies, and, for that reason, they were adrift. Many highly capable professionals were floundering, and he felt called to help them. I was inspired that one person took the initiative and was working so tirelessly, giving of himself to make his community a better place by using the skills that he learned throughout his career. I realized that the skills I had learned through my own career might prove to be useful, and I wanted to help.

Before staying home with my kids, I spent about twenty years working my way through my Human Resources career, learning how to source candidates, recruit, interview, and partner with businesses. I had most recently worked in a consumer-packaged goods organization, first in a manufacturing facility and then at the corporate level, supporting a sales department.

After prayerful consideration and with the support of my husband, I reached out to Bob directly, asking if I could volunteer with him in this endeavor. Bob seemed to have boundless energy and such a genuine heart for others. We met at the end of March 2021 at a local pastry shop for coffee, and he explained in greater detail how and why he started the Job Seekers' Garden Club (JSGC) of St. Louis. Bob was connecting and gathering people together for the purpose of getting people back to work, in jobs they would love.

An hour flew by, with Bob asking questions and listening to me with interest. We shared a bit about our own professional backgrounds and our families, and when we spoke of our shared Catholic faith, I felt sure this was a path that God was leading me to take.

I truly believe that being part of a community is one of God's gifts to us; to work together for a common cause lifts the spirit and brings meaning, which results in lasting happiness.

Following this meeting, I felt so excited that I was volunteering. I started reaching out to people in the group to offer help with their resumes, job searches, or interview preparation. I made introductions on LinkedIn and got to witness Bob in action. He met people for coffee, gave them encouragement, set up networking events like job fairs, and always had a kind word and smile on his face. Bob and his team of volunteers were so cheerful and encouraging, they welcomed me immediately and made me feel that my contributions were important. The best part about it for me personally was having a community again.

I was connecting with people from all types of professional backgrounds: from a recent college graduate trying to find their entry-level role to a senior executive displaced after over twenty years. They shared a common attribute; they needed someone outside their immediate circle of friends and family to listen to them and encourage them, as well as give them actionable tasks to help in their job search goals.

I made phone calls, met people for coffee, attended career fairs, and networked on LinkedIn. I watched numerous videos by content creators and experimented with my own LinkedIn profile, sharing tips and tricks to pass applicant tracking software. Some people just needed a few changes to their job search strategy, LinkedIn profile, or resume. Others needed introductions or help to find job openings. I was seeing a positive impact right away; I was using a part of my brain that I had not used in a long time, and I was meeting wonderful people through the work.

Through my previous experiences, I was able to contribute to my community without sacrificing my family. This gives me a deep sense of purpose and fulfillment. I also found an opportunity to accept a paid position on a part-time basis, using my skills to support and encourage others, which I would not have found if not for my volunteer work with the Job Seekers' Garden Club. I believe in blooming where you are planted, and in using your past experiences, good and bad, to learn and make life better for yourself and those around you.

Teresa Bishara is a proud wife and mother of two, with a lively cockapoo that brightens her home. After a successful career in Human Resources, she took a break to focus on her family and now works part-time, balancing professional and personal responsibilities. She still volunteers her services to friends and family, reviewing resumes and helping with job searches and interview preparation. Outside of work, she is passionate about reading and genealogy, exploring history, and tracing her family's roots. Since converting to Catholicism in 2015, Teresa's faith has played a significant role in shaping her life. She is also a member of the Daughters of the American Revolution (DAR), where she connects with others who share her love for history and service.

Please scan the QR code to connect with this author.

Nicholas Epps

The Calling to Dominate

Let's cut the fluff. There comes a moment in every person's life when they wake up, stare into the mirror, and realize they've been playing small. That moment—the one that grabs you by the throat and demands answers—smacked me straight in the face in 2019.

I was seventeen years deep in corporate America, grinding, hustling, chasing those titles, bonuses, and vacation contests companies hand out to keep employees content. I was "successful" by every metric society throws at you. A six-figure income, great benefits, and a very manageable travel schedule; but none of that meant a thing the moment my phone rang, and I got the call: My dad had a heart attack, died, and had his heart restarted on the way to the hospital.

A massive heart attack, followed by a medically induced coma. Doctors gave him less than a 10 percent shot of waking up. They told my mom to prepare for the worst. "She should have his last rites performed." Right there. That was the freight train moment. The slap I needed. The reminder that *tomorrow is not promised.*

Eventually, my dad didn't just wake up from the coma—he came back from the brink like a fighter. They called him the *miracle man.* But the fight wasn't over. He needed a sextuple bypass surgery. That's six arteries, for those keeping count. The doctors were only willing to operate on four arteries originally, because six was just too dangerous. Furthermore, they wouldn't even perform the quadruple bypass surgery unless he showed an improvement in both his physical strength and mental acuity.

That's when I dropped everything. As soon as my father was released from the hospital, I filed for the Family Medical Leave Act (FMLA). I moved my parents into my house. I became a full-time caretaker for my dad. I walked with him every day. We played chess to rebuild his mind. I was all-in on his road to recovery.

Guess what happened to my career? *Nothing.*

The company supported me. My team stepped up. The world didn't collapse because I put family first. And that changed me forever.

The Mission Shift

When FMLA ended and I went back to work, I wasn't the same man. I had a new lens, a new fire, a new mission. I had tasted what really matters. And I made a decision: I was going to retire at 40. Not talk about it. Not hope for it. *Do it.* I had the savings. I had the 401(k)s. I had the plan. So, in January 2020, I pulled the plug. I retired.

And for a moment, it felt incredible. I traveled. I spent time with my family. I laughed more. I slept in. There were no Zoom calls, no meetings, no chasing promotions. But comfort is a sneaky little devil. At first, it feels like freedom. But eventually? Comfort starts to feel like a cage. I had time—but I didn't have direction. I had space—but no mission.

And then, it started. That voice. That whisper in the back of my head… **"There's more."**

I had started a supplement line—something clean, no junk, built for people like me. But I knew it wasn't the bullseye. I didn't want to chase *income*. I wanted *impact*. So, I prayed.

"God, what's next? Where do You want me?"

And then it happened. People started showing up—random conversations, divine appointments—and they all said the same thing: "You should be a consultant."

Consultant? I brushed it off. I didn't want to be another suit giving vague advice. But the more I listened, the more I saw the gap. There's a massive canyon between small business and big business. Small businesses are drowning in noise, hacks, hype, and hollow promises. They're hiring "experts" who couldn't lead a lemonade stand to profitability. I knew I could do better. I knew I could bring real results, real knowledge, and real integrity.

So, I made the call: I'm all in.

The First Wake-Up Call

Let me rewind.

In 2018, before any of this happened—before retirement, before consulting, before the "miracle man" moment—I was standing at another crossroads. My health was a wreck. I was overweight and fatigued. I was sitting in a doctor's office with a death sentence. "If you don't lose weight now, you won't be around next year." The doctor pushed lap band surgery.

But I knew—and I mean *knew*—that wasn't the path for me. Something deep in my gut screamed, **"Don't do it!"** So, I went home, dropped to my knees, and begged God for direction.

The next morning? A text. It was a gym. My sister had gifted me three trial sessions. I didn't go.

The next day? Another text. This went on until I finally surrendered and walked into that gym. Nine months later—I was down 100 pounds. I had my energy back. My mind was clearer. My spirit was locked in. But I also hit plateaus throughout those nine months. I needed supplements, and every product had filler ingredients. Some products were proprietary blends that had just a pixie dusting of the important ingredients. The gym owner said, "Man, I wish there was a supplement line with only the ingredients you need, dosed properly! No filler or pixie dusting." Boom. That stuck with me.

So, we built it. A clean, no-filler supplement line built from integrity, not profit margins. I launched the product line out of gratitude to God—He had given me a second shot, and I owed Him everything. But when I prayed again —"Should I quit my job and do this full time?"—the answer came back clear: **No.**

So, I stayed with my job. And I realized I was making a real impact. I wasn't pushing paper; I was helping people—real people—rebuild their lives. Folks with credit issues, rejected by the system, got a second chance at obtaining a loan because of our programs. They now would have reliable transportation to get to work, feed their families, and turn their lives around. That gave me fuel.

God's Blueprint

From the outside, my journey probably looked like a zigzag. Corporate warrior turned caretaker turned retiree turned entrepreneur. But the truth? God had a blueprint the whole time. And I was just getting started. I said yes to faith when fear wanted control. I said yes to discipline when laziness whispered sweet lies. And, I said yes to purpose when comfort tried to seduce me back into sleep.

That's when consulting found me. Not because I wanted it. Because I was called to it. Seraphim Consulting wasn't about marketing platforms or ad strategies. Seraphim Consulting was about a mission. I wasn't selling growth—I was delivering *domination*. But not every business was ready for that. So, I created three non-negotiables. If a business didn't meet the criteria? We passed. We don't beg. We don't convince. We don't discount our value. We work with businesses that are ready for exponential growth—mentally, spiritually, operationally.

The Power Move: Risk-Free Trial

Now let's talk strategy. I knew I had the goods, the team, and the right system, but small businesses didn't know me and my company yet. I prayed: "God, what now? How do you want me to proceed?"

The answer: Offer a 30-day, risk-free trial. No fees, and no contracts. Let us run the ads, prove our worth, and if it works, let's roll.

I'll be real, I was scared. What if they just took the free trial and ghosted? What if current clients got mad? But then I remembered—God doesn't call you to play scared. So, we launched it. And it exploded. We stood behind our work. We put our money where our mouth was. And the market *loved it*. Clients came in waves, referrals doubled, and testimonials poured in. "You guys were the answer to our prayers." That's what they said, and they meant it. Because we weren't selling services, we were executing a mission.

Legacy Over Luxury

Today, I don't run a company. I drive a movement.

Every client's win has a ripple effect. When we help one business grow, we create jobs. We stabilize families. We inject life into local communities. That's legacy. And legacy doesn't come from playing small. Legacy is earned in the fire. That's why I tell every client, every team member, every person I coach:

"Stop playing small. Stop numbing your calling with comfort. Stop waiting for perfect conditions. Stop looking for permission. You're not here to survive. You're here to **dominate**."

Rise up. Get clear. Get aligned with your calling. Say no to the noise and yes to the mission. Because when you operate from faith, lead with purpose, and back it up with execution…

You don't just win. You dominate.

After a highly decorated career spanning automotive finance, pharmaceutical sales, and executive leadership, Nicholas Epps came out of retirement to pursue what he believes is his true spiritual calling from God—empowering small business owners through consulting. With a proven track record of record-breaking performance, he's led markets, shattered sales goals, and inspired teams at leading companies in the automotive, pharmaceutical, and rental car industries. From doubling territory revenue to launching products that redefined market share, his passion for excellence is undeniable. But success alone wasn't enough. A deeper purpose called him back to help others unlock theirs. Now, as founder of his own consulting firm, he combines corporate mastery with divine purpose to guide entrepreneurs toward fulfillment, profit, and lasting impact. This book is more than insight—it's a calling to action for anyone seeking direction, clarity, and purpose in their professional and personal life.

Please scan the QR code to connect with this author.

Tracy Mueller

This Little Light of Mine

"This little light of mine, I'm going to let it shine. This little light of mine, I'm going to let it shine. Hide it under a bushel? No! I am going to let it shine." As a little girl, I remember singing this song in my Sunday school class. It was a cute song with hand movements, and at the time, I did not realize that I would be hiding God's light in my marriage, at work, and with friends.

"You're here to be a light, bringing out the God colors in the world. God is not a secret to be kept. We're going public with this... Now that I've put you there on a hilltop, on a light stand— Shine!" —Matthew 5:16 MSG

Do you remember the temporary power outage in Paris during the 2024 Olympics? I will never forget the breathtaking image of the Basilique du Sacre Coeur (Basilica of the Sacred Heart of Jesus), which was the only light illuminating the entire dark city of Paris! This beautiful hilltop image was another reminder that God is the Light of the world.

Fast forward to January 2025; I always begin my year with a word. In the past, my words for the year have been intentional, empowering, and focused. This year, the word **light** was placed on my heart. I bought a journal for my devotions and wrote the word light in the center of the page. I did a deep dive into why the word is light. My friend shared with me how the moon reflects the sunlight. The moon relies on the sun for light! This was a revelation to me.

In the same way, I want to be intentional about shining God's light to other people. It is amazing how small gestures can have such a big impact on someone's day. Holding the door open for a struggling mom, sharing a genuine smile to a stranger, or congratulating a friend on an accomplishment. Those little moments of kindness could be exactly what someone needs to feel a sense of connection, joy, and hope. By intentionally acknowledging others, we create opportunities for positivity and shine God's light in their lives. As believers, the bible teaches us that we are designed to love one another and be a light to others in a dark world.

My parents have always been my greatest role models growing up and even more so as an adult. My mom is my biggest cheerleader. When I am struggling, she is my prayer warrior, and I have been on her prayer list since before I was born. Whenever I text her pictures of different accomplishments, she is the first to text back with praises and many exclamation points! I am so blessed to have such amazing parents, and I am so thankful that they are both still in my life. My father has been my hero since I was a little girl. I have his work ethic, and my dad is the humblest person I know. He is my business coach and is always offering his "two cents." My parents have taught me to be kind to those around me. No matter what is going on in your life, you can still bring light and joy to someone else. Our faith has brought my family through many trials, and God continues to bless us when we decide to let go and give it to Him.

"This is my commandment to love one another." —John 15:12-14

We are designed to love one another. That is it! There are different ways we can accept others and accept them for who they are. We are not perfect, just human. One of my spiritual gifts is to serve others. I do this through my church and non-profits in the area. It gives me joy to serve at my church and greet people at the door, welcoming the kids in classes, or serving our community.

My purpose in my daily, monthly walk of life is to be present and intentional in acknowledging those around me. Be present with my family, friends, and others that I encounter throughout my day. I need to learn to offer grace to those who may not have a light of hope or are struggling with life. A smile or greeting could make all the difference to a person and give them hope for a better tomorrow.

In 2019, I worked as a community connector for **The Connection Exchange**, a woman-owned business based in Columbia, MO. Through the company, I met new businesses in the St. Louis and St. Charles areas and scheduled a time to sit down with the up-and-coming new business owners and learn about their business. I would offer different resource experts to help their business be successful. I looked forward to sitting across from the business owners and seeing how excited they were to open the doors and begin this next chapter of their lives.

In 2020, many of the small business owners I had met had to close their doors; they were uncertain if they were financially able to reopen. I was unsuccessful in scheduling appointments for the company because we had the owners on Zoom instead of visiting their new space. One of the greatest joys about my role with The Connection Exchange was visiting the business in person and seeing the excitement in their eyes for their new venture. So, I pivoted and began reaching out to the small business owners I had met with before the pandemic. I told them about my network of experts throughout the St. Louis area and offered to connect them with any resources they needed to keep their business. A mentor told us during this time, "learn to insulate yourself as a business owner and not isolate yourself." So, I made sure to pass that wisdom along. I still keep in touch with a few of the owners I met during that difficult time.

In the summer of 2020, I sat across from a gentleman at a local coffee shop. His name was Bob Kolf, and he shared with me about his LinkedIn group and the vision he had for bridging the gap between job seekers and

HR recruiters. I was inspired that day and knew I wanted to volunteer with this non-profit organization. Job Seekers' Garden Club was creating an impact and building hope for our community. Fast-forwarding to 2025, I am actively supporting this organization, and they have provided hope and resources to many job seekers in the St Louis area.

My family and I had attended a church for over nineteen years. My husband and I were married there, both of my kids were dedicated to the church, friendships were made, and I had the honor of baptizing both my kids. When the church doors temporarily closed in 2020, we searched for a new church that offered sermons online. I have found an amazing church family because of the pandemic. I am so grateful because through that 2020 experience, I have developed such amazing friendships, and I feel spiritually filled by the messages.

In August 2023, I was blessed to join a family-owned business, Fresh Start Outdoors. I was acknowledged by the owner for my connecting and relationship skills and added to the team. I met the family in 2005 when our families attended the same church, and we were both part of a ministry called Parents with Young Children. Fast forward eighteen years, and I now had the opportunity to work alongside this amazing and talented family. Did I mention that all seven children work in the landscape business? As a brand ambassador for the company, my role has allowed me to connect with many incredible business owners and clients. Fresh Start Outdoors donates to several non-profit organizations in the area because we must make an impact in our community. I have a job where I love what I do. I feel appreciated and not "tolerated" in the company. I believe that God's purpose for me is to help entrepreneurs and business owners understand that they were designed for greatness. Once we step foot into our genius zone, the joy you will experience is amazing. You are using your talents.

A local radio station has a billboard that I occasionally pass on the highway. It always makes me smile. **Life is messy; I choose Joy.** I have days where I feel overwhelmed and just want to pull the covers over my head and have a pity party. However, when that feeling arises, I stop myself and realize I could be a shining light in someone else's day. People need joy in their lives because there is so much darkness in our world. Because joy gives us hope. We need joy. I have a God given purpose to spread love and joy to those I meet.

"May the God of hope fill you with all joy and peace as you trust in him, so that you may overflow with hope by the Power of the Holy Spirit" —Romans 15:13 NIV

This little light of mine, I am going to let it shine!

Tracy Mueller is passionate about people and making them feel included and seen. She enjoys helping job seekers, new business owners, and young entrepreneurs who desire to find their next opportunity or help them make a connection. We are all designed to shine and have a purpose in this world. Her role as a brand ambassador for Fresh Start Outdoors allows her to cultivate relationships and collaborate with companies in the area. Tracy is active as a greeter at her church, is a volunteer for Gateway to Dreams, and is an ambassador with Job Seekers' Garden Club St. Louis. She enjoys Zumba and loves naps. Tracy lives in St. Peters, Missouri, with her husband, two children, and her furbaby, Chewy.

Please scan the QR code to connect with this author.

Virginia Alexander

Choosing Time For Myself, I Found My Purpose

"For everything there is a season,
and a time for every matter under heaven…"
—Ecclesiastes 3:1

This is one of my favorite passages in the Holy Bible, and I think of it often, as it helps me get through life's struggles. A passage I was drawn to through music. There are many religious songs that refer to this passage, but my love for the passage came from a song by The Byrds ("Turn! Turn! Turn!"), and I have been singing it since I was a little girl. "*To everything turn, turn, turn. There is a season; turn, turn, turn. And a time to every purpose under heaven…*"

Music has always played an important role in my life. I was blessed to have parents who enjoyed music. My mom always had our kitchen radio playing while we kids did our chores. It made the work seem like fun! Often, a song would come on, and Mom would start dancing and singing with all of us kids. Such great memories were made! As I reflect on my life, I know that it's times like those and so many more that helped to create a strong foundation for my life's journey. Take so many memories like those, add love, nurturing parents and family, the passion I felt through music, and, of course, the Lord, and I had a winning combination of strength to fall back on when times were tough. And, like most people, there have been many.

So, to make it through the painful and just downright scary times, when I wonder if I'll make it through, I pray. I pray and I listen to music. Music—listening, dancing, singing, and performing—has always been my passion. It brought me through happy, sad, and rough times that I wasn't sure I'd get through. Like losing a job and wondering how I would pay bills, and having loved ones die (too many). I'm not sure what I would have done without music. There are many songs with beautiful meanings, and many of those songs are based on the love of God. Those are the ones that touch my heart. Take the song "Were You There?" as an example. I can't sing or even listen to that song without crying. The words and music are so powerful, knowing how much Jesus loves us. It is truly amazing! It wasn't until recently that I realized how much music and a strong faith foundation have saved me. Small blessings to miracles have seen me through those tough times.

To choose one time when my life felt as if it were in shambles due to the loss of employment for one reason or another is very difficult to do, because I have experienced job loss a few times. The worst time was when my husband and I were living apart. My husband was being transferred to another city with his company, and at the same time, my company had offered me an excellent opportunity. Given the opportunities, but more importantly, the fact that my dad had Alzheimer's and I wanted to help take care of him, my husband and I made a very tough decision—to have a commuter marriage. The situation worked fine for us because our love and commitment to each other were strong, and we saw each other almost every weekend. After a few years, my dad passed away, and I moved to where my husband was living, but that also meant I was jobless.

I took a couple of months off and then went on a job hunt. After several weeks of sending out résumés and going on interviews, I found a job! My husband and I were excited and thankful; life was good. Then, wham! My husband passed away suddenly. Given the grief and the stress of planning a funeral, and all the other responsibilities that happen at times like that, while trying not to fall apart, I forgot about my new job. When I called the new employer days later, they had a hard time believing what I was telling them, and they terminated me. My family and I decided it was best for me to move back to my hometown to be closer to my mom and siblings, which included a brother who was dying of cancer. That brother was such a blessing for me. Even though he was dying, he was there for me, and I was there for him. We had many beautiful conversations, and yes, we listened to music. He shared some of his favorite bands and songs. I shared some of mine. We often talked about spirituality and the existence of heaven, and grew closer than we had ever been. Music and God back in my life, another of life's blessings.

With all that, I still had to pay bills. So, it was back to the job hunt. In less than two months, I was offered three jobs in the same week! A feat only God could provide! I moved into my own place, but still saw my mom and brother as often as possible. A few weeks later, my brother passed away, making me even more grateful for our time together. For his funeral, he chose his own music—songs that were deeply meaningful. I say this with firm conviction—every time, every single time, that I faced events in my life that seemed to be dire, God brought me forward. He has remained steadfast through trying times and through good times.

Fast forward a few years... I was offered a job working for a fast-growing, innovative global company. I was successful and well-respected by 400+ human resources coworkers globally. Success and respect were great feelings! However, I was working sixty-plus hours every week. During busy times, I would work fourteen-plus-hour days and weekends.

I was exhausted and didn't have any time for a personal life. My friends strongly encouraged me to find something else. I would listen to the radio while driving home from work, praying for guidance. What happened? Songs came on the radio that gave me insight and strength. I would thank God while I listened, preparing myself to make a tough decision.

I asked the company to hire a part-time employee to help with the workload, but the request fell on deaf ears. I continued to work and pray. One day, another business cold-called me and offered me what sounded like a *great* position! Better salary, less stress, fewer hours...too good to be true? I pondered and prayed that God would guide me, and after several days, I accepted the position. I was excited, knowing I could put some decent money into savings, have a personal life again, start meeting people, and just live life!

That was not the case.

The company was not in good shape and assigned an additional role to me on top of what I was already doing. I was given responsibilities that I had no experience with and no guidance to understand them. I had gone from a company where everyone worked together to a company with minimal communication and minimal respect for their employees. I had made a mistake, blinded by promises too good to be true! I struggled to keep up with their demands and was working more hours than in my prior job. New leadership was put into place, and the new leadership gave me some ultimatums. I was overwhelmed. Friends told me the ultimatums were impossible to complete, that I should just quit. I've never been a quitter, though. Right or wrong, I'm not a quitter. I ended up meeting every single one of their ultimatums, and in a shorter period than required. But, in that timeframe, I also did some soul-searching. I looked in the mirror and saw a tired, worn out, unhappy person. I prayed to the Lord and found my answer. I did what was best for me and left that company.

That was scary! What did I just do? How was I going to survive? What would my friends think of me for walking away from a job? Negative thoughts were all that filled my mind. Which we all tend to do sometimes, don't we? I only shared my "unemployed" status with a couple of very close friends. After a few weeks of feeling ashamed and angry, I remembered to pray. I was still going to church, but I wasn't really "present in the Lord." **I became present**. I started taking walks, talking with people, and listening to my favorite songs. I talked with my priest, who offered beautiful words of comfort and prayer. I grew stronger and self-confident again and decided to take a few months off for me!

I didn't do much of anything at first, just chilled and enjoyed life. I connected with some old friends from other states. I cried a lot and made some great new friends who supported me and were truly there for me! One of those friends told me about the Job Seekers' Garden Club. So, I sought them out, only to find that a friend from the past who had worked with my deceased husband was strongly involved in that Club. She and several other people were so supportive of me. The people who lead that organization were truly remarkable and helped me find a new position. But, more importantly, *I found me again!* I was enjoying life and doing things that made me happy. I got back into photography, other hobbies, and, of course, music. I went out and listened to bands, went dancing, and sang with some bands. Through music, I met some great new friends. My soul was astir once again! Music is my basis for pretty much everything, including my reach out to God. I found a much deeper connection with my Savior as He guided me.

After several months of giving myself time, I dove back into the job hunt. I went through numerous interviews, even contemplating moves to other states, before finally accepting a position with a business in my hometown area. Is it the right place? I'm not sure, but it is a decent job, and whether I decide to stay or move on to something else, I know God will be there with me.

Those months off gave me time to understand that I am a good person, and I do deserve to be happy.

My dream? My desire?

I want to work in a totally different field. Somewhere I can give back in gratitude. Somewhere I can utilize my true talents—a passion for caring for people. I want to bring a positive outlook and happiness to other people. I've signed up for some veterinary classes and art and photography classes. I want to get back into music, either singing or as a talent agent. I've also become more involved in my parish and have gotten back into hiking and enjoying nature. It's great to have a life again. My family would want it that way.

If I were to offer advice to anyone, I'd say—take time for you! We all need to find ourselves and do things that make us happy.

This world really does need us to care for each other. One thing I know for certain: my Lord is there every step of the way. He never left me; I just needed to listen and allow *"Jesus to take the wheel."*

For it is so true—music can stir the heart, the mind, the soul. And where does music come from? God. As does everything.

Maybe now that you've read this, you will listen to the song "Turn! Turn! Turn!" by The Byrds (based on Ecclesiastes 3:1-8). *"To everything, turn, turn, turn. There is a season, turn, turn, turn. And a time to every purpose under heaven. A time to be born, a time to die. A time to plant, a time to reap …And a time to every purpose, under heaven."* God will fill your heart. We only need to trust and know. Oh, and listen to music. It will stir your soul!

God bless you all.

Virginia (Ginger) Alexander has over twenty years of experience as a benefits administrator/manager. She has worked with Fortune 500 companies, assisted in company bankruptcies, helped start-up businesses, and has shared her talents with charitable organizations. Outside of work, Virginia enjoys live music, sports—including baseball, hockey, and pickleball—photography, hiking, visiting historic state and national parks, and volunteering at church and charitable organizations. She has a strong passion for nature and enjoys sharing that passion with others.

Please scan the QR code to connect with this author.

Patrick Dolan

Finding Purpose in Prison

Since the beginning of time, men (mankind) have been trying to discover the purpose of their lives. Just imagine the first few thousand human beings and what they must have asked themselves—how in the world did we get here? What are we supposed to do?

Thousands of years later, we still ask ourselves similar questions. Why? Because we all desire to have purpose in life. Not just any purpose, but a meaningful purpose. Without meaningful purpose, life seems empty and unfulfilling. Feelings of anxiety, hopelessness, or even despair can take root.

It is incumbent on each of us to seek our own purpose. No one can do it for us. Frequently, we instinctively think of our occupation as our purpose. But is it? Should it be? Or, should your occupation be what you do in order to achieve your true purpose?

Keep in mind that your purpose in life should change as your responsibilities change. Major life events such as marriage, children, or aging parents will change your responsibilities. As they evolve, you should expect your purpose to change as well. If not, you are probably neglecting your responsibility and struggling to find peace.

Change can be very hard, especially when it is foisted upon you. But think about this: it is your responsibilities in life that give your life meaning. Maybe this unexpected or unwanted change is a message from God. Is he trying to get your attention? Could it be there is a more meaningful purpose awaiting you? One which will enrich your life and those around you? Consider this possibility.

To find purpose, I suggest you first wrestle with the age-old questions. What was the origin of the cosmos? How did life come into existence? Why these questions? Because, how you answer them should form the basis for discovering your purpose.

My observation is that each of us belongs to one of three categories. Theists, who believe all things were created by God or some other higher power. Atheists, who generally believe the Big Bang theory explains the creation of the cosmos. And that life randomly evolved over time. Lastly, agnostics, who throw up their hands and avoid tackling these challenging questions.

Theists often begin by contemplating why God created man. Then, more significantly, why did God create me? There are many books, most notably the bible, which can assist in this purpose.

Atheists, on the other hand, don't believe in God but rather that humanity is a random act of nature. They, therefore, must rely solely on their own intuition to provide a purpose for their life.

Finally, I suggest agnostics who are struggling to find purpose should begin by investing time wrestling with these age-old questions. Avoiding these difficult questions can often leave you feeling confused about life. Like atheists, you must rely solely on your intuition to find purpose.

As a Catholic Christian, I believe God is an infinite being. I believe God is the creator of all things in the natural world. Therefore, I believe God created mankind and all living creatures. God gave man dominion over the earth. God made man in his image and likeness. Meaning we can love, create, and choose to do good. No other creature shares these attributes.

I also believe God loves all men. He loved us into being. God is always present to us. He speaks to us through our conscience, our dreams, and our thoughts. He is always showing the way toward a life of purpose, peace, and joy. It is up to each of us to be receptive to his promptings.

So how do we find a meaningful purpose? I propose that we begin by identifying our responsibilities in life at the current moment. Our responsibilities almost always include putting someone else's interest above our own. This is the secret to having a meaningful purpose. Think about it: Our greatest satisfaction, peace of mind, and even joy often result from successfully managing those responsibilities.

Realize God made each of us as unique individuals. We each have strengths and weaknesses or shortcomings. Identify your strengths and develop them. Use them to fulfil your purpose. Do not make the mistake of focusing on your perceived weaknesses. Sure, you have them; we all do! Acknowledge them and get over it. Focusing on negative feelings about yourself causes unnecessary stress and anxiety. The result is that you feel overwhelmed, even helpless. This inhibits your effort to achieve your purpose. Focusing on weaknesses will overshadow your life if you let them.

I speak from experience. In my youth, I was extremely introverted and insecure. I had few friends. My hobby was stamp collecting, something I could do alone. I was nineteen before I went on my first date. To escape my self-imposed isolation, I focused on my part-time job at McDonald's. I often worked thirty to forty hours per week while I was in high school and college. This workload prevented me from making any personal connections.

I am still very much an introvert. Still uncomfortable when meeting new people, especially in large gatherings. It is still difficult for me to engage in casual conversations. At one time, I believed being introverted was a personality flaw. But now, I consider it merely a part of my personality. A characteristic. One of many which makes me unique. It is certainly not one of my favorite characteristics, but I am OK with it. I have learned to accept that trait as a part, a small part, of who I am. I no longer let it define me. I know that I am so much more than that.

It was as if this revelation set me free! I redirected my perception of this perceived flaw. I was able to overcome its hold on me.

Shortly before my forced retirement, I was asked to join a Christian ministry: Kairos Prison Ministry International, Inc. A Kairos team of volunteers goes into a maximum-security prison for a three and a half day weekend to minister to as many as forty-two residents. My initial reaction was, "Uh, no thanks." I couldn't imagine myself meeting with such a large group of strangers. And how was I, just an ordinary Christian with no teaching experience, supposed to "preach" about Christianity?

I joined the team with trepidation. Multiple team meetings were held in preparation for the weekend. At the first meeting, there were thirty-five or forty Kairos veterans. As usual, I was uncomfortable at first, but they enthusiastically welcomed me.

I discovered the program does not "preach" but rather uses talks, discussions, and chapel meditations to convey the Christian faith. By the end of team formation, I was fully prepared for the weekend. I was filled with my usual apprehension, but I was not going to let it stop me.

When the participants were first escorted into our meeting room, I observed their wariness at being there. Many of them did not come to learn about Christianity but for other reasons: getting out of their cell for several days, the chaplain or a former participant suggested they come, or to enjoy the bottomless basket of home-made cookies we bring with us.

More importantly, I noticed they were not talking to one another. They showed little or no emotion. All were wearing the same drab and well-worn clothing. I could sense the hopelessness and lack of purpose. I began to wonder what special purpose could one possibly pursue while in prison. I felt the despair of a life without purpose.

At the onset of the weekend, I spent about 30 minutes one-on-one getting to know the participant I was hosting. I served him coffee and cookies and clumsily initiated a conversation. I treated him as I would any guest in my home. This was unusual for him. In prison, no one pays special attention to you. When he realized that I was there to be his friend, he directed the discussion. He was pleased to have an audience, and I was happy that he carried most of the conversation.

Throughout the weekend, we sat with the participants, listened to talks together, and encouraged them to share their thoughts and feelings during the discussions. We had them draw posters. We went to chapel and heard meditations. We celebrated milestones. They sang Christian songs with enthusiasm and spirit. The Kairos team did not "preach." We simply shared with them the message of God's love and mercy and his desire to have a relationship with them. Their hardened hearts were softened!

By the end of the weekend, they understood that God loved them and would forgive them. A huge weight was lifted from their shoulders. Many of them experienced joy for the first time in a long time. They made new friends, the other participants, in the prison whom they can trust.

The transition from despondency to joy in just three and a half days was amazing to witness. At the closing ceremony, men who rarely discussed their feelings with anyone grabbed the microphone. They enthusiastically shared their experience with everyone there, including the guests, who were complete strangers. They told of the need to go back into the prison. They wanted to share the message of God's love and forgiveness with their fellow residents. They were actually evangelizing to their audience as they prepared to reenter the prison compound.

What changed in these men? The Kairos team offered them Christian love without judgment. But more importantly, they encountered the love and mercy of God. Possibly the first time for some of them. The weight of guilt had been lifted. They felt the gift of God's peace. They experienced joy.

Their lives were forever changed. Why? Because they discovered a meaningful purpose in their lives despite being incarcerated. They can be the hands and feet of Christ reaching out to fellow residents. Their purpose can be to serve others.

Driving home after my first Kairos weekend, I kept asking myself, "What did I just witness?" I concluded it was a miracle. Maybe a minor miracle, but a miracle nonetheless. I am convinced that the Holy Spirit was present throughout that weekend and healed their spirits. I have participated in fifteen similar weekends, and they all end with similar results.

Participants in a Kairos weekend often find a meaningful purpose in their life, even though they are incarcerated. They discover that putting someone else's needs above their own brings a special kind of peace and joy. I discovered that helping others find purpose in their life is a very worthwhile purpose for me as well.

One final thought. Develop an attitude of gratitude. Every day, take time to be grateful for something in your life. Make it a habit. There is always something to be grateful for. Then, on those days when life is a struggle, this habit will help put your difficulties in perspective.

Patrick Dolan is a Roman Catholic. His faith is the underpinning of his life. He is the third of five children. He is a husband, father of five, and grand-father of seven. Patrick spent his life in the St. Louis, MO vicinity, with the exception of six years spent in Breckenridge, CO after retirement. He is an active member of Ascension Catholic Church in Chesterfield, MO.

Patrick graduated from the University of Missouri-St Louis with a Bachelor of Science degree. Upon graduation, he entered the public accounting profession. After three years, he transitioned into the private sector. The majority of his career was in financial management with various manufacturing firms.

Patrick currently devotes a lot of time to volunteering for the Kairos Prison Ministry. He also enjoys traveling the back roads of the United States to discover the uniqueness of small towns in rural America.

Please scan the QR code to connect with this author.

Imani Robinson

Marriage: Purpose Not Perfect

Not exactly the ideal love story—for some. But it's ours.

Our love story: the Robinsons. Two imperfect and flawed people coming together for God's divine purpose.

Sredrick Robinson, a high school star athlete from Iowa, was on a full-ride scholarship to USC and was said to be headed for the NBA. Raised by a single mother with two older brothers, he had a firsthand taste of a lifestyle filled with drugs, sex, and rock and roll. Nicknamed "Snake Rob," he was no stranger to the streets and carried a persona both feared and respected. He navigated a world where survival was a skill, not a luxury, and emotions were buried beneath bravado.

Meanwhile, meet Imani Robinson—the oldest of seven siblings, a trauma-made rebel. A teen mom and the first to test the waters of independence, she believed she had to fend for herself. A creative soul, she sought solace in music, men, and misery, all built on a foundation of trauma. She traveled the world, searching for healing, leaving behind the true cure—her beautiful baby girl, her family, and God. Her journey was filled with emotional highs and devastating lows, often masking her pain behind laughter and lyrics.

Some would ask, *"How did these two come together?"* Well, I'm glad you asked.

After years of traveling and performing, Imani found herself weary—not of doing good, but of running. She longed to return to the spiritual foundation planted in her heart as a child. That search led her to St. Louis—a city known for birthing great artists and innovators, with a slower pace that allowed her to be just far enough from family while still engaging as desired. There, she found a great recording studio and a seemingly good man—a PK (preacher's kid) and producer. He became her husband, and she quickly moved her baby girl in, believing she had finally found her fairytale.

But soon, her dream turned into an emotional Alcatraz. What began as a fantasy quickly morphed into a nightmare cloaked in manipulation and control. During this season, she gave birth to another beautiful daughter, yet suffered abuse, betrayal, and a near-death experience that left emotional and physical scars. She barely escaped. In her heart and mind, she vowed never to marry again. Her trust in people—and especially in men—was shattered. The idea of love seemed like a cruel joke.

Then came Sredrick Robinson.

On a trip to St. Louis with his buddies, Sredrick decided to call an old friend who had moved from Iowa to Missouri years prior. He wanted to show his friends a good time, and that friend knew just who to call. That's how Imani entered the picture. At first, she was disinterested, still recovering from trauma and hyper-vigilant about her surroundings. She went along with the evening but barely engaged, her guard sky-high. By the time she made it home at 4 a.m., her phone was ringing. It was Sredrick.

Annoyed, she picked up, ready to shut him down. Before he could get a word in, she made it clear—she had long outgrown the booty-call era. After five minutes of lecturing him about class and respect, Sredrick softly replied, *"I just wanted to make sure you made it home safely."* Imani was speechless. After a pause, she gently said, *"Thank you,"* and hung up.

From that night on, they talked every day. Texts turned into phone calls, and phone calls into video chats. Conversations got deeper, laughter came easier, and walls began to crumble. Soon, Sredrick relocated to St. Louis, believing something real and worth fighting for had begun.

Their journey was not an easy one. Before tying the knot, they went through extensive premarital counseling, facing hard lessons and deep self-examination. They had to look themselves in the mirror and confront the baggage they each brought. Together, they brought nine children into their union—four daughters and five sons—along with a whole lot of trauma, trust issues, and past wounds.

Trust. That was the biggest hurdle. Imani had two children by two different men. Sredrick had seven children by five different women. The struggle was real. Their reality wasn't glamorous, but it was honest. They wondered: *How could they build a life and support their family?* Both were educated, passionate, and determined—but their pasts made certain opportunities hard to come by.

As they continued counseling with Pastor Rod Walker, they grew closer to God and each other. They realized their past did not define them—God was a God of second chances. And third. And fourth. They began to truly believe that He would provide.

But faith without works is dead. They needed action. They committed to making Jesus the Lord over their lives—not just in word, but in action and attitude.

They prayed for direction, and soon, God led them back to their passion—serving youth in their community. They started by hosting safe spaces for young people to gather, have fun, and engage in community-building activities. They offered snacks, mentorship, and encouragement. What started as a handful of kids turned into dozens.

The deeper they grew in faith, the more involved they became in church. Then, an opportunity arose—one that would change everything.

A door opened for them to reopen their cleaning business, **Sparkle Like Diamonds**. This time, it was different. This time, they were building something together, not just for financial security, but for ministry. They employed people from under-resourced communities, providing jobs while discipling those in need. They created a culture of grace, dignity, and excellence.

Contracts came and went, but God's peace remained steady. His Word was engraved in their hearts. They were truly living out their faith— together. Business became ministry. Cleaning homes became touching hearts. They used every mop, broom, and opportunity to reflect Christ.

After a year, Sredrick was offered a position at a children's home. He worked tirelessly to provide for his family. But despite his honesty about his past and holding a master's degree in human services, he was let go. The past, it seemed, still had consequences. Paperwork couldn't erase prejudice.

But God was not done. Shortly after, a new opportunity arose at another children's home—this time, with better pay and excellent benefits. It was more than a job—it was a divine setup.

At the time, they had only one vehicle. They did whatever was neces- sary, including waking up the children at midnight to pick up their family hero from work. They made sacrifices, knowing the long nights would one day lead to brighter mornings.

Meanwhile, Imani was taking online college courses, advancing in ministry leadership and development. She completed her master's degree in psychology while still managing the cleaning company, serving in church, and being a hands-on mother. Her days were full, but her spirit was fueled by purpose.

Life was moving forward, but challenges persisted. A leaking roof in their apartment. Over half of their income going to child support and

health insurance. Another two job transitions for Sredrick. And then—
a miscarriage. A silent pain, carried deeply and privately. Yet, they pressed on.

What kept them going?

A solid foundation in Christ, a supportive church family, and an amazing marriage coach. Their coach, who was also their pastor and spiritual father, didn't just mentor them—he trained them. He taught them to know the Bible, follow the Bible, apply the Bible, live the Bible, and, above all, obey the Bible.

For twelve years, Sredrick and Imani served faithfully under Pastor Rod Walker before being ordained together as pastors. Today, they serve as Pastor and Co-Pastor of **Love In Action Inc.**—a ministry dedicated to being *"the church without walls."*

All the past pain, hurt, injustices, and bad decisions? They were all part of a greater plan—**God's divine purpose.**

Love In Action is more than a ministry. It's a **movement**. It provides resources, care, and empowerment to under-resourced and vulnerable children and families throughout St. Louis, Metro East, and even to 25 families in Ghana.

That global reach started with one family.

A family that had relocated to Ghana seeking a fresh start and cultural reconnection found themselves trapped in an unexpected web of difficulty—limited resources, no support, and looming desperation. Through a divine connection, they were referred to Love In Action. What began as a one-time act of compassion became a divine calling.

Sredrick and Imani guided that family through every step of returning to the States—coordinating travel, helping with documentation, offering emotional support, and creating a reintegration plan. Through the process, they saw a need: families who had tried to return to their roots needed help returning to stability. Love In Action stepped into that gap and, before long, became known as **repatriation specialists.**

One family turned into five. Five into ten. Today, twenty-five families in Ghana have received assistance—spiritual, emotional, and logistical—through the faithful hands and hearts of Love In Action.

From city streets to global outreach, their love story isn't just about romance. It's about **redemption.**

It's about **legacy.**

It's about **obedience to God's call**—no matter how unlikely the path.

Through every storm, God has remained faithful. Their story is living proof that broken people can be healed, that wounded hearts can love again, and that God can use anyone for His glory.

If you want to learn more about Love In Action and follow the work God is doing, visit **www.loveinactionstl.org**.

Imani Robinson is a multifaceted professional dedicated to faith, service, and community empowerment. As the founder of Love In Action, she serves under-resourced children and families while advocating for social change. A wife, mother, and godmother, she balances family life with her impactful work as an author, public speaker, singer, pastor, and human rights consultant.

Her book, It's *My Absolute Pleasure*, guides readers in service and giving. Passionate about wellness, she introduces Redlight therapy and ionized water to her community. With a doctorate in divinity and certification from DeVos Urban Leadership Initiative, she is committed to spiritual and societal development.

Alongside her husband, Imani is raising her godson, showing resilience after the tragic loss of his father to gun violence. Known for her warmth and compassion, she continues to uplift others through faith-driven leadership and advocacy.

Look for Imani's new book—coming Fall 2025.

Please scan the QR code to connect with this author.

Betsy Simpkins

You Do You

"You do you!"

This phrase was the last thing one of my good friends, advocates, business partners, and collaborators said to me as we hung up the phone. So, with that said, this is a story about me—a once broken, now put-back-together, strong, beautiful, wise human whose life is a testament to the goodness of God.

It's the age-old question: What is the meaning of life? Why are we here?

We spend our lives in relationships, jobs, places, and events. It's a journey—a beautiful, messy mix of problems, deadlines, mountaintops, valleys, and scenic moments. We're all heading toward our own promised land, a place created for our enjoyment and purpose. And yes, there are giants along the way. But with God, those giants are no more than grasshoppers. Remember, David conquered Goliath not with a sword, but with five stones and the confidence that God was on his side.

I suspect that you, the one reading this, have asked similar questions. Maybe that's why you picked up this book—to draw inspiration and find clarity for your own journey. My prayer is that, through my story and the stories of others like mine, something powerful will rise within you. That you will begin to discover who God created you to be, because once you do, you'll never want to be anyone else.

God has already laid the trail before us. So, step forward, not because we're enough, but because **God is**. If we look closely, we'll see the path illuminated. He factors in every failure, provides for every need, and presents us with opportunities that are there for the taking.

My story begins in 1970, born into an affluent home in St. Louis, Missouri. But it was far from perfect. I never experienced a "normal" family. We had dysfunction—at its finest. My mom was a single parent, a broken woman trying to figure out life without the tools she needed.

I know many of you can relate. It's hard, isn't it? There are no perfect parents, but having even one who is present, grounded, and whole makes a difference. I knew my reality wasn't ideal, but it was mine. And to cope, I learned to dream.

My dreaming happened on a swing in our basement—a cleverly hung seat from the rafters. That swing was my sanctuary. I would get lost for hours, imagining a home filled with love, laughter, and faith. My dream home had a mom and dad who led with love. I believed in God, even though I hadn't met Jesus yet.

As I grew up, my dreams became more focused. I imagined being married, having children, decorating a cozy home. I wanted to create what my mama couldn't. I found joy working with children, and by age fourteen, I had a babysitting job every weekend. I loved it.

It felt so natural to go to college and become an Early Childhood Educator. I landed my first teaching job in 1994, and as a young married mama, I became "Mrs. Simpkins, first-grade teacher." I was living the dream. I was checking all the boxes—marriage, motherhood, a fenced-in yard, a steady career.

It was during this season of dreaming that I met the man I would fall madly in love with. He was kind, funny, and had a heart that made me feel safe. We built a life together, and he became the father of my children. I was head-over-heels, filled with hope that we would create the kind of home I had once imagined from that swing in the basement. Though our story eventually led to divorce, I want to honor him here, as the father of my children and a part of the foundation God used to grow my family and shape my journey.

But then the terrain changed. And it was rough.

I was checking off one goal after another, determined to blaze a trail and always in a hurry. It made sense, it went with my life, it seemed so perfect. Mrs. Simpkins, Early Childhood Educator! Fun, but firm. Creative and full of a million ways I was going to change the world.

One child at a time.

Slow down, Betsy…but slowing down was not on my radar. My dream? Check, check, check.

But—then comes disillusionment. Or, to stick with the path analogy… get ready. The terrain ahead is not for the faint of heart. **Buckle up, buttercup!**

Let's go back to where my dream began, on a swing.

That swing was a soothing escape, where I would get so lost in my dream that I'd forget the horror I was living in. I spent hours planning the life I wanted to create, and in so many ways, that swing helped save my life. It was there I learned to hope.

But what I didn't learn was how to deal with stress.

Now I was married. I had a mortgage, a child, a husband, and even a fenced-in yard. I came home to housework, responsibility, and an extremely busy little boy named Andy, who was my entire world. The creation of a human being that my little girl heart had dreamed about so many years before.

He was my busy little toddler, and I was going to empower him to reach his full potential.

Hold on… this is harder than I thought. I need to escape. But where?

I remember the moment like it was yesterday. *One drink. That will help.* As I reached into the refrigerator, a very small voice I was trying hard not to listen to whispered, "This is not a good idea." I quickly pushed it away with an arrogant, self-righteous attitude: *I am better than my mom. I'm not like her. Nope. I want relief, and I'm going to get it.*

Life. Stress. Decisions. Mistakes. Jobs. People. Places. Things. I had gotten what I wanted—my dream had come true right in front of my eyes. So why was I so miserable?

Baby number two came in 1996. I was in my second year of teaching and now had a little girl, a sweet bundle of joy with a completely different personality. This passionate, red-headed baby named Sarah was stubborn. She was sassy. And she gave me a run for my money. I quickly learned to empower her with small choices, to give her a sense of control, all while keeping up with a four-year-old who had the strength of Samson.

I needed relief.

In 2001, my journey took another turn. I had moved school districts and was once again ready to change the world—one child at a time! Two kids, a fenced-in yard, an established career—I had everything I wanted. Check, check, check.

Slow down, Betsy.

That same year, after browsing some display homes for decorating ideas, we made an impulsive decision and put money down on a lot. We were going to build our forever home. That year also brought another job change. After seven years of teaching, I was finally going to my dream district.

I was home. I had arrived.

In 2003, we welcomed our youngest son, Caleb. I named him after the Caleb in the Bible—strong, bold, and full of faith—the one who entered the promised land with Joshua. He was my third child, and another check off the list of dreams fulfilled.

In 2005, I gave birth to my fourth and final child, Rebecca. Her name means "to bind" or "tie firmly," and she was the last beautiful piece of the family I had always dreamed of building.

I remember it like it was yesterday. The night before Good Friday, 2014, my oldest child, now twenty-one, came crawling into the room because his leg hurt so badly, he couldn't walk.

A week later, we had a cancer diagnosis.

I was running around, trying to make sense of what was happening. My coping skills at that point were heavy medication. I didn't see a problem—after all, the doctor knew what she was doing. Medicine was the answer, and I was functioning just fine. My house was in order. My kids were provided for. But a cancer diagnosis? That was too much.

How could You, God? How dare You? I needed relief.

This story isn't about my son's cancer diagnosis. It's about finding purpose.

We all live with different circumstances, each of us born with a unique set of gifts and talents, intentionally placed there by our Creator. We gain wisdom and depth through the experiences we endure—some fun, some painful.

It's taken me a long time to understand this: I was created for one thing—to stay in close relationship with Jesus.

He sends people to help guide me. He gives me His Word to grow in wisdom. He's gifted me with a beautiful, specific combination of talents and trials, and He has never stopped walking with me.

On December 20, 2017, I surrendered. And began, once more, the journey in front of me—one small, small step at a time.

Everything had been stripped away. I began to learn that my identity comes not from a title like teacher, mom, wife, or friend… not even from the possessions I had.

My identity lies in being a daughter of the Most High God. So I trust God and do the next thing.

Perseverance, stewardship, consistency, and willingness make an excellent vessel. God turns ashes into beauty. He weaves our mistakes so well into His plan that sometimes we blame Him for the very tragedy He's redeeming.

One small step led to the next, and today, as a real estate professional, I feel like I'm walking in my calling. Every job, every failure, every success—every twist and turn—has brought me to this moment. God has woven it all into a beautiful tapestry.

It's more than a job. It's a ministry. It's purpose. It's walking with people in transition, helping them find home, just like I longed for as a little girl on that swing. I haven't arrived. I'm still human, still learning, still silly and whimsical, full of dreams and ideas. But now, I slow down before I move forward. I pause and ask, "Lord, what do You want me to do next?"

If you're confused or unsure how to get from point A to point B, take your time. Ask questions. And if it doesn't feel right, it probably isn't. God is waiting for you to invite Him into the process. Sometimes the tasks He gives seem small or even meaningless. But remember, He trained David in the fields long before He placed a crown on his head. That same God took the most overlooked son, the shepherd boy with a sling, and made him king. And from David's line came the King of Kings.

His name is Jesus. And I wonder… have you asked Him?

My children are my miracles—my teachers—and proof that no season is wasted in the hands of a faithful God.

Romans 11:29 says, *"God's gifts and His call are irrevocable."* No matter how far you've wandered or how badly you think you've messed up, your purpose still stands. And *Esther 4:14* reminds us: You were created for such a time as this.

So, if you're standing at the edge of something new, if you feel uncertain or afraid, remember this:

Jesus is the Author and Finisher of your faith (*Hebrews 12:2*). He made you. He knows you. And He's just waiting for you to ask: **"What do You want me to do next, Lord?"**

Because that's where purpose begins.

Betsy Simpkins is a passionate encourager, teacher, and real estate professional whose life is a testimony to the redemptive power of Jesus Christ. A former early childhood educator turned purpose-driven entrepreneur, Betsy is called to guide and inspire the younger generation. Her heart beats to see youth rise, thrive, and succeed—one step at a time. Through her own journey of struggle, surrender, and restoration, she has learned that identity is not found in titles or accomplishments, but in being a daughter of the Most High God.

From the swing of her childhood dreams to the front doors of homes she now helps families walk through, Betsy carries the joy, wisdom, and whimsy that come from walking closely with Jesus. Her life is proof that no season is wasted, and that God truly does weave beauty from ashes.

She still asks daily, "Lord, what do You want me to do next?"

Please scan the QR code to connect with this author.

George Walker

Suit Up, Show Up, and Work Hard

"You are braver than you believe, stronger than you seem,
and smarter than you think."
~A.A. Milne

If there is anything that the recent global pandemic has taught me, it is to trust my gut and follow my instincts. My best friend, who always worries about me, would introduce me as a "Professional Job Hopper" whenever I would meet someone new and they asked me what I did for a living. And who could really blame him? I have had many different jobs. I think I was just waiting to find where I belonged and my purpose in this world.

My very first job began when I was a high school sophomore. I was fifteen years old in 1998, and I wanted a car when I turned sixteen. My parents told me I would be responsible for paying for half of my car, the insurance, and all the upkeep. I didn't really know what I wanted to do; I just knew I did not want to work in the fast-food industry like many of my friends and others our age. There was a skilled nursing facility down the street from my house that was looking for a dishwasher. Seemed like an easy enough job. Little did I know that this decision would come full circle for me as an adult.

I worked at that nursing home for over seven years. I would work part-time during the school year and full-time over the summer, all through high school and college. I fell in love with working with seniors. It felt like going to work with one hundred extra grandparents. Most of my time there was spent in the kitchen or dietary department. I was a dishwasher, server, and prep cook. I also worked in the activity department during my last couple of years there.

After college, it was time to get my first "big boy" job, and I became a high school English teacher. I had had such a wonderful high school experience, and when I needed to declare a major in college, becoming a teacher just seemed like the logical next step. I knew early on in my teaching career that I could not and would not teach forever. I taught for seven years, but in that time, I worked at three different schools and took a short break each time I left.

Unfortunately, teachers are not paid very well, so I always had a side hustle. Usually waiting tables and bartending during the evenings, weekends, and summer breaks. It was at one of these part-time bartending jobs that I found something else to try. One night, I stayed after the bar closed, talking and drinking with my boss, the owner. She was looking for a buyer because she wanted out of the business. "That sounds like fun!" And in a few months' time, I purchased the business and began operating my very own neighborhood bar and restaurant. I have never worked so physically hard in my life. The great thing that came out of this experience was that I was able to sell this business just twenty-three months later for a significant profit. This profit allowed me not only to adopt my beautiful son but also to stay at home with him for the first few years of his life.

I then went back into education but not as a classroom teacher. A friend of mine worked for a non-profit in St. Louis that helped underprivileged youth. My role was to manage before and after-school programs for students at multiple St. Louis public elementary schools. I didn't stay long in this position. A little over a year after starting, I left to purchase another restaurant.

This restaurant was in the next neighborhood over from where I lived. I naively thought that I would be able to manage the business the same way I had done before. Grow the business and sell for a profit in just a few short years. I was mistaken and ended up closing this business in less than two years, taking a significant loss.

What was I going to do now? Looking for work again, I became a General Manager for a pizza chain that was opening new stores in St. Louis. I only lasted nine months before I made the decision to go back to working with seniors.

I started working as a Business Office Director for an assisted living and memory care facility. I worked in this position for nine months before I left that facility to work as the Community Relations Manager for a private Home Care company. This position opened up a new concept that gave me the "sales bug" while working with seniors and their families. I left this company in less than a year, opting to work as an Assisted Living Sales Counselor for Friendship Village.

I really felt like I had found what I was supposed to do when I started working at Friendship Village. I felt supported, important, and valued. Friendship Village felt like home. I started this job in the beginning of April 2020, right at the beginning of the pandemic. I knew it would be challenging, and I welcomed that challenge. My job was to sell assisted living and memory care apartments to seniors and their adult children, but they were not allowed to enter the building for a tour due to the pandemic restrictions. I had to become creative and started conducting most of the selling over the phone, through email with floor plans, and provided virtual tours. The worst part was when I would move a new resident into the community, I couldn't tell their family when they would be allowed to visit as we did not know when it would be safe due to potential exposure risks to the elderly. The occupancy of my building was less than 75% when I started in April of 2020, and by July of 2021, it was 100% occupied with a decent waitlist. For the first time in a long time, I was thriving and excited to go to work every day. So, what do you think happened next?

Yes, I decided to leave. Not that I was unhappy, but it was the appropriate time for my family and me to move out of state, near a beach; something that we had been planning to do for some time. My family moved to Naples, Florida, where I began working at another continuum care retirement community as a Sales Director. I enjoyed my time in southwest Florida, but fate had other ideas for me. In January of 2023, my mother was diagnosed with a terminal illness, and my family and I decided to move back to St. Louis to be near her. I accepted a position as the Sales Director for a senior living community upon moving back.

After just three weeks, my previous boss called and said, "George, I hear you're back in town. I have a crazy idea I would like to speak to you about." A few weeks later, I was back at Friendship Village in the newly created role of Director, Talent Acquisition. They wanted a "sales approach" to recruiting. The pandemic has hurt many different businesses and industries, especially when it comes to finding reliable, qualified employees in elder care. My previous boss understood something about me that I didn't truly grasp about myself; they believed in me and my abilities, which allowed me to believe in myself.

I got to work, building this new position at Friendship Village. I reallocated funds and built the department from the ground up. When I arrived, much of my budget was being used to boost job openings on Monster, Indeed, and other similar job boards. Through much research and determination, I was quickly able to find a different programmatic partner, which increased the efficiency of my department's budget tenfold. My department went from spending around $14,000 per month on ads to just $3,000, and the quality of candidates I was finding were generally a much better fit.

Building the recruiting department involved handpicking my recruiting team. The philosophy and best practices I implemented were to take a sales approach and to be proactively recruiting. I started an external business development process for my team, requiring each of my staff to host an event every quarter and attend multiple off-site events every month. I also began and grew a partnership with the internal marketing team at Friendship Village, using our combined resources to revamp the "Careers" portion of our website. We created job-specific testimonials and promotional videos, as well as blogs, all of which could be sent out to prospective candidates. I implemented a new applicant tracking system that was more cost-effective and user-friendly for my recruiters and found an employee referral software that increased our employee referral program, making it easier for current Friendship Village employees to recruit for us.

After just fourteen months in this role, I was promoted to Senior Director, Talent Acquisition. I attribute this promotion to having new, fresh, out-of-the-box ideas when discovering and understanding how to attract top talent. My team and I hire approximately fifty-two new employees every month. In less than two years, I was responsible for saving over $1,000,000 in Friendship Village's operating costs. With fewer open positions, reliance on outside agencies and overtime had been minimized while enabling Friendship Village's communities to increase revenue with a full staff, something they were unable to do with the previous staffing challenges.

I helped build a better culture amongst the staff too, as evidenced by the reduction in the company's consolidated turnover rate, down to 37% from 46% since I was hired. Because of this decrease, the average employee's tenure increased. The average employee stays at Friendship Village for close to five years, an incredible number for a workforce whose makeup is 90% frontline employees. My hard work and dedication resulted in a nomination for and selection as the 2025 *St. Louis Business Journal's* HR Hero Award.

I have learned that fate will lead you to where you should be while providing many opportunities along the way. With each role I took on, what always remained consistent was to suit up, show up, and work hard, learning everything that you can from everyone that you can, and be ambitious. Don't let fear stop you from walking away from a job that is toxic, boring, or something you have outgrown. Every time I left one job for another, I always received a title bump and more money. You will find your place, even if you are not looking for it; even when you are not expecting it. A place where you will be free to grow, learn, thrive, and succeed. Be sure to tell your direct supervisor what is next for you. You may be surprised what the future has in store for you. Go after what you want!

George Walker was born in Long Beach, California, but calls St. Louis, Missouri, home since he moved there with his family when he was eight years old. He is passionate about helping people inside and outside of work. He is married and has three children. He goes to the beach every chance he gets; it's his happy place. When not working, George loves to read, listen to music, dance, travel, and experience new things with his family. His favorite thing to do is attend concerts and Broadway shows. He has lost count of how many concerts and shows he has attended. George has such a positive and infectious attitude that other people want to be near him. He wants everyone to know that great things happen when you suit up, show up, and work hard.

Please scan the QR code to connect with this author.

Erica Blomgren

Just Go for It!

Most of my career is more of a love story than a tragedy. Even the pandemic had some profoundly positive effects. But with reflection, there is certainly disruption that happens among the career journey, even without ever switching companies. A twenty-five-year career loyalty is a journey of disruption in and of itself. For me, it is one where new hope rises from change, and disruption is part of minimizing stagnation.

First, let's hit a few key points on me. I am an only child. Of an only child. Of an only child. All not by choice but by battles of infertility. And while I have three beautiful children, as genetics would have it, my road to parenthood started on a rocky path. Six years into the journey to start our family, and multiple losses later, our first son was born in 2009 to my husband and me. Our second child followed in 2011, and our family was completed with a third child in 2014. Becoming a mother of multiple children was my lifelong dream, and it was also a generational dream filled with emotion.

Now, let's intertwine this thing called work into the picture. I was offered and accepted a professional job before finishing my undergraduate degree in business and marketing at the University of Missouri in Columbia (Go Tigers!). Sure, I had done the lifeguarding and babysitting roles, but this was my first real job. I was headed into an office and could not be more excited! I chose to become a "recruiter" back when no one understood recruiters or recruiting agencies. In fact, when discussing potential opportunities, my dad said to me, "Companies have HR departments for that sort of thing, *and* this feels like it could be a pyramid scheme." Ironically, the logo of our company at that time was a pyramid, but I digress. The interview involved a half-day job shadowing, and I could see from the first moment that these were like-minded people; competitive individuals in pursuit of making a real difference. It felt like home even before I finished my first day.

I started with our organization, where I still reside today, as a bright-eyed college graduate ready to recruit IT professionals and make money so I could live on my own and go out in the evenings with friends. It was a simple life, and the motivations were pure and modest. As an only child, I was painfully shy and mostly a rule follower; thus, I did what I was told at work and home (my mother may challenge this). This served me well and, with some great partners and mentors, I thrived and was promoted to sales after success in the recruiting ranks. Sure, it was a grind, with moments of failure and questioning and what felt like lots of time in the office, but overall, it provided for my humble motivations and ability to make a difference in the lives of others. Good co-workers saved me in the most challenging moments.

Sales was a bit scary for a shy, only child, but recruiting gave me just enough confidence to give it a try. After a few failed attempts to avoid the opportunity, some of those great work partners pushed me and saw things that I didn't see in myself. As women, we hold ourselves back traditionally. I was traditional.

It was a great move at first, early success and opportunities to bring others along with me. But a few years into sales and three failed pregnancies, my fourth pregnancy resulted in a healthy child and changed things up. Office time was no longer my first priority, nor was being the top in sales, and I wondered if those areas in my life could ever co-exist. As I prepared to go back to work after maternity leave, I investigated options to work differently, as the hours I was working before were not going to work as a new mom. It was a bold moment for me and one of many disruptions. I put together a business plan to work four days a week in a company that had only approved this concept once before, and only for one singular person, a great mom, mentor, and friend of mine. I also worked for a company that valued in-office time more than most and still does! I proposed a compressed schedule and came to terms that this may not work. If it wasn't approved, I was prepared to break up my professional love affair. A decision that was tearing at me, but the tiny blue eyes of my newborn had me ready to do what I needed to do. After some negotiations, my plan was conditionally approved, and I felt a new hope and new life. I was going to be able to continue with my purpose of affording others with growth and opportunity, while being present at home. I was so very committed to meeting my expectations because those Fridays with my new son were worth the world to me! Perhaps, those worlds could in fact co – exist! **A bold move, followed by change, and inspiring so much hope for my future simply because I asked for it.**

There were often tears (from a girl who was taught to not cry in public) when I missed milestones at home because I was working. A work trip that required me to miss an event at school or home could also send me into a tailspin. And there were times when I questioned where I was supposed to be in life. I even journaled often about this, asking the Lord for answers. There is a little phrase often shared between my husband and me in these deep discussions, during times of questioning, *"the Lord always provides."* And while the answers are not always with full clarity in the times when I am searching, He does provide clarity. My husband has also pushed me in these times of searching, when I didn't like the course of the career road I am traveling, to take ownership and change the direction myself. I like to think that I have urged him the same way. We both have a strong belief in controlling what you can control, and I've often shared the quote once shared with me, *"Life is 10% what happens to you and 90% how you respond"* (Charles R. Swindoll). One of those bumps came in a work travel request that conflicted with my son's mid-week birthday. I was given honest feedback that I needed to make it happen when I requested to miss the scheduled event. I begrudgingly agreed and ended up having a successful work trip and a successful birthday party the following weekend. The point is that not all my asks have gotten a yes. It's not a perfect story, but no love story really is.

With some bumps along the way, success continued. After twelve years in the organization, I interviewed and earned the title and role of leading the operations for the St. Louis market. The Director role is where I found the craziest amount of stress, along with the most professional fulfillment I've ever had. At one point, I was leading a team of eighty-five individuals serving a regional marketplace and winning in the market-place by adding new clients and growing relationships each and every year. As a team, we promoted leaders to move across the country to run their own teams, and the St. Louis market became known for its talent pipeline. What it meant to me was that there were opportunities for people who had become some of my closest friends to make a great life for them-selves and their families. I was witness to marriages, new homes and cars, babies, and so much more because coworkers dedicated themselves to our organization through great attitudes, relationships, and hard work. How lucky was I to be able to advocate and provide growth and opportu-nity for those who were my best friends?! This is where I realized that my true passion and purpose were around advocating and pushing others, the way I had been pushed for the better. Making an impact by providing growth and opportunity for others, as it had been provided for me.

Commence pandemic. We were abruptly at home with a kindergartener, a second grader, and a fourth grader. And it's important to mention that my incredible husband of twenty-one years is also in sales, selling private aircraft globally. By the way, good luck winning your kids over that you have the coolest job ever when your husband sells airplanes! He is also the best salesperson I have ever met in my life, which is an interesting trait when it begins to manifest itself in your teens.

My company began to operate our recruitment business from basements and kitchen tables across the area. And surprisingly, companies invested quickly in additional personnel to keep their own businesses operating, an unexpected business opportunity amidst the tragedy. *Boom!* We were the best of the best in quickly finding personnel to solve business needs, as a large team of recruiters with history in the market that spanned decades. We did just that, putting people looking for work into positions to earn an income. I was afforded the opportunity to fulfill my true purpose for people in my company, and people we were placing, giving growth and opportunity for others. While I was working upstairs, I could hear the sweet sounds of my husband teaching our youngest child how to read at the kitchen table. I will never forget that moment. I will also never forget making lunch with our party of five daily, taking walks with the dog together, and checking homework every evening. I won't forget the daily drop-offs and pickups at my parents' house so they could be the homeschool teachers for one grandchild, every day. And bringing home the daily treats they baked up in Grammie's kitchen! The moments and memories made during the pandemic were those that last a lifetime. It was finally the perfect marriage of my desire to successfully climb the career ladder *and* be the present mom I've spent my whole life dreaming about. It was bliss.

When the time came to come back into the office and the kids were fully back at school, it left me in a quandary and caused gut-wrenching reflection. I had more tears and questions than my journals could hold. I was battling financial questions, sleepless nights filled with worry, and so much emotion. After many conversations with family and friends, I was acutely aware that my time had come to hang it up and break up this nineteen-year career. To try something new. Again, I was emboldened to take a stance. But this time I didn't have a proposal or a plan. I just had a desire to be more present at home than I could be if I were in an office early and late each day. I had bold conversations with my supervisor and others I trusted at work again, even with the risk that the decisions could end this professional love affair. I was honest, but I was also realistic. Some tasks needed to be completed in person, I knew that fact along with what my desires were. I had conversations that led me to flexibility in exchange for travel. I was afforded an opportunity again to try something new and see if I could win in a different way. I became a national leader for a team in the transportation industry, much of what could be done virtually with a new opportunity to see different places of the world. **A bold move, followed by change, and inspiring so much hope for my future simply because I asked for it.**

In the years that followed my promotion, I have been afforded additional opportunities to lead and grow, while also being the mother, wife, daughter, and granddaughter (yes, I am lucky enough to still be a granddaughter too) that I want to be. As I reflect upon finding my purpose through my professional career, my advice is to be bold. Don't be afraid of change. Take control of your path while being realistic with yourself about what matters most. There is so much out there that this world has to offer, but you have to ask for it. And as females, we sometimes need an extra reminder not just to ask, but to really go for it!

Erica Blomgren, an Indiana-born Hoosier, was raised in Missouri, where she is currently residing with her husband of twenty-one years, three amazing children, and a golden retriever. She is fortunate to live just miles from her parents and childhood home and has a "family first" philosophy. In her spare time, she loves to be on the water with family, attending youth sporting events, or reading a good book. Erica seamlessly blends her career ambitions with her commitment to those she loves the most.

Please scan the QR code to connect with this author.

Amanda Kendall

Embrace the Disruption

There are so many uncertainties in life, but the one thing that is certain is that change will come, and normally, change happens when we least expect it. Change can often catch us by surprise.

My entire life has been marked with one disruption after another. My family moved five times within the first ten years of life. My parents divorced when I was five years old, with my father moving out of state; my father battled alcoholism and lacked parenting skills, to say the least. I got married young (best decision of my life), had two beautiful biological kids, and later adopted two sweet kiddos. Another disruption came when my daughter was just eight years old and was diagnosed with a brain tumor. My husband would later battle kidney and Lyme disease.

Disruption has always found a way to my doorstep. What helped me through every challenge that came my way was to simply embrace what was happening and walk through it. We either get to be active participants in our journey, or we become the victims. Victors face challenges head-on! Whether uncomfortable, hard, sorrowful, or dreadful, it doesn't matter. Disruption is all the same—after all, it is disruption. Disruption is new, unfamiliar, and can suck! Embrace it, face the fear head-on, and don't allow it to consume you.

In 2020, I found myself in a very unpredictable, unfamiliar situation. We, as a nation, faced a major disruption. I went from a full schedule of hustling in between work, personal commitments, and my kids' school and sports activities to a dead halt. Everything had shut down, everything had stopped, and no one was going into the office. Going out in public was extremely limited, and there certainly were no extra activities. In the chaos of facing the unknown, I found myself being still for the first time in years. I took this time to personally reflect all the way back to my childhood. I reevaluated my passions, my desires. I reflected on every area of my life that brought me energy, as well as the areas in my life that were emotionally draining me. I had certainty within my role at work—my career was comfortable, familiar, safe. I was so grateful for the relationship that I had with the founder of our company. He supported me in working from home prior to the pandemic, while raising four children, two of whom had been recently adopted. I had grown so much in my career and my personal development while working at the brokerage firm. I experienced four promotions within four years and reached the ceiling of what my career field could offer.

While my career had extensively accelerated, and the achievement felt great for a moment, I found myself unchallenged. I knew there was no next move—I was at the dead end. The choice was to stay and be content, do what was comfortable, or pursue what was possible. I knew change would potentially come with disruption, along with a disruption in my income. Change would also come with a disruption in my flexibility. Being stagnant within a career comes with a cost, too. I talk to people every day who are burned out in their careers and are very aware that they need to make a change, yet they're unwilling to take a chance on themselves. Most people have become comfortable with being comfortable. They stop challenging themselves, they stop growing personally and professionally. We all get one life, and we get to decide what legacy we leave and what standard we are setting for those around us. Are you inspiring the world around you? Have you given up on yourself? Have you set your own limits and restrictions? Let's be honest with each other. No one is stopping any of us from progressing in our careers or personal lives; we often are the ones who put on our own restraints.

After years of being with the same company, I decided to remove the restraints that I had put on myself. I decided to take a chance on myself, which, honestly, felt uncomfortable at first. I drafted my résumé and a cover letter and applied to multiple job boards. I was unsure if I was ready to take a step of faith or not. Was I ready to be open to a new career? I decided to explore what was possible. A few weeks after I began my job search, a recruiter reached out from a financial firm in St. Louis asking if I was open to having a conversation.

After several conversations, a vision ignited a desire within me to partner with a company that believed that bringing impact to the lives of other people was a top priority. It wasn't just about how much money they could make; it was more important to help people become more financially secure, to develop people in their careers, and see them live their lives by design.

From an early age, I was raised in an environment where community service and giving back were a priority. I had seen lives changed by someone reaching out and helping another person, and I knew that if I could find a career that aligned with that vision of impact, with the desire of bringing change to the lives of other people, that the rest would be history.

Here I am, almost three years after starting my business, and I have never looked back. Not once! While change can be scary, new, uncomfortable, and unfamiliar, change can also feel igniting. Over my career, I have talked to thousands of individuals who have found themselves in the middle of a career disruption that they were unprepared for—laid off or intentionally pursuing other avenues. I often ask people, "Who is the one person in your life that you were able to lean into to be coached and developed?" They normally look at me with a blank stare. Finding people who have invested in you professionally, personally, or spiritually is a rarity. Many companies offer a growth track, claiming to coach and develop you within a career. However, finding a company that will create a plan of action and a pathway to be developed while putting action behind words is another thing. I have absolute conviction that every person deserves a career path. To all the women reading this and thinking, you're talking to me! I see *you*!

Women desire to be shown what's possible; women also prefer a high level of communication and detail. Creating a career for yourself where you have the control makes a huge impact to you and your family. If you have settled for what's available to you in this season and lost the vision to see what's possible, I want to encourage you to challenge yourself.

If you find yourself in a place of disruption in life, don't lose courage and strength. God always has a plan, and sometimes it takes disruption to make room for your true purpose to be revealed.

It was through the heat of the pandemic that I spent time reflecting on my career discussions and my spiritual life. My family had plans of moving to Tennessee, so we booked a trip, met with a realtor, and were ready to put an offer on a house (that we *loved* by the way). We quickly found out that a move wasn't what God intended. We encountered another disruption and decided to stay rooted locally. In that time frame of pausing, waiting, and praying, we sought the Lord's will in our lives. We felt that another disruption would come, and we weren't exactly sure what it would be. We went from attending a large, well-organized church with a ton of people to planting a church. I never imagined that we would be pastoring, and now here we are ministering to the lives of others weekly. God knew that there was a purpose, and he had a plan all along. I had to remove myself from making all the decisions and trust that the Lord knew what was best for us.

Doing something new, unfamiliar, and uncomfortable can feel daunting. I remember having so many answers and questions through our transition. What do you do when you walk a journey for the first time, and no one is around to give you the answers you need? I had to learn to trust in God. Proverbs 3:5 says to *"Trust in the Lord with all of your heart and lean not on your own understanding; in all of your ways submit to him, and he will make your paths straight."*

I believe that life is worth living, that each of us has been given a unique skill and gift. Going to bed tired, waking up tired, driving to an office, and dreading the day should not be the norm. There are tools available that can assess your strengths and areas of interest to help you determine a direction in finding a purpose. I would remind you that you deserve a career where you can thrive and be fulfilled. I hope that you challenge yourself to dream and pursue what is possible!

Amanda Kendall is a wife and a mother to four beautiful children. She has a bachelor's degree in theology and a bachelor's degree in business management. Amanda is a public speaker, development coach, growth partner, and market leader. When not doing ministry or working, Amanda enjoys spending time at the beach, traveling with family, spending time outdoors, and investing in the lives of others. She fully believes that God deserves all credit for anything good within her. Her husband is her loudest cheerleader, her partner in life, and her best friend. Amanda's four beautiful children are her "why," and she loves them very much.

Please scan the QR code to connect with this author.

Jake Kline

Buy a Ticket

"Are you ready?" my mom asked. "Yes, let's get it over with," I responded. We descended the stairs from the main floor to our basement. As we walked to our destination, the concrete floor made my bare feet feel as if we were wading through water. We opened the washing machine lid and dug in, wringing the water from our clothes as we carried them out of the basin. The agitator on our washing machine went out, and we needed to wring out the extra water in the clothes before placing them into the dryer. My fingertips began to lose color as they continued to interact with the water. Meanwhile, the detergent seeped through the cracks of my hands. The smaller clothing articles swam around the basin, retracting to the walls of the washing machine as we plunged our hands into the water.

It was a dry and windy winter, which withered away the moisture from my hands when exposed to the cold air. The temperature had been below freezing for some time, and my hands stood no match for the elements. My dried-out hands would crack and bleed. The water from the washing machine infiltrated the cracks, reopening the cracks and causing them to bleed. To prevent blood droplets from getting onto our clean clothes, we pushed our palms out while our fingers pulled back, wringing the clothing in a retracting motion. Between the swooshing of the water, my mom pointed out, "This is why you go to college. This is why I want you to have a career versus two jobs. Don't live paycheck to paycheck." We fished out the remaining socks and closed the lid with a resounding echo.

Ten years later, the stage was set for the prophesied chapter in my life. I had timed my college credits so I could spend time with friends I made along the way. Each of the school organizations I was involved in were personal interests of mine. It was a welcome pace in comparison to the past seven semesters of college. After finishing my Spanish minor, my final semester was academically committed to my economics major.

On March 5, 2023, my friend and I were doing another all-nighter, where we would stay up until 5 a.m., mostly doing schoolwork. My friend turned to me, asking how he could see what credits he had completed. I said "Sure, I'll show you." The website showed the requirements necessary to graduate. On my digital transcript, most of my boxes were checked off as completed, since it was my final semester. As I scrolled through my transcript, I exclaimed, "I found it." In my peripheral vision, my friend was concentrating on a sports game score. My eyes were not distracted when they landed on two unchecked boxes that showed incomplete.

I thought it was a mistake. I enrolled in enough economics classes, didn't I? Where did I go wrong? I walked through each credit on the transcript, matching a class and semester to it. My econometrics class did not count for both the required and additional credit categories; it would only count for one of the two. My blood drained from my back as if I had taken a cold shower. My fingers started to freeze up.

"Can you show me where that website is?" My body unstiffened as I turned toward him.

"Yeah, not a problem." As I walked him through the process, my mind was elsewhere. I was ten weeks out from graduation. With three clubs and four classes, I did not have time to spare. I could not get the funding for another semester; this was it. There was no other way but to jump into a class halfway through the semester. I would have to bring my efforts to another level. I did not come this far to fail.

I called the night early and tried to gather myself for what was next. My health and response being the only two things I could control. It was 3 a.m., so there was nothing more I could do until I woke up. I took a shower and sent an email to my advisor for an emergency meeting. My advisor set up two reading classes where I could finish my remaining three credits. It added an extra 1,700 pages and required me to write five essays, a daunting task with less than six weeks left in the semester.

Down the stretch, I had issues with concentrating. The work had become monotonous. When I worked in the dorm halls, I noticed parents helping students return home for the summer. In the academic buildings, I could see graduating students pose for photos along sets of stairs or verdant plant life. I needed to reduce the distractions. In the study room, I turned my desk parallel to the windowsill, so my back was facing the one window where students walked by, significantly assisting me with the reading classes.

With less than two weeks left, I still had 1,500 pages to read, work with clubs, and my Spanish linguistic test. The deck felt stacked. To help myself out, I negotiated the deadline for the final essays to be due at 7 a.m. on Monday, May 8, a little over a day after my graduation ceremony. One night, I sat down at my desk. To clear any doubt, I rummaged around for a sticky note and tore the top sticky note off the stack. I inscribed "I will graduate." I held the sticky note up to the lamplight and palmed it into my planner. I admired it for a moment and turned off my lamp.

Graduation day started at 11 a.m. on Saturday, and I was up and running off of adrenaline. After some photos with friends, I headed towards the auditorium, where I took the time to appreciate the feeling of graduating. A black gown draped across me with an honor cord resting gently against my neck alongside a strap holding a medal for cum laude.

The ceremony came and went. When I got back to the hotel, I knew I would not graduate without passing the final reading class, even though I had already walked the stage.

I spent another night in silence, pulling quotes together for the final three essays of the game theory class. I read some small articles and finished the first and second essays. Around 3 a.m., I was feeling very tired. The screen light had a nice warm feel to it as it shone on my face. The text itself seemed to have less meaning with each character. Regardless of the looming deadline, I felt very calm. I caught my eyes shutting several times in a row. It was not the first time I felt like napping on a long night. I pulled myself together and reminded myself of what the purpose of that night was. I finished my final essay at 6:04 a.m. I graduated.

Oddly enough, it was only the first part of my mom's lesson I had completed. I earned a degree in economics, and I was going to use it. To my surprise, my school organizational work and education were not enough. During one of the applications I submitted, there were people with MBAs applying to the same role. It appeared that other students also believed their education would speak for itself when it came to being hired. It felt as if the train of opportunity had left the station, and I was caught sleeping in the station because I had overlooked the importance of internships. In college, I assumed they were only for earning money over the summer, in which money was never a concern with my low expenses. With the pandemic, experience opportunities were not abundant, and my spring school workloads were never light.

The hiring managers did not get back to me instantly, so I researched industries and discovered ways to be relevant in some of my career interests. I continued to interview for jobs, but my lack of working in a professional setting seemed to get in the way of the experience-based job market. With each rejection, I evolved my cover letter and resume writing. My family began searching for job opportunities for me; however, none of them worked out. By the end of the summer, my family seemed defeated in the search. The job search made me feel inadequate at times, but I knew the timing between the employer and me was misaligned at that moment.

I attended local networking events and was referred to one where their purpose was helping people find jobs. The group was known as the Job Seekers' Garden Club (JSGC). The Garden Club showed me that anyone can be unemployed regardless of age or experience. It was not reassuring, but it showed the importance of reinventing yourself and how it is never too late to find a new opportunity. The Garden Club emphasized job rejections are not rejections of you as a person, maintaining a positive attitude toward the search. At each meeting, there would be a presenter and sufficient time to engage with other attendees. The best part for me was the elevator pitch we had to give each meeting, since it helped me consolidate what about myself and my skills I wanted to share with others in the room. After all, it would let people know who I am, what I have accomplished, where I came from, which goals I have, and why I am at the event.

One Sunday at church, my priest told a story about a man who wanted to win the lottery. The man prayed on it each day; however, he never won. The man eventually lashed out at God, exclaiming, "Why won't you let me win the lottery?" God replied, "Then buy a ticket."

I decided my ticket was helping people. In the past, I tutored friends and strangers in over twenty-five different subjects. This time, I offered resume and cover letter writing advice, which eventually landed jobs for some of my close friends. At this point, I would go to networking events with the mindset of not finding a job but helping who I can, from professional development skills to business model consulting. I found purpose in utilizing my skills to grow together with those around me. I began to lose myself in helping others. Through service, I remembered how effective I could be in working to identify and achieve goals.

In September 2023, I found a role where I could thrive and develop. The interview process did not go through four rounds; there was responsiveness on both sides, and it was personable. During my first day of training, we met with our senior management team in a conference room. Each person was given the opportunity to talk about themselves as they went around the table. My training class was a little nervous, explaining themselves in depth or very little. Thanks to attending over six JSGC events, I stood up with a clear voice and introduced myself, covering my background, what the company and I could accomplish, and enough time for a little joke.

If you ever find yourself on a path that you did not expect, learn to accept that your path may be different, despite being able to achieve the same goal. You may set out with an end goal, but find out the journey itself taught you more. Each of our timelines is different in when and how we come across our milestones. If you are consistent, you will find success. When you put yourself in a situation where you continue to learn from each attempt, it makes it hard for others to doubt you and, more importantly, for you to doubt yourself. My education did not give me my purpose; rather, the summer of 2023 showed me how I can ascend to the next level.

Jake Kline is a Saint Louis native who prioritizes his time with his family and friends. As the big brother of three siblings, Jake could not be more thankful. Jake earned a degree in Economics and a minor in Spanish from Truman State University. Jake continues to volunteer with the Job Seekers' Garden Club, now as treasurer, as well as a board member with Junior Achievement, a non-profit helping kids with professional development and financial literacy. You may see Jake on roller skates or in shoes practicing hockey, but the same cannot be said for ice skates. When he is not working up a sweat, Jake enjoys reading and playing card games. He laughs often because sometimes the world is too serious. Jake enjoys setting other people up for success so they can reach their potential.

Please scan the QR code to connect with this author.

Angela Russell

Defining Myself Outside of My Title

One morning, the CEO of our company invited me and many of my colleagues to a virtual meeting. As I logged in, I had no idea that my life was about to change. In that meeting, we learned that due to redundancy after an acquisition, we were no longer going to be part of the company—mass layoffs. My thoughts became a blur, my mind racing with questions about what this meant for me, my family, and my future. As the CEO and Human Resources team spoke, it was as if all I could hear was the muffled, unintelligible voice of an adult from a Charlie Brown cartoon.

I was shocked. I was what was known as a company loyalist, someone who stayed with one company for years to continue that upward progression and growth through the company. I had assumed that after the merger, my colleagues and I would be given opportunities for growth. I had been holding on, waiting for what was to come, believing in a future within the company. I had envisioned career progression, new challenges, and an expanding role. But instead, I was faced with a void, an uncertainty that left me reeling.

When meeting someone new, we often ask, "What do you do for work?" Our jobs become intertwined with our identities. As my mind raced and the weeks passed, I began to wonder, who am I without my work and job title? This confusion was unsettling. I didn't know how to introduce myself anymore or explain what I did in those polite conversations. It felt as though a fundamental part of me had been stripped away.

I had poured years into my career, developing skills, gaining experience, and taking pride in my contributions towards the success of the company. My work was not just about a paycheck; it was about purpose, direction, and self-worth. Without it, I felt lost. Who was I outside of my role? What was my value if I wasn't contributing to a company's overall success in the same way?

Determined to regain my footing, I began networking, creating connections, and treading in the rough job market waters. Initially, I approached networking with a single goal in mind—finding a new job. But as I spoke with people at the networking events, something unexpected happened. The conversations began to shift away from resumes and open positions and toward more profound topics: our lives, our passions, our dreams beyond work.

The more I listened, the more I realized that I wasn't alone, and other people had faced similar crossroads. Some had changed careers entirely, discovering new passions they never had time to explore before. Others had built businesses, turned hobbies into professions, or found fulfillment in community work. These conversations opened my eyes to the possibility that my career, though important, was not the sole measure of my identity or success.

At work, my purpose had been to communicate company initiatives, values, and missions to employees, helping them connect the dots and see the bigger picture while providing them with the tools and resources they needed to succeed. I had found fulfillment in creating clarity and fostering engagement. But now, I asked myself a deeper question: What was my purpose outside of that job? What was I truly meant to do?

The question haunted me. During the 2020 pandemic, the world was forced into an unexpected pause, giving many of us time to reflect on our lives—our passions, our goals, our sense of purpose. For me, that reflection was forced upon me when I was furloughed, suddenly deemed "not essential". That label stung. I had spent years pouring my energy into work that I believed mattered—building connections, fostering communication, and helping employees feel engaged with their company. And yet, when the doors shut, so did my role. If the work I did to connect people was no longer considered essential, then I had to ask myself a deeper question: *If I wasn't essential to the company, why was the company essential in my life?*

That thought stayed with me as I found myself with more free time than I had in years. I used my daily walks with my dogs not just for exercise but for clarity, allowing my mind to wander as I considered what truly mattered to me. I took online courses, brushing up on skills, determined to make myself better, more valuable, more prepared for whatever came next. In the back of my mind, I kept telling myself that this was just a pause, that eventually I'd be called back. And when that happened, I'd return stronger than before. And sure enough, that call came. I stepped back into my role as if nothing had changed, picking up right where I left off, diving headfirst into my responsibilities.

But something *had* changed.

At the time, I didn't fully recognize it, but in hindsight, I see it clearly—I had pushed aside the very reflections I had during the furlough. The same thoughts that had urged me to reevaluate my path were buried under the weight of deadlines, meetings, and the daily grind. I was back in motion, spinning my wheels, caught up in the relentless pace of work. And just like that, the opportunity to pause and reassess my life was lost. It's easy to lose sight of personal aspirations when you're buried in the trenches of routine. When every day feels like an urgent to-do list, passions and goals are the first things to get sidelined. When we get back into our safe and comfortable routines, we don't allow our future selves the chance to grow because our purpose and passion are put on the back burner.

But reflecting on ourselves—our purpose, our values, our direction—isn't just a task to check off. It's uncomfortable. It's daunting. True self-reflection forces us to confront our fears, insecurities, and the possibility that we might not be living in alignment with who we want to be. We must dig deep, peeling back the layers we may have ignored for years. What if we don't like what we find? What if we realize we've been on the wrong path all along? It's easier to stay busy, to distract ourselves with work, obligations, and the noise of everyday life, than it is to sit in silence and truly listen to what's within us. But avoiding those hard questions doesn't make them disappear. They linger, waiting for a moment of stillness to resurface.

Several years later, I found myself in an eerily similar position—except this time, there was no promise of a callback. This time, it wasn't just a temporary pause but an abrupt ending. And with it, those questions I had once pushed aside came rushing back, louder and more demanding than ever.

Now, the reflection wasn't just a fleeting moment of self-awareness; it was an urgent reckoning with my future. The same questions I had once pondered in passing now demanded answers. What truly brings me fulfillment? What is my purpose beyond this job? Who am I when the title is stripped away?

This time, I couldn't afford to ignore the questions.

One day, while having a conversation with a woman I had met through networking, she asked me a simple yet profound question: "What is it you want to do?" Without hesitation, I immediately thought about getting back to work in the line of work I had always done. It was instinctual, returning to what was familiar, what I knew best. But then, something shifted. That question sparked a thought: "What else can I do?"

I had spent so many years defining myself by my job title that I hadn't seriously considered alternative paths. What if I explored something new?

143

What if I took this moment of uncertainty as an opportunity for reinvention? It was a terrifying yet exhilarating realization. For the first time, I allowed myself to think beyond the conventional and entertain the idea of doing something different—something that aligned even more deeply with my values and passions.

I started journaling, documenting my thoughts, fears, and small victories. I wrote down a list of items in my life that had always brought me joy—speaking to others, storytelling, creating meaningful connections. I thought about the times in my career that had left me feeling truly fulfilled. Surprisingly, they weren't necessarily the biggest achievements or promotions; they were the moments when I had made a real impact on someone else's journey. Because of those connections, a light grew in me while watching them succeed and grow, improving their own lives.

I realized that my passion wasn't just about corporate communication or telling the company's story, but about connection itself. I found fulfillment in helping others—whether by offering career guidance, mentoring, or simply listening to their struggles. I understood that my purpose was bigger than any one job title; it was about uplifting people, empowering them to find clarity, and helping them navigate their own challenges.

As I explored new opportunities, I found myself drawn to spaces where I could make a real impact. Whether through writing, coaching, or community engagement, I wanted to inspire and support others. Slowly, I began to redefine my identity—not by my job, but by my ability to connect, support, and uplift those around me. I attend networking events with a new purpose—connecting with people.

This shift in mindset did not happen overnight. There were days filled with doubt and frustration, moments when the job rejections stung more than I expected. But every conversation, every connection, and every small step forward reinforced my belief that I was more than my career. I got back into volunteering, another passion I had before the nine-to-five took all my time. I reached out to old colleagues, not to ask about job leads but to genuinely reconnect and see how they were doing.

With time, I began to embrace the idea that our work should serve as an extension of who we are, not define us entirely. A career is a platform, a vehicle through which we can express our talents and values—but it should not be the sole source of our identity. We are multi-dimensional beings, capable of growth, change, and reinvention.

This journey of self-discovery taught me that we are not defined by our careers but by the values we uphold and the impact we make. Losing my job was not the end of my story—it was the beginning of a new chapter, one where I could truly align my work with my deeper purpose.

As I continue forward, I do so with a renewed sense of direction. My purpose is clear: to give, to connect, and to inspire. Not because of a job, but because it is who I am.

Now, when someone asks, "What do you do?" I no longer define myself by a job title. Instead, I share what drives me. I tell them about my passion for storytelling and for helping others navigate their own paths. I talk about the journey of self-discovery and the realization that purpose is not found in a job description—it is found in how we choose to show up in the world.

I know now that while careers may shift and change, our core purpose remains. It evolves, grows, and adapts, but it is always within us, waiting to be discovered and embraced.

This transformation has given me a new perspective on success. It is not measured solely by a paycheck or a title but by the positive impact we have on others. I have learned that life's transitions, even the most difficult ones, can be opportunities for growth, self-discovery, and reinvention. And with that realization, I move forward—not with fear, but with confidence in the person I am and have become.

Angela has an adventurous spirit and a deep love for exploring new places and cultures. She and her husband of ten years, Joel, are on a mission to visit all 50 U.S. states and explore at least one new country each year. They make their home in Foley, Missouri, where they enjoy the company of their two dogs, Gaby and Mack, their cat, TomTom, and a small flock of chickens.

A lifelong learner, Angela thrives on new experiences, whether experimenting with a new recipe, taking a class to learn a new skill, or channeling her creativity into an art or home project. She embraces a fulfilling balance between professional dedication and personal passions, making the most of every adventure, whether at home or across the globe.

Please scan the QR code to connect with this author.

Cheryl Zink

Steps in Faith

In March of 2019, I left my corporate job. There was a rare opportunity to volunteer to leave and receive a generous severance package. During my twenty-three-year career with a global telecommunications company, I had several leadership opportunities, leading eight different call centers. When I left, I was the Senior Manager over Fraud Operations for all wireless and landline call centers. By September 2018, when corporate announced the severance packages, I had reached a point where I was no longer growing professionally. While I worked with some top-notch people, the work could be toxic, and it was impacting our culture. I had drifted away from using my growth mindset and had let the work begin to impact my positive outlook. When the company announced the severances to over 40,000 employees, I knew immediately it was my opportunity to leave. I had prayed for a way out; in my mind, I thought I was unlikely to qualify for a package given my responsibilities and leadership. I honestly felt like God was speaking to me, saying, "Now is the time, take this step."

Over the previous twelve years, our family had been attending a church that challenged us, stretched us, and grew our faith in ways we never thought possible, and we became true followers of Jesus Christ. It is because of our faith that I truly believed, without a doubt, that God would provide when I walked away from my secure, high-paying career. I still needed and wanted to work, and I didn't know what my future entailed, but I did know that I would be alright, so it was time to take this first step. In the last several weeks before I left my career, I read a devotional to prepare myself for the next chapter of my life. *100 Days to Brave*, by Annie F. Downs, proved to be very critical to my transition. In my notes, on the one hundredth day of reading, I wrote:

> "Oh God, thank you for always showing up. I needed direction, and you pointed me to this book. I needed clear assurance about my next steps, and you gave them to me time and time again with messages in my 100-day journey, and for the timing of everything that has happened... most especially the timing starting in September and still happening with each day and step forward. Thank you, God. I will make you proud and give you the GLORY." 6/8/2019.

With the encouragement and recommendation of my very dear friend, I decided to pursue an opportunity to learn about real estate investing. Upon my retirement, I knew I would pursue starting my own business rather than seeking a position with another company. After time off with family, I began to release some of the negativity that had surrounded my career over the last year. Through prayer, reading the bible, and reading my 100-day devotional, I was able to quickly let go of old stress. I gave it to God, and I looked to Him for my next steps.

I attended seminars, meetups, and networking groups. My friend had used this avenue as a vehicle to leave her own corporate career, and she knew someone who was leading a three-day workshop. I hired him as a coach to teach me how to wholesale houses, and he became my teacher, my mentor, my coach, and my friend. Real estate investing (REI) was not a lifelong dream. In fact, being self-employed wasn't either. I just knew it was time for me to leave my corporate job, and I knew God would provide and lead the way. I pursued REI because I needed a path, I needed to take a step toward something.

Over the next several months, while following what I learned from my coach, I also spent hours each day reading the bible and books on self-development. I had never read the entire bible, and I wanted to read it cover to cover, looking for where it would lead me, what it would teach me, and what my unique purpose is in His world. I wanted to know the path I was supposed to be on. I knew my relationship with God and my mindset were both critical and interrelated, as well as vital to my future success. So, I prayed, read, and took steps forward.

In 2020, my husband and I joined a mastermind and met other like-minded entrepreneurs who wanted to learn, grow, and collaborate. It was in this faith-based group that we looked at what we wanted our life to look like, not just our business, but also our dreams as a family and followers of Jesus. We explored our why, our purpose, and how everything fit into our new business. We took another step of faith, and we began to write out our visions. During our quarterly meetups, we shared what was happening in our lives that kept us from living our dreams and fulfilling our why. We dug deep. We shared our hopes and our hearts, and we cried. I cried with our fellow boardroom members while learning about their journeys, feeling their pain and joy, and I got uncomfortable sharing what was standing in my way. One of those obstacles was not knowing my purpose, while another was having a large mortgage that kept my husband tied to his job. So, over Thanksgiving 2020, we downsized and moved! This was our first step toward financial freedom.

Accountability was my word of the year for 2020. It was the first year I had picked a word of the year. Taking **accountability** for our financial freedom meant moving into a smaller home, in an older subdivision, and releasing ourselves from our large mortgage. The mastermind group was supportive and caring. Each time we met, we had personal breakthroughs. We accepted hard truths in our lives, and we took steps forward. Through reading the bible and hundreds of other books about Jesus, life, mindset, and purpose, and through reflecting on my journey, I was gaining wisdom. I was successfully wholesaling and flipping houses, and setting larger goals for the following year.

In 2021, my word of the year was **Believe**. I continued to pray daily and **believe** God would lead us to what our youngest son needed from us as parents as he was growing, changing, and challenging our thinking. I needed to trust God with our son and believe He would lead the way as we navigated some coming-of-age challenges. I had been focusing on mindset, and I wanted to trust and believe my business would grow and allow Mike to leave his job. I also **believed** I had a bigger purpose. I was beginning to understand that my purpose was not to join a huge, earth-shattering non-profit organization that would save the world. By the end of 2021, our mastermind group had experienced a huge loss with one of our coaches unexpectedly passing away. His passing had a substantial impact on each of us individually and as a group.

Over time, I had grown to know and understand God's universal purpose for each of us (know Him, try to become like Him, follow Him, share Him). From there, I continued to search for my unique purpose. First, I went back and assessed my skills. When we joined the mastermind, they asked us to send out an email asking for help from friends on identifying our unique genius zone. This, with my spiritual gifts survey, reinforced my belief that I was on the right path to using my unique gifts to help others. I needed to continue to trust God and **believe** with each step that I was going to continue to discover my purpose.

As we entered 2022, my word of the year was **Be Still**. *"Be still and know that I am God."* Psalm 46:10. My husband had left his corporate job, and we just passed the three-year marker in our business, while homeschooling a senior in high school who was turning eighteen and getting ready to make his own way in the world. I prayed daily. I needed to trust my son as he was now an adult taking his own steps forward and leaving home to travel the world. By April of that year, to share our knowledge and empower women in real estate investing, we launched a monthly meetup and co-led this with my friend, who brought me into this business.

In 2023, my word(s) were **Be the Light**. It was our fourth year in business, our three sons were all doing well, our business was growing, and many things in my vision were happening. Although we celebrated our wins, we never settled in; we continued to challenge ourselves and reach higher. I was clear with my vision, but I still wasn't sure about my purpose. I picked **Be the Light** because I wanted to use what I learned and share with other people, shining a light into their lives. I wanted to focus outward, not inward, and show others love. I had read a couple of books that were very convicting: *Everybody Always,* by Bob Goff, about loving everybody always, not just people who are easy to love, and *Unoffendable,* by Brant Hansen, teaching humility and gratitude. These are challenging lessons for most people but are important lessons for all of us. These books weighed heavily on my mind, and I wanted my words to be a reminder of these lessons. I did not know at the time that I would be introduced to a light later in the year that would significantly change our lives for the better.

Everything has a season in life, especially as entrepreneurs. Contractors change, industries shift, and costs and prices change. With this, so did the mastermind group. The loss of our coach over a year earlier had taken a toll on our group, with people leaving and people joining. In a group where we often got very personal, it no longer felt like a safe space. We were outgrowing the group. Our mastermind had been amazing and had served its purpose; we had a life vision, we had been removing roadblocks, we had been holding each other accountable, and we had set big goals and were surpassing them. It was time now for us to take the next step and leave the mastermind.

In December 2023, we began using a light therapy product and found such great success with the product that we became brand partners in the network marketing company, LifeWave. We bounced into 2024, loving the new product and casually enjoying our new small business. I chose my word of the year, **Connect.** I was connecting people to our incredible health and wellness product. On the surface, nothing in our new business venture seemed to align with our goals, so we slowly stepped into it. We didn't want the distraction of a new business, but we loved the product, and we loved the leader, so we followed where God was leading us.

Throughout 2024, we took steps forward on our journey with LifeWave. We were five years into owning a real estate investing business while starting a new venture. I was reviewing my purpose, vision, and goals regularly. I had grown comfortable with accepting that my purpose did not need to be earth-shattering, though I was still open to the possibility. The more I looked at my purpose, the more I found that I was truly living it and fulfilling it. While it may not be earth-shattering, we were impacting over 500 people in just over a year, and we were continuing to grow.

My word in 2025 is **Serve.** With this shift of mindset and new business, I was now serving others. My husband and I are now senior directors, and we have helped hundreds of friends, family, and acquaintances, growing our own team to over 500 people. We **serve** people with improved energy, sleep, strength, reduced inflammation, and a variety of health and wellness concerns. We have enabled people to impact their health using a holistic approach. We have helped people turn their passion for health and wellness into a small, successful business. We are serving. And our big, hairy, audacious goal is to impact 100,000 people. That's kind of earth-shattering, isn't it?

Over this six-year journey, I discovered my purpose. It has been building the entire time I was searching for it. It may not have sounded earth-shattering, nor like I would reach the masses. But I believe I will, with my goal of reaching 100,000 people. My purpose is to live to glorify God by reflecting Jesus in all that I do—through my actions, generosity, and love. My purpose is to share Jesus, help others experience healing and wellness, and use the resources God provides to bless those in need. I am committed to leading with faith, building a thriving business that empowers others, and creating financial freedom to give abundantly. In my marriage, family, and community, I strive to be a light, offering encouragement, connection, and support. Every day, I walk in faith, steward my gifts wisely, and trust God to guide my path.

Cheryl is a devoted daughter, wife, and mother of three incredible young men. Passionate about helping others, she actively serves in her church, goes on mission trips, and sits on the board of a local real estate non-profit. She co-leads a monthly real estate investment group of empowered women, sharing her experience and expertise with other investors. As an entrepreneur, she and her husband own multiple businesses. They love helping people optimize their health and well-being through cutting-edge phototherapy technology. Cheryl loves to catch up with friends over a hike rather than a cup of tea. Her goals are to hike 640 miles leading up to the Mammoth March twenty-mile challenge, and to hike all national parks. Cheryl loves to read books on personal development, using what she learns to help her team. She believes strongly that words matter and impact everything we do. So, choose your words wisely!

Please scan the QR code to connect with this author.

David Marks

Discovering Me

I know today, in my heart, what my purpose is. It's to wake up inspired and enthusiastic to be *me*. That sentence right there gives me life now, because I used to wake up and dread the day. I didn't know who I was, didn't know what I was doing, and honestly, I didn't feel like I mattered. But today, I do. I know I matter. And how I got here is a story I'm grateful I get to share. Looking back, my journey has been a blessing, even though there were long stretches of time where it felt like anything but.

I've always known I was adopted. I didn't know who my biological parents were or why they gave me up. My adoptive parents were kind, they loved me, and they truly did the best they could. After they adopted me, they had two kids of their own. I never felt like they treated me differently. They tried hard to make me feel like I belonged. But no matter how much they tried, that feeling that I didn't quite fit in never fully left me. I'll never forget the first time I felt it—deep in my gut.

It was the first day of middle school. I remember walking in and seeing groups of kids I had gone to elementary school with. But now, they were talking and laughing with kids I had never seen before. Kids from other schools. And I remember thinking, "How do they already know each other?" It was like I missed something, like everyone had been invited to something I didn't even know was happening. That day planted a seed in me—a belief that I didn't belong, that I wasn't good enough, and that I was always going to be left out.

That feeling just got worse when I got to high school. And then, right before I turned fifteen, my adoptive parents got divorced. That rocked me. Here I was, already feeling like I didn't fit in anywhere, and now my home life was falling apart too. There wasn't any real guidance. No structure. No emotional support. I started hanging out with the wrong crowd, and by sixteen, I got a job at a pizza place. That's where a coworker asked me if I got high. I had never touched a drug in my life, but I said yes. I wanted to fit in. I didn't want to be the odd one out. I smoked weed for the first time and felt like I finally belonged somewhere. It felt like I had found my people.

From there, it escalated fast. By seventeen, I was smoking crack in North St. Louis. Between sixteen and twenty-six, I used any drug I could get my hands on. Weed, acid, mushrooms, cocaine, alcohol—you name it. I loved how psychedelics made me feel like I wasn't different. Like I wasn't broken. I used because I didn't want to feel. I used because I didn't want to be me. I hated being me. I used because it was the only way I knew how to survive emotionally.

During that time, I believed I was going to use drugs and drink for the rest of my life. I truly didn't see another way. I thought God handed out a good life to others and just skipped me. I would see people who had money, nice houses, relationships, stability—and I'd wonder why God didn't show up for me like He did for them. I barely graduated high school. I went to a tech school for auto mechanics and just scraped by. My self-worth was in the gutter. I didn't believe I was capable of anything more than barely surviving.

Then, at twenty-six, something happened. My family staged an intervention. I didn't hide my drinking, but I did everything I could to hide the drugs. Somehow, they knew. That intervention saved my life. I got sober and started going to AA meetings. I stayed sober for seventeen years. AA changed my life. But looking back now, I can see that even in sobriety, I still didn't feel "normal." I still didn't fully feel like I belonged. I just adapted to the alcoholic personality instead of the addict one.

I remember always wanting a girlfriend. Even when I was using, my friends would ask me why I didn't have one. They'd say, "You're a nice guy." And I'd say, "I don't know." Truth was, I didn't feel lovable. I didn't feel attractive. I didn't feel like I mattered enough for someone to want me. I was stuck in deep, deep self-pity, and I didn't even realize it.

My last two years of using were a nightmare—*LIVE* and in person. And my first six months of sobriety? Same nightmare, just different scenery. I had used drugs and alcohol to numb myself from everything. Once I got sober, all those feelings I had buried came bubbling to the surface, and I had no clue how to deal with them. I saw a therapist around six months sober, and I'll never forget what she said. She looked at me and said, "You finally look like a human being. When you first came in here, you looked like a zombie." That moment stuck with me.

I started making AA my social life. That's where I met my first girl-friend in sobriety. She told me later she was flirting with me, but I had no idea. She didn't have a car, so I gave her a ride home—and one thing led to another. I had never had a woman be physically attracted to me before. I didn't care that she was eleven years older and had two kids. I felt wanted. Eventually, she moved in with me and my brother. Later, we got our own place and lived together for about two and a half years.

Eventually, I realized the relationship had run its course. I moved back in with my brother and met my future wife on a dating site. We dated a year and a half, then got married. I learned so much about myself in that marriage. Mainly, that I got married because I wanted to fit in. I wanted to show up to family events and say, "This is my wife. These are my kids." I was trying to belong. But the marriage was not healthy. It felt like a dictatorship, and she was the dictator. I was never happy. She'd belittle me in front of others, especially family, and I started to hate her. I wasn't living. I was just surviving—again.

After that divorce, I started looking for love again. I was still in AA, and a woman asked me out after a meeting. At first, I said no. I thought she was crazy based on her share during the meeting. But she kept asking, and eventually, I said yes. We went out for coffee, ended up sleeping together, and just like that, I was in another relationship. She moved in after six months. I wanted kids, she didn't, but I stayed anyway. For a few years, we were content. We fixed up the house. I moved my business from the garage to a retail location. Life was stable… but not fulfilling.

Then came 2021. I got involved in personal development. I joined a mastermind with other entrepreneurs, people who were building serious businesses. Some were multi-millionaires. What stood out to me was how spiritual they were. They talked about mindset, purpose, healing childhood wounds, all the stuff I had been avoiding. My girlfriend would come to retreats but didn't want to do the work. She'd come along physically but wasn't in it mentally or emotionally. I tried to get her to join the journey with me, but it just wasn't her thing.

In the summer of 2024, I finally found my purpose. I kept hearing other entrepreneurs talk about theirs. About their families, their businesses, and how they felt like they were born to do what they were doing. I still felt lost. I had no idea why I existed. I didn't feel a deep connection to anything. That's when I heard about 75 Hard. I decided to do it—not to prove anything, but to find out what I was made of.

I was two weeks into the program when I realized the woman I was with was not my person. I started to see how self-pity was running my life. It was keeping me stuck—personally and professionally. I looked at her one night and said, "I'm not happy." I loved her, but not the kind of love that builds a life. We were two depressed people living in a messy house. She moved out two weeks later.

After I finished 75 Hard, my whole life changed. I started studying self-pity and how it works. I learned it's not just sadness, it's a cocktail of shame, low self-worth, hopelessness, rejection, and anxiety. I began to understand how it shaped my entire story. Around that same time, my adoptive parents gave me the records they had from when I was adopted. One note in particular hit me hard; my birth mom didn't want anyone to know I existed. That crushed me.

I worked through that pain with my therapist. She explained adoption trauma. How babies can feel the absence of their birth mother. How those feelings of abandonment get wired into your nervous system. I started realizing that my whole life, I was trying to prove I was good enough. Trying to matter.

One Saturday morning, I felt this deep pull to reach out to the adoption agency. They were closed, but it didn't matter. I took action. Monday came, and I started the process. The court unsealed my records. I got a non-identifying report. My birth mother was twenty-three, my father twenty-five. They talked marriage, but split up before I was born. She gave me up to protect my well-being. That line right there helped me start to heal.

After that, I doubled down on personal development. I became emotionally aware. I stopped needing to feel "ready" to go after what I wanted. I stopped waiting. I started believing. I knew that whether or not I ever met my birth mother, I would be okay. I wasn't attached to the outcome. And then the agency found her. We've exchanged a few emails. I know her name. That's it. But I'm at peace.

Today, my purpose is simple: Let go of what doesn't serve me. Let go of the emotions that try to hijack my peace. Let go of being attached to outcomes. I still want to get married. I still want to have kids. I want my business to own the building it's in. I want to build a legacy. But I'm not desperate. I believe life gives you what you believe it will give you. And now, I believe I'm worthy.

I meditate almost every day, fifteen to thirty minutes. I can see the life I want. I can feel it. And that gives me confidence to take action. My business is doing better than ever. I believe the woman I want—someone younger, emotionally healthy, and excited about building a life—is on her way. I believe we'll get married and have children. Not "if," but "when." Same goes for business. All the things I've dreamed of, I believe they're coming. I just have to keep showing up as me.

David Marks is the owner of Quality Auto Repair, Quality Auto Sales, and Lease A Quality Auto—three businesses built on the values he lives by: trust, integrity, accountability, and transparency. But more than an entrepreneur, David is someone who believes the most powerful thing we all want is to feel appreciated. His life hasn't been easy, but every challenge has shaped his purpose: to wake up inspired and enthusiastic to be himself. David lives a healthy lifestyle, exercises regularly, and fuels his days with adventure. He loves camping, hiking, kayaking, golfing, and swing dancing. Personal growth is a big part of who he is. After overcoming addiction and rebuilding his life, David now lives with intention, lets go of what no longer serves him, and trusts that everything he wants—love, family, and business success—will show up at the right time. His story is real, and so is the heart behind it.

Please scan the QR code to connect with this author.

Karen Schindler

Helping People Achieve the American Dream

For as long as I can remember, family and society have always told me to do good in school, study hard, and go to college so I will find a good job, a good career. My parents were teen parents who faced many uphill battles of their own and wanted the best for me.

After high school, I attended a local business school that taught real-world applicable career classes. The school had a job placement service that helped me obtain a job with a local property management company. The job required that I get my real estate license at the ripe old age of nineteen. I worked as a leasing agent, helping people find the apartment they wanted within a 1,208-unit historical complex. I learned that I loved helping people find a home! However, I felt limited working at only one complex. If a person didn't like the complex I was working with, I couldn't offer suggestions to other complexes. I was also broke, making barely enough money to live on. It was time to change that.

I started looking at other career options and opportunities to improve my career path and make more money. I discovered that I needed to go back to school and finish my college degree. I was fascinated with houses and home design, and I wanted to learn how to build houses but was told that wasn't something girls do. I remembered how Mr. Brady, from *The*

Brady Bunch, was an architect, designing an interesting office building on the television show, and that was what I would do. I applied to a prestigious architectural program at a large university in a neighboring state and was accepted. Since my state didn't have a public college that offered an architecture degree, I was able to get in-state tuition reciprocity, making that program affordable.

After two years of working in classes that I discovered I did not like, such as engineering and math, it was clear I would need to change majors. However, the business management major meant my in-state reciprocity would end, and I would no longer be able to afford that out-of-state college. I decided to move back home to St. Louis, getting a job at the same apartment complex I had been at previously, this time as a purchasing agent in the maintenance department. I worked full-time during the day and took college classes at night. This routine eventually led to me being able to successfully graduate with a Bachelor of Science in Business Management with honors! I was the first person on my dad's side of the family to graduate college, and I just knew red carpets would be rolled out and top dollar job offers would come flooding in. Guess what? The top dollar job offers never came, and the new offers I received would pay little more than what I was already making. I did take a new job offer for a position leasing commercial real estate that paid a little bit more than I was making prior to completing my degree. Society, school counselors, and my family had all said that if I worked hard and obtained my degree, I would have a great career with amazing opportunities. I was starting to realize that wasn't always the case.

Once it was evident that my dream job wasn't going to magically appear, I decided to take a proactive approach. One of the things I did was reach out to a friend of a friend who was a real estate agent to see if she would do an informational interview with me to learn how she forged her path to success. When I worked up the nerve to make the call and set up the informational interview, it went great. The Realtor shared with me many of the steps she had taken to create a successful entrepreneurial path for herself. She invited me to shadow her on appointments after I got off work, where she was showing homes to buyers. It was an exhilarating experience! It was exciting to be back in the realm of helping people find where they wanted to live without the limitation of one neighborhood or complex. It was perfect. I knew real estate was what I wanted to do and that I would be good at it.

When I thanked the Realtor for allowing me to do the informational interview and shadow her, I told her that she helped provide clarity that I was going to be a successful Realtor... after I was able to build up my savings, buy a bigger car, and get licensed again. The Realtor wasn't having my excuses. She saw something in me, a spark, a passion for helping people, and knew that I could be successful. She invited me to join her team as her Buyer's Agent and become my mentor, working with her buyer clients for a shared commission structure. At that time, this was an almost unheard-of concept. It was fun to be on the innovative side of the industry, to be a Buyer's Agent, and be an integral part of a successful team.

I was unsure as I felt it was too soon, I wasn't ready, I didn't have enough savings…the reasons not to accept her job offer went on. Like any good mentor or coach, the Realtor listened to my objections, guided me, helped me find answers and solutions, and helped me build a financial pro forma to determine what actions I needed to take to move forward. Ultimately, I accepted the position of Buyer's Agent on her team. As a single twenty-three-year-old with $800 in the bank, I signed up for my salesperson pre-licensing course and gave my two weeks' notice to my job at the apartment complex. I was ready to take control of my own success.

The very first buyer I showed homes to on my own ended up writing a contract on one of the homes. Within the first six months I was making nearly twice what I had been making at my previous job. Life was grand. I loved helping people. I loved helping people find their new house, to make it their home. I loved seeing my clients' joy when they visualized their kids playing in the yard and growing up in their new home. My career in real estate gave me the gift of helping people achieve the American Dream of home ownership. Working in real estate gave me the opportunity to work for myself, where my only limit was me. A career that allowed me to bring home more money than either of my dads made. About five years into being a Buyer's Agent on a team, I felt a prompt that I had outgrown my role and was ready to branch out on my own.

I worried. I fretted. I lost sleep. I was still young, just twenty-eight years old. I had just purchased my first house. How could I possibly leave the team that had helped launch my career? Then, disagreements with the team leader about work-life balance or compensation would surface again, and it became clear that going out on my own was the only solution. After months of worry and sleepless nights, I left the team and became a solo agent at a different franchise. Life was good, and I learned that I did have what it takes to be successful on my own terms. It didn't take long for me to be back on track, finding my own buyers and sellers to work with and finding more success than ever. All those sleepless nights and worries were in vain. I made it all on my own. I was able to build upon my already successful career and maintain my lifestyle.

A new, innovative real estate franchise came to town, and soon, I was managing that office and helping grow that brand. After a few years, I joined up with a group of other successful Realtors, and together, we opened our own franchise location of that innovative brand. Together, we grew this branch into the St. Louis metro area's most successful single office in the number of agents and the number of buyers and sellers served. I grew my own team, becoming the top team for the brand in the area. As the years passed, I became a parent, partnerships ended, and I found myself completely burned out of the industry. I was tired of working nights and weekends and wanted to have a better work-life balance before my daughter finished high school and moved away to college. My family and I had bought a lake house, and I was tired of leaving my family and friends floating in the lake so I could go show homes to a buyer or negotiate a contract.

After twenty-three years in the real estate industry, I left and went to work at a large national bank, helping oversee the funding and construction of affordable housing complexes throughout the USA. It was a rewarding cause that made a difference in the lives of many people. However, I was so far removed from the people my work was impacting that I felt like a cog in a machine. I felt that the corporate world was not for me. As great as that financial institution was, and the impactful work that was accomplished, it was hard to work for someone else after twenty-three years of being self-employed and owning my own businesses. After just a few years with the financial institution, it was time for me to once again take control of my own success and move back into entrepreneurship. I wanted to personally know the people my work was making a difference for. I wanted to meet the people who I was helping, know their stories, talk them through their fear, and help them wake up to their own power.

I took a leap and became a Career Ownership Coach. I work with people who are going through career transitions to help them explore opportunities for self-employment and business ownership. Using a series of tools, worksheets, assessments, and coaching calls, I help my clients get back in touch with their dreams. I help people discover pathways they hadn't seen before or hadn't previously explored to see how the path of business ownership can help them achieve their goals and dreams.

I love helping people, like the married mom who had just lost her job at a major corporation. I loved helping her wake up to her dreams of owning her own business. She had always wanted to work for herself and didn't know where to start. I was able to help her visualize her roadmap for her next chapter of success. There is nothing more rewarding than watching her grow her home services business into an asset she can build and grow and get her children involved in when they are old enough to work.

I loved helping a gentleman who had been a road warrior account executive for a national supplier and was exhausted from living out of a suitcase to grow someone else's bottom line. He was so tired of traveling and had no idea what else he could do. He thought his only option was to retire. After six months of retirement, he was going stir crazy and ready for a new challenge. I helped him explore possibilities and options, and he ultimately decided to open a company that handles shipping and logistics for small to medium-sized businesses. His business helps his customers save money and experience improved customer service, and he gets to utilize his business-to-business (B2B) sales skills to build his own business while no longer having to travel for work.

These are just two of the many success stories I have been a part of. I love the impact I experience, helping people take control of their own success. My career has come full circle. I started by helping people achieve the American Dream of home ownership, and now I help people achieve the American Dream of business ownership. It is an honor and a privilege to help my clients make their dreams become reality.

Karen Schindler brings over twenty-five years of business experience to her coaching practice. She coached and consulted her clients to achieve the American Dream of home ownership. She managed a real estate office for one of the most successful franchises in the region, increasing the production and profitability of that office by 56%, and then opened her own real estate franchise that grew to be the single most successful office in the St. Louis, Missouri, metro area. While leading these offices, she learned the joy that comes from helping others start their own businesses and successfully launch their careers. After doing just about everything one can do in real estate—broker manager, broker owner, salesperson, property management, investment property owner, principal and general contractor on condo conversions and rehabs, commercial banking, and construction risk management—she launched her Career 2.0. Karen helps other people explore career options and realize their American Dream of self-sufficiency through business ownership.

Please scan the QR code to connect with this author.

Sandra Fernandez

Finding Freedom and Purpose

"For I know the plans I have for you, plans to prosper you and not harm you, plans to give you hope and a future." —Jeremiah 29:11

As a child, I was fortunate enough to grow up in a family with two parents, an older brother, and a younger sister. I was the middle child. I could relate to Jan from the 1970s sitcom, *The Brady Bunch*. My older brother was born with mosaic Downs syndrome, a rare form of the disease. He was a fun, sweet kid, but he needed extra time and attention from my parents. My sister and I were less than two years apart and loved to play together. We were a happy family with many good memories.

I was lucky. Pretty normal. I did what was expected of me. I got good grades in school, went to college, met a boy, fell in love, and got married. We both had typical corporate jobs. We worked long hours, saved up for a home, had kids, enjoyed life with friends. We were happy to the rest of the world. But then it happened. Divorce. It was difficult, but we worked hard to make sure our boys knew they were loved despite the hardships.

I moved out of our home and got a new place for me and my boys. I bought a townhome and started over. I was now a hard-working, single mom, working longer hours to excel in my career and earn promotions and accolades. I was good at what I did. I worked as a regional hospital Food Service Director and Registered Dietitian. I had a great team of over five hundred employees and forty-five managers, located in seven area hospitals. We made your typical old, bland hospital food on ugly trays into room-service-style quality meals with huge success. It was truly remarkable. Patients liked the food and gave us glowing reviews on our surveys. It was the pinnacle of my career. Life was good. I had a great job. I had even met a wonderful man I would eventually marry.

My now husband and I moved in together after a few years of dating. Remember the townhome I purchased when I divorced? It was now 2014, and the housing market was still recovering from the downturn that had occurred five to six years earlier. My townhouse was worth less than what I paid due to slow home sales and massive foreclosures. I did not want to lose money, so I decided I'd rent it out until it appreciated, regaining the value it had lost, so I could sell it. There was only one problem. I didn't know anything about being a landlord. I had no history of real estate. Being resourceful, with years of management and project management, I knew I could figure it out. So, I rolled up my sleeves, did my research, and got my first rental up and going.

Little did I know this was the seed that started what would be my future, my second career.

After a few years, the hospital system went through several changes and reorganizations, budget cuts, and my position was eliminated. I had to change roles, which was a demotion, but I was thankful to still have a job. Then corporate and healthcare politics headed south. I saw the writing on the wall and planned my escape. I was too proud to get fired. I had built a successful team that I was very proud of. Working together, we had accomplished much over the years, completely transforming hospital food service in our Metropolitan area. I would not let corporate have the upper hand. I was going out *my* way. I can hear the Frank Sinatra song now...

My career had amounted to twenty-five years of hard work and long hours. The last few years were sixty to seventy hours a week, on call 24/7, and it was hard to turn off work when it was Mom and family time. I would work until about 10:30 p.m. every night, after the kids went to bed. I was also helping take care of my eighty-five-year-old father suffering from advanced Parkinson's. I had given my career my all, and I'd had enough. I had no idea what I would do next, and I needed the income and benefits. I didn't want to move to another company to work the same long hours. I was done with the corporate grind. My family was more important. It was time to leave.

I had one rental up and going. Could I obtain more rental properties, make more money, build a retirement? Yes. Yes, I can.

Now well into my forties, I was no spring chicken. But I had experience, tenacity, and many years to go before retirement. And I wanted to spend more time with my boys before they grew up and left for college. I was *motivated*! I was ready for change and up for the challenge.

But how?

I bought two more rental homes that were small, modest, nearby, and easy to manage. My formula worked on the first rental, so I duplicated my process. Rinse and repeat. The problem now was that I was out of savings and couldn't get any more loans. An Angel showed up to help. I had become good friends with the mother of one of my son's friends. We met and had gotten to know each other while sitting at football practices and trying to stay warm on cold Missouri fall afternoons. She was a Realtor, a Real Estate Investor, and her husband was getting ready to teach his first weekend bootcamp on wholesaling. She told me I should attend so I could learn how to find properties off market and make money "flipping" them, so I did. It was like drinking from a firehose! There was so much to learn and so many amazing ways to make money with real estate. I had found my niche. I was hooked and ready to jump into real estate investing full time.

I crafted my exit strategy at work. We were required to give thirty-days' notice, so I figured out my timeline, my finances, how to get health insurance coverage, and I set my exit date. I was excited and apprehensive. I'd worked for my company twenty-five years. It was a huge leap of faith in myself, financially, and for my future. And it was totally worth it.

Financially, I struggled the first few months. I had saved up money, but starting a business wasn't cheap, and the money went fast. I had to get creative quickly. I took a pay cut that first year, but I was ok, and we didn't starve. I had freedom and was making my own choices, building my business. My second year in business, I had exceeded my corporate income! I was doing well wholesaling, had started rehabbing houses, bought more rentals, and became a licensed REALTOR® to save money on commissions when I sold my homes. I was doing it all and loving it. Rentals would become my retirement income. Rehabbing homes was what I enjoyed most and where most of my income was generated. I also enjoyed helping people buy and sell their own homes. My rehabbing experience really helped me show my retail clients what a good, or not-so-good, home was. I had working knowledge of repair costs, could recommend reliable contractors, could navigate inspections, assisted with negotiations...all of it. Having one foot in retail real estate and one in off-market real estate gave me a good advantage in working both sides of deals. I was even recognized by my brokerage as a top-producing new agent within my first two years of being licensed. I was making it happen.

Then it hit. The pandemic. Shutdowns.

Luckily, real estate was considered essential, so my contractors and I could keep rehabbing. But my clients weren't buying or selling. Everyone was scared in the beginning. Then, regulations let up and businesses reopened. The real estate market took off! Most agents had their best couple of years during that time. Home prices soared, multiple offers, interest rates low, prices went nuts. It was a frenzy of fast home sales. It seemed great, but it was hard for home buyers and sellers to wade through all that chaos. You'd show up to an open house, and police would be directing traffic. It was wild.

After the pandemic settled down, the markets began to change again. Interest rates rose, and there were fewer homes on the market, resulting in slow sales. People didn't want to give up their great 2.5-3% interest rates. I was no longer wholesaling, but my son was, so we shared leads and worked together buying, selling, and rehabbing.

Another trend became obvious to me in that aftermath. People were becoming more aware of the harmful side effects of food additives, drugs, and accepted medical treatments. More natural foods, ingredients, remedies, and treatments were becoming popular, and there was a push for fewer toxins and additives in foods. I saw more and more people turning to "alternative" treatments, therapies, and methods.

As a former Registered Dietitian, I was always a proponent of whole foods over nutritional supplements in a can. I began eating less processed foods, came to love essential oils, was fascinated by energy techniques, and became certified in Reiki. I saw remarkable results with Reiki, including my own husband, who had a serious, precancerous skin condition that reversed.

I was becoming a student of the more natural methods to live by. I began making my own laundry soap, natural household cleaners, and mastered making homemade sourdough. I was making and selling small batches of bread for friends when I had time.

I was also introduced to a wellness technology company called Lifewave by a dear friend. Knowing I was having serious knee issues and that I prefer more natural healing methods, she shared this remarkable little light therapy patch that boosts your own body's stem cells, the God-given ability for our body to heal itself. Today, I go on eight-mile hikes, I have more energy, and my hot flashes have disappeared. I saw this as another way I could help other people. I love sharing how it eliminated my knee inflammation and discomfort, and so many other things without medicine, injections, or surgery. And the company pays me a nice income for sharing this, and helping others feel their best and discover their gifts.

I believe that if we truly love what we do, it doesn't feel like work. Looking back, I find it ironic and incredible that such a devastating and life-changing event, like my divorce, led to an even better career, giving me freedom and more flexible time with my family. I have faith—faith in God that he has a plan for me and my family. We are all here for a reason. I know when one door closes, a better one opens. I still work a lot of hours, but they are *my* hours. I get to choose and accept or decline the work. I'm my own boss, I get to choose my projects, owning the good and the bad. I now choose who I work with, declining meetings, jobs, and people that aren't matched to my highest and greatest good, and that of my family.

We create our reality. I created true freedom for myself and helped people along the way. And I love helping people. I used freedom to name my first two companies. Freedom from my former corporate career feels good. Freedom to run my business my way feels good. Freedom to help others and see the good that comes from that work. I find myself back in health and wellness, while working real estate into the mix. My life is better than ever. It's all about better living.

What's *my* purpose? Helping others. That's it. And I do it in more than one way. Including through my children. Seeing that I helped create intelligent, independent, and self-sufficient adults is so incredibly satisfying. I'm so proud of them.

I'm still on my journey, discovering how I can help others. But the journey is mine, and I love how it's shaped up so far. I love the adventure of it all, discovering me and why I'm here. I'm grateful to my husband for his undying patience and letting me be myself, discovering my gifts and purpose on this earth. Surround yourself with good people. My husband is a good one, a blessing to me. My angel on earth.

Sandra Fernandez is a licensed REALTOR®, Real Estate Investor, and Wellness Advisor. She lives in O'Fallon, Missouri, with her husband and their four sons. Sandra holds a Master's degree in Medical Nutrition from Saint Louis University and worked twenty-five years as a Registered Dietitian and Food Service Director. After a divorce in 2009, she discovered the wealth potential of rentals and real estate investing, sparking her second career. Sandra remains passionate about helping others through real estate and health and wellness.

Sandra has been featured in local real estate publications, magazines, and podcasts, and co-founded a local meeting focusing on women investing in real estate. She has volunteered for years and served on the Board of Directors for Lafayette Industries, a regional workshop for adults with disabilities.

Sandra published her first book, *Rental Wealth*, in December of 2024.

Please scan the QR code to connect with this author.

Tom O'Reilly

Finding Passion Through Education

I've worked at so many different jobs, and I've tried so many separate careers. But for about the last thirty years, my work, either professionally or what I have volunteered to do, has typically involved working with young people or children within learning environments. I served as a houseparent in a dorm for kids with special needs. For twenty-two years, I taught toddlers and older children how to swim. And for the last twenty-four years, I have been teaching religion in our parish. It has been a rewarding journey, helping and participating in the education process for so many young people, especially kids. I can only thank God our Father, and Jesus his Son, and the intervention of God's Most Holy Spirit in seeing me through so many challenges in life.

I was six or seven years old when my parents were introduced to the very new terms of "learning disability" and "dyslexia," and their fourth child had it. My diagnosis added an additional stress to our family on top of the other dysfunctions that our family was trying to deal with. It turned out that there was a reason why their son was such a bad student, not behaviorally, just academically. That there was a reason why the boy spelled cat as T-A-C and did not even get the C correct. That it wasn't a discipline problem at all, like they and others had thought.

Starting school in kindergarten, I was excited about going. There were many of my friends starting that same day. One who I walked to school with, another kid I didn't know too well at the time, but we would become great buds, and then there were two others. Generally, school went fine, but at the end of the school year, I was the only one of my friends who had to go to summer school. As a matter of fact, I was the only one of my siblings who went to summer school. I didn't quite get the learnings.

Despite my academic struggles, the local public school system believed in me and promoted me to the first grade. I didn't go to the same school as my older siblings, a brother and two sisters. They went to the parochial school in our parish. I went to the brand-new elementary grade public school.

Despite this very new and modern school, the results were pretty much the same as before. And like before, the school district showed their confidence in me and promoted me to the second grade. But thank God my parents intervened. Looking at my report cards, they decided that, given my record at school, I wasn't ready for the second grade. My parents made the choice to hold me back that year. I wasn't really happy about it, but it was the correct thing to do at the time. Later on in life, I was grateful that they had the courage to do the right thing out of genuine concern for their son, versus what might have been the easier thing to do. But they thought that it was a discipline problem, so they sent me to the parish school, thinking discipline would fix me. It really didn't. Every day, my teacher would send a note home with my sister to give to my mom. And every day for two weeks, I would get a spanking from my mother.

I didn't get my first spanking until I was about five or six years old, not that I hadn't deserved one prior to that, but because of a relatively mild birth defect. Once our family doctor told my parents that I could be paddled like my other siblings, I got my very first swats on my bottom.

After two solid weeks of being paddled, I cried and told my mom that I couldn't take it anymore. She let me return to the public school. I could see the frustration in my mom's eyes, and she said that it didn't seem to be working. So, she called the principal at the public school, and I started back the next Monday morning. It didn't turn out too badly, as one of my friends, who had missed a lot of the previous school year because of his health, also had to repeat the first grade. We were in the same class together.

After that second year of first grade, my parents were introduced to those new terms, "learning disability" and "dyslexia." It was a new concept for my entire family. My parents tried to understand what it meant for me to have dyslexia, and my two sisters were somewhat sympathetic about it. I don't believe my brothers quite got it. To them, I was just sort of dumb.

After discovering I had a learning disability, I had to go to a school in the district with a class that worked with students who had various learning disabilities, which didn't help build up my self-esteem. My largest challenge in life, like for so many other people, was what I thought about myself. An ever-declining view of myself was a chain that kept growing more difficult to bear as I got older. I became afraid of making close friendships with other people, especially other kids. I was afraid that the other kids might discover what an all-around loser I was, or at least, what I thought I was. I was afraid of other people seeing how dumb I was.

Growing up, I hated school, but I loved it as well. I loved the environment, even though I always felt like an outsider to some degree. There was an excitement about the environment. I could always feel the excitement that I still feel today. To me, the education was the horrible part. For many people, education is a pathway with many gates. A way of getting someone from where they're at to where they want to go or what they want to be. But to those of us with various learning disabilities, education is a fire-breathing dragon, just waiting to gobble you up, to destroy its victim.

With courage, this monster can be defeated, overcome. It took me a long time. I was in my thirties when I finally learned the tricks and skills to beat my learning disorder. Some people have asked me, "Why should I carry on the contest so long?" "Why not surrender to the situation all around me?" Because down deep, I knew that I was smarter than my school and academic records showed. I didn't need to prove that to others, but I did need to prove it to myself.

I barely graduated from high school, and over the years, I made many starts at the local community college, in which I was only moderately successful. I did accumulate some college credit over the years, but nothing significant. My grade point average was always at or around 2.0. That was not what I was looking for. But it was faith that motivated me forward. Faith in God our Father, faith that He created me better than what other people saw or didn't see in me. That I wasn't alone on this journey, this trek, this pilgrimage that we call life. Over the years, that little voice inside of my heart told me that I could do it, I could learn. But it took surrendering my life, all that I was, and all that I hoped to be, to discover my own learning style to finally learn how to learn.

In my thirties, I gave it one last try. I offered this last effort to God and His Son. This time I promised Him that I would do my part by studying and reading the material as I had done before. I would try to stay on a more consistent schedule and timetable. And that I would work through the paralyzing fear that was always a barrier between where I was and what I wanted to be. Then, I would place it into God's hands and trust Him with the rest that was needed to succeed. Especially those things that were out of my control. My life began to change, I started to see things that I hadn't before. And I began to discover my own learning style, the way I studied and took tests, and so forth. Prior to this, I studied and took tests the way that we were all taught to do it, how we studied, and how we took our tests. Going from point A to point B, on to point C, and so forth. Often, I would find myself stuck and not able to move very fast through the assignment or test. I would get nervous or in a flux because I was trying to learn too much in a small period of time, and would find myself so overwhelmed.

A change came when I was learning the lines to an entire play in one week. I found that I could learn those lines in a relatively short period of time. Then, once I learned the part, I could experiment with it and sort of shape my part within the proper limits established by the play's director. The role would be mine to perform competently, confidently, and comfortably. I realized that I could use those same techniques in other fields of study with more academic success. I wasn't just creeping through classes as before. My grades were improving. My G.P.A., which had always hovered at around 2.0, started growing to the 3.0-3.7 range. It was amazing how God's intervention helped me to see myself in a whole new light.

My only regret was that I was already in my thirties when I learned how to fight against my learning disability. Because of life circumstances, I wasn't able to complete my college education. But regardless of the outcome, I was able to face my dragon and all the negativity that I had grown up with and put that monster in its place. The loser attitude that I had grown up with didn't have quite a tight hold on me as it once did.

In our lives, we all have a call, a vocation. A mission from God, as the Blues Brothers tell their audiences. That call or vocation is quite different for each one of us, whether you are male or female, young or old, or even of varying ethnic makeup. That call might be a religious call to be a priest or nun. It might be a secular calling. The most common vocation for most human beings is as a spouse or a parent. But for some, and I suppose that includes myself, there are a few of us who are called to a single life. To serve the Father and our neighbor in the best way that we can. In so many different capacities.

I grew up in what is classically referred to as a dysfunctional family. But I am so much indebted to each member of my family for whatever there is that is good in me. So whatever successes I've known in my life, I thank God and the family that I grew up with.

Tom was born on a Friday in 1958 and grew up in the small town of Florissant near St. Louis, Missouri. The fourth child of Donald and Bernice O'Reilly, Tom was a Shriner's kid, treated for a birth defect (bilateral hip dysplasia). Between kindergarten and high school, he changed schools about nine different times (never once moving from his family's residence). Tom earned a technical diploma in mechanical and architectural drafting. He has worked in many different positions, but most notably as a residential counselor with special needs students and as a swim instructor.

Tom is single and regularly attends Sunday church services where he sings in the church choir and is part of a men's scripture study group called "Men's 55." He keeps a personal journal and occasionally likes to share excerpts from it with others.

Please scan the QR code to connect with this author.

Laura-Lee Whitelaw

Purpose Reimagined

If you've known me for any length of time, you've heard me joke that my life was like a Spanish soap opera—big drama, lots of trauma, and more plot twists than you can count. I jokingly laugh when I say it, not because the pain, emotional, and mental anguish wasn't real, but because I've finally learned how to reframe the chaos. I've looked for the lesson, the good, and the hope within it all.

I never thought I'd be starting over at fifty-four years old. After nearly two decades of loyal service to one company, I walked away in 2018. No backup plan, no new opportunity waiting, I just couldn't continue working under the circumstances I was being required to work in. My soul was tired. I was doing the work of six people, working eighty-hour weeks for a forty-hour paycheck, and being told I wasn't meeting expectations. I was crying constantly, my health was crumbling, and I finally said enough—I'm DONE!

At first, I thought I'd finish my degree in one semester with just twenty-five credits left to go for my Bachelor of Arts (BA). Then re-enter corporate America confident and more "marketable." After getting special permission from the dean and advisory counselor, I completed my twenty-five credits in one semester and graduated with a trifecta of honors! I'm good to go! But rejection after rejection made me question everything. I was fifty-seven years old, with decades of experience and an incredible work ethic, but I couldn't even get one job interview. I was applying for jobs that I was clearly qualified for and overqualified for, and no one was going to roll the dice on a 57-year-old, regardless of the BA, the decades of experience, and the dedication. My confidence was shattered.

I took odd jobs—helping friends, caring for a man with dementia (which changed me), working for a plumbing and septic company (which taught me so much), and eventually, answering a Craigslist ad for a real estate photographer. This decision would be the one that, while it didn't work out as planned, created an opening for all that I am blessed with today.

My mom was an amateur film photographer, and photography had always been a part of my life. I almost always have a camera with me. While attending Webster University to finalize my BA, I took a photography class. It helped me rediscover my creative voice. When my professor asked me to use some of my photos in his future classes, something changed in me. I found some confidence and belief in myself that maybe, just maybe, I was good at this. I started exploring the options and opportunities and found the ad for the real estate photographer. This was a whole new world, but I jumped in with both feet. I was looking to learn the trade and improve my skills to become a valuable addition to the company that gave me an opportunity. I did everything asked of me, and then some, to grow.

There were the proverbial "red flags" while working for this company. No practical training, just yelling after the fact. The operating process one day didn't apply the next. There was no support for any need. I carried more expenses than income. I was trying to hang in there to gain as much knowledge as possible. I was starting to think, "Hey, why don't you branch out on your own?" A scary and exciting prospect. Just as these thoughts were becoming a part of my daily routine, I stumbled upon a course on starting your real estate photography business. Curious and skeptical, I emailed the company to get more information and the potential return on my investment. After a couple of back-and-forth emails, each with the signature of the creator of the training, I responded, "Yeah, right, this is actually you." The response back was, "Yes, it's me. Here's my cell number." And it was!

I was traveling to Texas for a horse clinic and couldn't take my horse at the last minute. I then thought, "Well, this is the course creator's hometown. Let me see if I can pick his brain on the business that I was still contemplating." The instructor and his top staff graciously spent four plus hours answering all my questions. When I left their office, I had a sense of renewed hope and belief that I could actually do this! I was going to do this!

On my drive home from Texas, Legacy Real Estate Photography & Media was born. My company name, my logo, my mission, it all came to life on that twelve-hour drive home. I felt like I was finally stepping into a life I had always imagined. Legacy Real Estate Photography & Media launched in January of 2021. I offered everything a media company would offer, even though I only knew how to do photography at that time. I was still learning how to do cinematic videos and hadn't yet started studying for the FAA certification that is required to fly a drone. I figured I could fake it until I made it.

Then cancer struck me, again. In April 2021, I was diagnosed with breast cancer for the second time. When I shared this devastating news with my husband, the first thing I said to him was, "I don't have time for this shitake or !#$%." I had finally found my purpose, and now I felt like I was being forced to hit the pause button! Surgery, chemo, and radiation were part of my daily life until November of 2022. Exhausted and plagued with chemo brain, I was constantly feeling like the village idiot with a foggy brain, dealing with forgetfulness and frustration at my current situation and circumstances. I was fighting to feel human while still moving my business forward. Some days felt hopeless, but I didn't want breast cancer and all that went with it to define me. I wanted to decide how my life was going to be, so I had to learn to reframe, pivot, and be intentional with my choices, actions, and decisions.

I was blessed through the real estate photography course, finding a tribe of amazing like-minded people who became my safety net. People who I could lean on and learn from. People who lifted me up and believed in me, even when I didn't. I remember the first time I showed up to a weekly call with this tribe of people I so lovingly revere today, and shared that I didn't have my FAA certification yet with no date in sight, a member challenged me. I was still in a deep fog from chemo brain, and studying felt impossible. That member pushed me to set a test date that night! I blurted out, "OK, four weeks from tonight!" And so, it was game on—I had to buckle down and study. Despite having to repeat the same lesson many times to help retain the information, I passed my test! That loving push helped me to conquer my fear, my insecurity, and my disbelief in my ability.

In 2023, I relaunched my business. It was slow in the beginning. I was fatigued all the time still, trying to extend myself some grace that being back to the powerhouse I was before would take time. I reminded myself to be patient. Patience, for me, is a four-letter word. Patience is a struggle for me, especially when it comes between me and something I want.

They say you always remember your first! A feisty little redhead was my first client and is now a dear friend. Jamie wanted both photography and drone footage. Neither of which I had done for a real client before. I had only practiced. My husband came with me to the photo shoot for moral support. Taking the photos was easy for me, with no stress. However, the thought of using the drone to capture the lake and community center made me want to vomit. Using the drone was challenging with the FAA rules I had to follow, and I didn't want to embarrass myself with a crash and burn or something equally horrifying. I told my husband, "I'm just going to tell Jamie they wouldn't let me fly it." My husband reassured me that I could do it. As I sat to breathe and compose myself, I could hear the voices of my tribe in my head and John Wayne saying, "*Courage is feeling the fear and saddling up anyway.*" So, I did it! I put the drone up into the air, and it is a source of pride and accomplishment far beyond any monetary payment I received that day.

Today, I love what I do. Even on the hard days, because it's mine. I get to decide and choose the culture, the mission, and the vision. I get to stay in alignment with the core values that are meaningful to me and not someone else's agenda. I am proud of the business I've created, the work we are doing, and the impact on the lives we touch: our clients, employees, and community. My business has a philanthropic element in that we donate 4% of every purchase. Last year, we donated $1,100 across eleven charities. This year our goal is to triple that impact. My workdays are long, and some days are hard, but I go to bed feeling fulfilled, grateful, and deeply proud of the life I'm building for myself, my team, and our community. This is a new experience, one I never honestly felt during all my years in corporate.

Now, at sixty years old, and after many speed bumps, disappointments, and the need to reinvent myself with more stops and starts than I can count, I feel like I am finally living my life with intention and purpose. During my last eight years, I have known burnout, disappointment, discouragement, and questioned my own worth. I can also share that with the right mindset and support tribe, you can rise above, reimagine, and build your life on your own terms.

If you're standing at a crossroads, let this be your sign: It's never too late. You are never too old. Just take action and keep driving forward. Wishing you well on your journey!

Laura-Lee Whitelaw is the proud founder and owner of Legacy Real Estate Photography & Media. After forty-plus years in corporate America, she is now living her dream life. Her business launched in 2021 and relaunched in 2023 after battling breast cancer for the second time. Legacy offers top-tier media services while donating 4% of every sale to charity: Operation Underground Railroad (OUR) (2%) and the client's charity of choice (2%). Laura-Lee's company reflects her core values of excellence, dependability, integrity, and humanity. Every stop on her journey has been a testament to her grit, grace, and desire to have an impact on those around her. Now, at sixty years old, she is living life on her own terms. Her joys and drive in life are to empower other people to believe it's never too late to start over, that anything is possible, and to create a legacy that makes you proud.

Please scan the QR code to connect with this author.

Karen Glavin

Free to Be!

I am watching a 30-year dream come true! How can it be 30 years since I started Glavin Hypnotherapy Plus, LLC? It sounds impossible. However, I am so excited for this next chapter of my life.

You know the quote from Dr. Martin Luther King Jr., "I have a dream…" Well, it was not exactly a dream. I had been hypnotized by my brother, who had become a certified hypnotist after quitting smoking and was helping me deal with what was beginning to be a very difficult time in my life. He had done four sessions with me. After one of the last two sessions, I opened my eyes and heard, "The world needs to know about this." It was like a dream, off and on. I would wonder if that came from me or the Holy Spirit. To this day, I believe it was the Holy Spirit.

You see, I had been blessed to be a stay-at-home mom and had some amazing times with my children when they were young. I always thought this was who I was supposed to be, a mom! However, life was changing, and I needed help.

Hypnosis allowed me to release what was causing my issues of not functioning in life, allowing me to begin making the changes I needed to heal emotional trauma and help raise my children on my own and to do the best job I could for them.

I became a single mom raising four children, having to create an income, which required a lot of healing, growth, and changes in me. I knew I could not be the person I had been for my children back then, and I started the process of where I am today!

"The Lord will fight for you: you need only to be still." Exodus 14:14.

Personal growth is significant to me. It's an everyday activity for me to make sure I am becoming the woman God wants me to be for my family, my business, my church, and his kingdom. Jeremiah 29:11 states, *"For I know the plans I have for you,"* declares the Lord, *"plans to prosper you and not to harm you, plans to give you hope and a future."*

I know life can be hard, difficulties come and go. There were unexpected direct challenges that stopped me dead in my tracks quite a few times. However, to move forward, you must get back up, brush yourself off, and move on. Sometimes I just wanted to sit in denial. I did it for a while. It was easier than doing the work needed for change. I also know that denial may be good for the time being, but I could not stay there; I was missing out on so much that life had to offer.

My relationship with Christ is very important. It has been since I was a small child. I grew up Catholic and went to a Catholic elementary school. I made sure that my children also received all their sacraments before we left the church.

As the years moved on, I began attending a Non-Denominational Church where I learned about scripture and what God was calling me to do. I was led to a Divorce Care program that my church wanted to offer. We offered the program twice a year, and I led the program for eighteen years. The church still has the program running. I had a wonderful opportunity to support hundreds of people going through this very difficult time in their lives. It seems weird to say that; however, what I learned, I was able to continue to heal right alongside the participants. I once read that the teacher learns the most. I believe that. I also read that God does not *"call the qualified, he qualifies the called."*

I don't know about you, but I put statements like that on my refrigerator. I read them repeatedly until I believed them. Wow, that statement is so true. God took this single mom of four, stressed to the max most of the time, trying to run her own business so that she had the flexibility to be there for the kids when they needed her, and who is dyslexic, to be able to move through life to where I am now. My mind is blown, and I am so grateful.

As I was raising the children, I did not have a lot of money, I was not able to invest in myself or my education for my Hypnosis business. I knew what I knew from the certification programs I had taken and the books I read. I used that, and my clients had a lot of success.

In 2019, I decided to sell my house and move into an apartment with a friend where we had fewer responsibilities and could enjoy our lives more. I had some extra money and bought some nice furniture for this new stage of life.

I also decided it was time to invest in myself. I took quite a few classes to help me grow in my business. They not only helped me learn new techniques but also allowed me to realize the work I had been doing was good and valuable. It was nice to know that I had been on the right track.

A major health scare and pandemic hit shortly after taking the classes, and life changed. One of the things was that you could not go to conferences. However, a hypnotist in New York City offered a conference via Zoom. She had invited speakers from all around the world. I connected with a coach and hypnotist from Australia. I kept all her information and decided I wanted to work with her someday.

The next class I took was a Peak Performance Mindset Program that works with athletes and high achievers in sports, business, and any other area of life. The instructor had that same coach from Australia speak in part of her program. I was able to talk to her and then signed up for her public speaking and coaching programs. One thing I never wanted to do was public speaking. I hypnotized others to overcome the fear of public speaking; however, I was good where I was! Have you heard that the fear of public speaking is one of the biggest fears, other than death?

I decided it was time to overcome my fear of public speaking and allowed myself a hypnosis session so I could now sign up for a class. I am now an SMJ Certified Public Speaker from the SMJ Coaching Institute. The program is not your average public speaking program, getting up in a room full of people with your PowerPoint, etc. It is a program teaching people to speak publicly for ninety minutes without notes and Power-Point in front of large groups of people at conferences. Ok, sure, I can do that. (Sarcasm for sure.) I took the class, and I will admit that I took it twice because I have dyslexia. I was very surprised that I enjoyed the class.

I went on to become an SMJ Master Coach with the SMJ Coaching Institute, too. When I started this program, I was asked to take the Myers-Briggs Personality Test, and it came back to say that I should be a coach. I laughed. I did not see this one coming! I now know that I have naturally been a coach all these years. I have been blessed to have been invited into a Master Class program that allowed me to continue my education.

What a joy it has been to continue growing and watching the changes in my business. I have taken how I worked for the last thirty years and made minor adjustments. I love having success in helping people eliminate the root causes of their life challenges. When you eliminate the root of the problem, there is usually no need for the problem to continue existing. Seeing a client's face change from being so heavy to joy in a few sessions warms my heart. To see an athlete, who was afraid to go forward because someone on social media made fun of them, become a national champion is amazing. Or watching a 67-year-old adult male who loved distance cycling complete California's Death Ride (104 miles over six mountain tops) in approximately eleven hours, after having just recovered from six broken ribs, blows my mind.

We have minds that can heal; whether we do it daily with where we are focusing or what we are focusing on, or using hypnosis, we have massive abilities to heal and change. I am a walking and talking example of it.

What a privilege it has been to be a small part of someone's life, whether it be an athlete or someone afraid to step out and open a business. My heart is full.

My kids have moved on; my family is growing. Two of my sons are married and have beautiful families. It is so exciting every time I think of those grands, whether it is my two bonus boys or all the grandbabies. It is so exciting, every time I think of my grandchildren, how blessed our family is. My insides go all a flutter. I always heard about the love a grandparent feels for their grandchildren, and now how cool it is to be one! I never expected to feel anything like this.

I have decided to move forward with my business. However, I still hear the words in my head, and *"the world needs to know about this."* I have created Redeemed Hypnosis. This is a protocol that can help other hypnotists, mental health professionals, and sports psychologists with their clientele and patients, which could be sold across the USA and, why not, around the world.

Through the creation of Redeemed Hypnosis, I can continue to fulfill what I believe is one of God's purposes for my life. I still get to enjoy this next generation of my business and a new chapter in my life. All these changes are happening the way God wanted them to *"for such a time as this,"* Esther 4:14.

I have been blessed beyond words to be able to work with thousands of clients, to help them move quickly past their challenges in life, knowing that God trusted me with his people. Now, I welcome the opportunity to affect thousands on top of thousands more people in the future with Redeemed Hypnosis. *WOW,* just *WOW!*

I absolutely love Redeemed Hypnosis's tagline! FREE TO BE!

Thirty years with Glavin Hypnotherapy Plus, LLC, which she retired from in 2025. She enjoys helping people make changes in their lives. and become FREE to BE, which has led her to her newest tagline for her protocol with Redeemed Hypnosis.

Karen is pediatric certified and has been working with children since 1996. She is also trained as a Peak Performance Mindset Coach, Timeline Therapy, as well as other approaches. However, Karen says, *"It makes sense to me to help clients eliminate their problems at the root level, with no band-aids, and allow clients to move on with their lives."* That is why her protocol, Redeemed Hypnosis, was launched.

Karen is a certified SMJ Coach and SMJ Speaker with the SMJ Coaching Institute.

Karen's goal is to help her clients be FREE TO BE!

Please scan the QR code to connect with this author.

Randy Jenkins

Crafting Beliefs

Articulating a "Life Purpose" is challenging. My wife insists my love language is "Acts of Service." I never thought about it much. I have, however, thought about it since the pandemic. Michaelangelo would remove "that which is not the Purpose." Sherlock Holmes would "eliminate the un-purposeful." I'll follow their example.

My Career

*"Making a living and making a life that's worthwhile are not the same thing. Living **the** good life and living a **good life** are not the same thing. A job title doesn't even come close to answering the question. 'What do you do?'"* —Robert Fulghum, *It Was on Fire When I Lay Down on It*

My job is not my purpose. It is how I acquire resources to live. I am a "Greek in Rome" in the business world. There are great companies and less-than-great companies. *"Careers aren't built on companies. Careers are built on relationships."* —Steve Jobs.

My Family

In November 2021, Dad passed away. The following February, we lost Mom. My wife's brother passed away in May of 2023. I lost count of the number of cousins, classmates, and friends who left us during the pandemic. My wife had four children when we met. I was an insta-dad, a stepdad, a bonus-dad, and finally a Velveteen Dad (based off *The Velveteen*

Rabbit by Margery Williams). Now: "Grampa" to ten grandchildren. These roles have shaped my life more than any others. The family we formed in 1994 has changed. Relationships have blossomed. Relationships have faded. Kids aren't kids anymore. They made new ones. Some of our grandchildren will start families soon. The pandemic affected several friends and family members more than it affected the two of us. One granddaughter graduated high school in 2020. Her classmates rarely saw each other that spring, until their July outdoor ceremony. Her elder sister completed her USAF basic training in January 2020, and we attended. Watching America's youth prepare to serve inspired us during much of the pandemic. Birthday parties were skipped. How will this generation see the world? I serve my family, even long-lost cousins I may connect with during a genealogical spelunking adventure. However, it is unfair to delegate the responsibility of my life purpose to my family. I gratefully consider familial interactions privileges, not entitlements. Imposing expectations on extended families often strains those relationships and can create conflict. We've seen that happen in other families, and work to avoid it in our own.

My Tribe(s)

The Lord gives us families. He lets us choose friends. Humans prefer small groups. Treat neighbors better than you treat friends, co-workers, or extended families. Make new friends. Change jobs. Ignore extended families. Changing neighbors requires moving or hoping your neighbors move. Moving is expensive, and "hoping" is not a great strategy.

Teenagers implement tribalism proficiently. They get more "sense of Self" from friends than from family. Right before we're born, we're each in our own, perfect Universe, experiencing God-like, responsibility-free existence. Discomforts are quickly communicated to the Universe, and the Universe responds with sustenance, comfort, and good feelings. This Universal relationship continues after the Universe expands beyond mom's womb, and now the Universe provides numerous dedicated servants to us. This arrangement exists for some time until we speak your first words of "Mama," "Dada," and finally: "No."

Next, caregivers begin the loud, messy, painful, and complex process of socializing us. Our Universe starts off as "Mom" and later turns into anyone we see. It's still like that, but we don't control it. Thanks to these caregivers, we begin our journey to become civilized members of society.

Newborn babies are selfish, narcissistic tyrants. Consider their initial existence. Who can blame them? We reinforce that identity because they cannot exist without caregiving. I've heard parents say, "If they weren't so darn cute, we'd take 'em back where we got 'em." They're kidding. Probably.

Parents experiencing their children mature is painfully rewarding. We recognize the passage of time and perceive its acceleration. We wonder if we did enough. We consider how they may (mis)behave in society and how society will (mis)treat them. It's a jungle out there.

That's why people gravitate toward tribes. Observe children's behavior as they become teenagers and grow into young adults. Tribalism is in our DNA and is now, in this post-pandemic world, more predominant than I can recall in my lifetime.

I am an Eagle Scout. Inept at most physical sports, Scouting provided the community I lacked by not excelling at sports. Interesting forms of entertainment involve groups of people: *The Lord of the Rings* Trilogy, *The Hobbit*, *Mean Girls*, *Yellowstone* (the series), *The Sopranos*, even *Monty Python and the Holy Grail*. It's entertaining and fascinating to observe other relationships because **we can relate**. We **must not** deny our tribal nature. Don't take it for granted. Don't ignore it. Occasionally, review and re-evaluate your tribal associations. Tribe mindsets and norms can quickly devolve into group identities. You can lose yourself by depending on tribe for your "sense of Self." Don't allow group ideologies to craft your very personal and precious belief system. This leads to identity politics, or delegating your beliefs to mob-think, which is a foremost toxic issue in society today.

"Two of the behaviors that set early humans apart were the systematic sharing of food and altruistic group defense. Other primates did very little of either but, increasingly, hominids did, and those behaviors helped set them on an evolutionary path that produced the modern world." —Sebastian Junger, *Tribe: On Homecoming and Belonging*

We evolved from other primates **because** we stick together. It will be ironic if these behaviors ultimately lead to our species' demise. I won't align my life's purpose with any specific group or community. That's too risky. My tribes won't determine my purpose for Me.

My Purpose

Four things comprise the Human Condition: thoughts, emotions, behaviors, and beliefs. The first three create the Cognitive Triangle. Thoughts flow into feelings, forming underlying emotions. Emotions inspire or excite behaviors that we think about. We do things and observe others doing things. We may reflect on the "doing." This is chaotic. Beliefs lubricate our Cognitive Triangle's Engine. They help evolve this mental and emotional chaos into self-control. A healthy belief system lets us ride the Cognitive Triangle Roller Coaster. "Keep your hands inside the car, and don't get out until the Ride is over."

Our behavior impacts others. What a person thinks or feels, as well as their beliefs, is no one else's business. It's human nature to poke our noses where they don't belong—into other people's business. Socrates illustrates this point while telling the story of the Ring of Gyges to Glaucon in *Plato's Republic*.

Emotions are born in **fire**. Passion, anger, joy, sorrow, delight, fury, etc. All may lead to the owner to be hot under the collar, warm hearted, even cold hearted.

Behaviors allow us to interact with things, people, and the world around us—**earth**. Move a rock. Drive to work. Clean the fridge. Turn on the TV.

Thoughts are like **air**. Think big thoughts. Think you can fly. Imagine the vastness of the Grand Canyon. Consider the grandeur of a sunset, or what you will.

Beliefs are like **water**. Fluid. Malleable, yet with a constant volume. While we should challenge our beliefs, don't subject them to whimsy, nor cause them to boil over because of rogue emotions. When the water in pipes freezes, pipes burst. When water boils, steam expands quickly, also damaging any container. Beliefs too closely enmeshed with thoughts and emotions are dangerous, perhaps catastrophic.

No human mind is immune from propaganda. Therefore, we **MUST** believe **something**. **Something** is our propaganda buffer. **Something** is magnetic energy guiding our moral compass. We may choose **our beliefs** and should mindfully evaluate extant beliefs as well as monitor when a belief unconsciously changes. Freezing beliefs makes us hard-headed. Allowing beliefs to mutate due to intense emotion may evaporate them, making way for some poorly considered belief to sneak in and take root. Emotionally boiling beliefs away creates a void for **something else** to subconsciously take their place. Schools teach Mark Antony's *"Friends, Romans, countrymen…"* speech for a reason—beware "mob mentality." The mob's expressions shift from "Noble Brutus!" to "Noble Antony" to "Noble Caesar!" Each expression indicates a fleeting belief, without a second thought. Can "mob misbehavior" be far behind? Read *Julius Caesar* for yourself. Jesus has a similar story—tried and convicted by the mob.

Here are four questions:
- Does Satan exist?
- Does God exist?
- Do I believe in Satan?
- Do I believe in God?

Equating the existence of God/Satan into a corresponding belief focuses all attention on the physical world and sets aside the possibility of "Something Greater." Nietzsche, Dostoevsky, Kierkegaard, and Sartre are all strong proponents of existentialist thought. Coupling existentialism with a belief in God begets believing you're Him. I don't want that job. However, I won't shirk my responsibilities. Therefore, I see four questions and not two.

"Does Satan exist?" Well, yeah. Our human minds need to logically explain all the bad things we see in this world, and Lucifer is as good a scapegoat as any. Watch the news or peruse any social media platform, and be inundated with emotionally charged, mostly "bad news."

"Do I believe in Satan?" Nope. Beliefs govern my Cognitive Triangle's operation. Icky beliefs gum up the works. When the Apostles' Creed is recited at church, should we ask at the end, "What about Satan? Do we believe in him, too?" Probably not. As such, I acknowledge existence without incorporating that extant thing into my Spiritual Beliefs.

"Do I believe in God?" Indeed. Jordan Peterson says, *"I tend to behave as though God exists."* A gentle way of saying: that's none of your business, but I won't misbehave.

My Life Purpose: Believe in God, Every Day.

I could not articulate that idea pre-2020. I believe in God. However, I won't take God for granted. Repeat. Every day, I:

- Recognize there's "something else"
- Acknowledge it's "not all up to me"
- Set narcissism aside
- Let God guide my thoughts, feelings, and behaviors.

Simple. Not easy.

Finally: "Does God exist?" Many years ago, I was part of a study group with Royal Satterlee, a retired minister who had discovered New Thought. After one of the lessons, someone asked, "What if we advance to the point where technology shows us the story of Jesus was only a story?" This question would be poorly received in many churches. Royal, well into his eighties, experiencing the mid-stage impact of Parkinson's, removed his eyeglasses and plainly responded, "It wouldn't make any difference. The Idea of living a Perfect Life is something worth Believing in." He put his glasses back on, and that was that. I felt he'd dodged the question. Royal, wore a pressed shirt, tie, and dress trousers for this gathering in his home, as he couldn't get out much.

Today, I see Power in his answer. "It wouldn't make any difference..." How much mindless rejoinder around the existence of God/Satan do we blather on about? If someone would like to have an argument about existentialism, point it out for what it is. Propose there are other ways to think. Allow for the existence of something that we do not believe in, as well as a steadfast Belief in something we can neither prove nor disprove worldly existence. For the sake of our Belief System being akin to our Moral Compass, how else do we want to live? If this moral existence is all there is, as Melvin Udall (*As Good as It Gets*) said, "*What if this is as good as it gets?*" Well, what if it can be better? The material world is not my Spiritual measuring tape.

Traditionally, a career gives a working man his purpose. Ladies, more in their families. Teens in friends. Gender lines have blurred recently. Each day is important. New things happen every day. "*To me there are three things everyone should do every day. Number one is laugh. Number two is think—spend some time in thought. Number three, you should have your emotions move you to tears. If you laugh, think and cry, that's a heck of a day,*" Jimmy Valvano was correct.

Find your moral compass, higher power, God. Laugh, think, cry, repeat. Take regular Spiritual Inventories. Form that habit and let that be your Life's Purpose.

Namaste.

Randy Jenkins was born in a small railroad town in Northeast Arkansas, just West of the Missouri Bootheel. His mother kept a letter he wrote in the third grade, where he said he wanted to be a writer. Regrettably, that never happened. Randy even avoided certain masters' programs because they involved writing a thesis. To that, he said, "No thanks." This is Randy's first attempt at publishing. He thanks you for reading.

Please scan the QR code to connect with this author.

Melanie Claborn

Grace and Grit

The streetlights flickered on around the parking lot. I stumbled my way to my car, feeling chilled on that warm summer evening. Leaning against the metal of my car door, I asked the question, "How do people make money?" I saw a familiar black Mercedes, his car, driving toward the exit and watched the taillights blink as he stopped. Maybe he didn't mean it and was going to turn around and come back. The fleeting hope was dashed. He didn't turn around but instead turned on his blinker. The winking light turned left onto the blacktop street and grew smaller and smaller. I watched silently as the only income for our family drove away into the night. A hard knot of fear formed in my gut. I was now alone and with three children to care for.

I tried to find a job. As a stay-at-home mother and wife for fifteen years, I was not marketable. I prayed over many resumes and filled out countless applications. Crickets. The temp agency in our area wouldn't even hire me. I had been out of the workforce for too many years. Turns out volunteering and teaching home school don't count with corporations. I kept lowering my sights until I began looking for any job! I found a job as a hostess making $9 an hour at an upscale restaurant in Brentwood, Missouri. It was a beautiful place, and I was grateful for a job. It was soothing to go there, and the managers were kind and accommodating. I served tables at Maggiano's for six years.

We were technically homeless as we had just lost our home to a short sale and needed to be out. My father took us in, except, he said, for the dog. I gave our boxer, Daisy, my friend and running partner, to a nice couple, and we all missed her terribly.

Having previously enrolled in college with only one year completed, I continued the classes and worked hard to stay on track. My little six-year-old girl was good and played near me in my basement "office." She is precious to me, and I hated that I was always leaving her to go work. She lost her dad, and then Mom disappeared into constant work. I clung to the dream of finding a way to be a work-from-home mom so I could be with her, like I was there for the boys. The two boys, who were older and a little less dependent, came and went as they had activities and work.

One evening, my middle child was cruising through the pantry and staring into the refrigerator; he came out empty-handed. I asked him if he needed something. His reply was, "Mom, I'm never full; we just need more food." At fourteen and seventeen years of age, those two boys each had the proverbial "hollow leg." They were always hungry! It bothered me, and I felt bad. So much so that I drove over to the WIC office on Page Avenue. I needed help with providing food, and yet I didn't want to walk into that building. Signing up for help was humiliating. I never thought I would be in that position. But both boys were growing and required bigger shoes and clothing often. They were good kids. They prepared lunches, did their own laundry, and helped with their little sister.

With my boys' assistance, somehow, I graduated college! In the same month of graduation, July of 2012, I also made the last payment on over $140,000 of debt my ex-husband left with me. To save as much money as possible, I gave my Honda Odyssey minivan back to the bank and drove a small sedan that my brother paid $500 for. He was so kind to give the car to me! Following the *Pro Rata Plan*, created by Dave Ramsey, I worked hard to save up a small stash of money to offer to the next creditor in hopes of settling a debt. I had a long list of debtors, and it took proactive work on my part to keep my goals in mind. To accomplish my goals, we had a strict schedule, and I scheduled everything, including lots of prayer and reading! My time was divided between time with the kids, time with my dad, saving money, working three jobs, and negotiating with creditors. Life was a full-time endeavor, and I was determined to get off assistance and get out of debt. I did it in four years while taking college classes and working. The day I made the last debt payment was a glorious day! The kids and I celebrated with thankful hearts, pizza, and desserts!

My degree was in elementary education, and I soon realized that I took a pay cut to teach school. I continued serving tables. During the next summer, I searched for a company that would hire an ex-teacher. I became the children's editor at a Christian publishing company and found out very quickly that I was a terrible editor! I tried, but I missed items I should have edited. My boss would go through my manuscripts and mark them up with a red marker. The manuscripts seemed to come back bleeding red everywhere! Thankfully, they wanted my teaching knowledge and hired a copy editor just for me. I stayed three years with marginal improvement. I'll never be a talented editor. It's just not my skill set, and I've embraced that.

During those three years with the Christian publishing company, I also took classes on real estate investing and began working toward new goals. I don't recommend jumping into two new careers: two learning curves of high intensity at the same time were brutal! One morning, I dropped my daughter at school and went to a property that had an inspection. The inspector was notorious for making investors paint the chain-link fences. With my roller, a pan, and shiny silver paint, I arrived early and began the long process of painting the entire backyard fence at 7 in the morning. I finished just as he was arriving, and my rental passed the inspection. Now I had to get to work. I hurriedly changed into a business skirt and top and bent down to buckle the slim strap on my dress shoes. Horrified, I stared at the splattered paint from the fence that was all over the front of my legs and feet. There was no time to go home; I had to go to work that way!

While juggling all these necessary activities, I found out that not everyone was cheering me on. Each person is given a dream, and if they act on it, the dream will become reality! But your dream was not given to others, and they may not understand what you are doing and the life you are going for. That's OK because the dream was given to you, and you must protect it and nurture it. The adversity was good for me. Adversity pushed me to strive harder, to present questions to people of whom I would not usually ask questions. Adversity drove me out of my comfort zone, made me trust God, and pushed me to my destiny!

My brother was not happy about my real estate career. He often criticized and said harsh words. I had to separate myself from him to stay positive. It affected me, and I felt, at the time, that my life could be summed up with a subtraction sign. My losses were large, relational, and painful. My ex drove away in 2008; my oldest son moved to Canada to marry a young lady in 2010; my other son went to live with his dad in 2012, and I feared what would become of him. My brother quit talking to me in 2015, and I lost his love and support.

It was seven years of hardship, but today, I am thankful for every loss and every hard day. My father and my sister were my champions at that time, and they helped me stay on track. My father was my first investor, and my sister and brother-in-law were my second investors. I had a dream, and I was shakily moving toward my dream and my goals. Scared but persistent, I pulled from somewhere within to find the grit to keep on. I was doggedly following the plan my coaches and I had created. They kept encouraging me to keep my focus on building the new life I was making and to forget the losses behind me! Eventually, I was able to do that and move forward with solid confidence, seeing only the goals and the freedom I would soon have!

One day during this tough season, my sister and I were driving west on the highway. The sun was setting, and I marveled at the beauty. I realized I could still enjoy life! Sunsets, my children, friends, and family were free, and it was a liberating realization! Setting losses aside and enjoying my life was a must! I incorporated other musts, like taking full responsibility for where I was in life. I was 100% responsible for where I was when my ex-husband drove away. I couldn't blame him for my circumstances; and I must never lie or deceive myself about people or circumstances.

Problems are just opportunities to grow. While my external situation was still not lovely, and I lived in my father's unfinished basement (with the occasional mouse), a mind shift took place. Challenges became opportunities. I realized my dream of becoming a real estate investor and left my job on March 3, 2017. In the three years of juggling both a full-time job and a new career in real estate, I had learned how to renovate properties and to wholesale other properties. I began to see my life as fuller with fantastic new additions of skills, friends, and grace! I found my purpose: to be there for my little girl like I was for the boys; to grow and improve as much as I can; to forgive and love without conditions; to walk humbly with my God wherever He would lead me.

Today, I am developing land in Wentzville, Missouri, for an Assisted Living campus of four residential homes that will each hold sixteen residents. In helping both of my parents navigate care and end-of-life issues, I realized America needs to change the way we deal with our seniors. In most care homes, the care worker to resident ratio is high (1:16 is what Missouri says is good, but many homes are often over that mark).

We must take care of them as they took care of us, with attentive love and respect. Thousand Springs Senior Living is patterned after the Greenhouse model of care, including a low caregiver-to-resident ratio, allowing time for friendships based on dignity and respect. They will live in a home-like setting. They can enter the kitchen anytime to request a meal or a snack, and it will be served up hot and fresh. No strict schedule, just relaxed living with lots of interaction to keep cognitive skills high and keep friendships growing. We are small enough that we can bring in their personal hobbies and help our seniors feel even more at home. I'm so excited to build this, and we should be opening the first 8,700 square foot ranch home in November 2025! There is a great need to be filled, and my team is ready and willing to serve!

Melanie is a native of St. Louis, Missouri. She has three children: one is a law enforcement officer, one is an apostolic evangelist, and the youngest graduated from Urshan College in 2024. Melanie is a graduate of Stockton Bible College (1987) and Western Governors University (2012) with a BA in Education. She began her real estate investment career in December of 2013 as a student of Robert Kiyosaki's Rich Dad Real Estate Classes. She left her publishing job in March of 2017 to go full-time into real estate. Melanie also passed the real estate licensee exam in 2017.

Currently, Melanie has completed over 300 renovations of various levels, has sold over 475 properties in the last ten years, and owns eleven rental properties. Melanie loves to network and create joint ventures with other investors. She is presently mentoring new investors and is excited to experience the thrill of the deal with them!

Please scan the QR code to connect with this author.

Alexis Thiele

From Loss to Light

"You get what you give," my father told me in a final personal video—words that would become the foundation of my purpose. In the years since his passing, that phrase has echoed through every twist of my journey: through grief, career disruption, spiritual awakening, and ultimately, into a life of purpose.

The Beginning of a New Decade

The year 2020 will forever be etched in my memory, not just as the year I turned forty, but as the year my world was turned upside down. Like countless others, I was not immune to the impact of the global pandemic. I lost one of my closest friends, my son's godfather, and suddenly, it all became painfully real. The pandemic disrupted lives, shattered plans, and forced us all to survive uncharted waters.

My husband and I manage several real estate-based local businesses. We run a ten-man crew rehab company that has remodeled over 350 homes locally, a property management company overseeing nearly one hundred doors, and a rental maintenance company for investors. We also have a personal portfolio of rental properties and have rehabbed and sold approximately fifty properties of our own. The pandemic put the brakes on everything—material delays, limited tenant interactions, and a standstill in acquiring new projects due to social distancing and fear.

I vividly remember the day the shutdown hit. Within hours, we lost a $40,000 contract—the first of several. The abrupt halt created a financial and emotional spiral. We were not prepared for that kind of revenue loss. We had employees depending on us, not just our own family. A face-to-face industry had suddenly lost its most vital element: human interaction.

The Loss of My Anchor

Throughout my life, I navigated turbulent waters, and my father was always my anchor—steady, supportive, a safe harbor. His unwavering presence was my lighthouse in the darkest nights.

In October 2020, life dealt me another devastating blow. As energy never dies, my father is, not was, my best friend and mentor. He was diagnosed with Stage 4 lung cancer. After fourteen years of battling COPD, the added weight of cancer became too much for his already fragile body. Pandemic restrictions meant limited hospital visits. Only one designated visitor—my mom. Weeks passed without in-person contact when my brothers and I needed him the most. On December 31, 2020, the hospital allowed him to return home. On January 6, 2021, he passed away.

That date held national significance for reasons beyond my personal loss, but to me, it is seared in my heart for something much larger. My father's death left a void I could not imagine filling. I felt spiritually and emotionally lost. My anchor was gone, I was adrift.

Spiritual Struggles and Rediscovery

After my father's passing, I found myself questioning everything I had believed. My relationship with God became strained. I stopped talking to Him altogether, careful not to question Him openly but harboring a deep sense of confusion. My spiritual journey was at a significant stall, not in rebellion, but out of confusion and pain. It was in that silence and darkness that the first seeds of purpose began to sprout.

I began to see that my father's love was not just in his words—it was in how he lived. "You get what you give" was not just a phrase. It was a divine reminder, a guiding light from him to me. Slowly, I began understanding that my purpose was tied to the legacy he left and the lessons he quietly taught me and my brothers.

The Blessings of Love and Family

Love is such a blessing. I am so grateful for the gifts God and the universe placed on my path to help me heal. My husband, a man committed to building a well-lived life for our family, saw my light fading. He stepped in, gently pushing me (even when I resisted) back into life and business. It was not fast or easy. I cried. I struggled. I floated aimlessly. But he stayed beside me.

We have two sons. One son is headstrong and determined. Guiding him is both a challenge and a reflection of my own growth. Our other son, named after my father, is pure light. He is love in pure form. Wise beyond his years, he consistently reminds us that we are all loved. He is a vessel of God, a daily reminder that Spirit is within us.

Finding Hope and Support

By the end of 2022, I found what I now call my tribe. My husband introduced me to a mindset coach and spiritual guide, Mike Kitko, from Inner Wealth Global, an entrepreneur empowerment organization that raises global consciousness. I resisted at first. I did not want to talk about my struggles or admit my pain or insecurities. But on January 6, 2023, exactly two years after my father's passing, Mike reached out to me. Believing in divine timing, I said yes. No coincidences.

Through Inner Wealth Global, and with the loving support of my family, I began to speak to myself with kindness. I reconnected with Source. I also worked with a gifted hypnotherapist, Karen Glavin, who helped me release internal blockages and finally embrace self-love. I had been living in distraction and insecurity—avoiding being seen, avoiding growth.

Surrounded by others who had faced profound struggles, I found strength in shared vulnerability. People with big successes and heavy burdens became mirrors, showing me I was not alone. I began stepping out of the darkness to bring light to others. What had been building inside me—energy, compassion, and spiritual strength—was not meant to be held in. It was meant to be shared.

Cultivating New Passions

I was exploring new passions. I began studying human design (which I am positive will be a lifelong following for me), spiritual development, and embracing more digital tools for our business. This renewed mindset helped our family not just survive but thrive in a post-pandemic world.

I had been so dependent on the life I lived before that I never truly met myself. The pandemic, with all its chaos, became what I now call an invitation. I deepened my connection with my spouse. I slowed down. In the stillness, I began to meditate and turn inward. I discovered the presence of God within me and the spirit that surrounds us all. I began to reconnect with the earth, barefoot in the grass, under the moon, in the sun; the same earth that nourishes our bodies and pulses with energy beneath our feet. That grounding reminded me I was never alone, even in silence.

I surrendered to the pain within me and released it. I opened my heart to love and allowed the tears to fall as I heard God whisper, "You are worthy."

As I faced the darkness of grief and long-buried trauma, I realized how those wounds had been blocking my growth. In healing, I discovered my spiritual gifts—the ability to sense and shift energy, to facilitate healing. Initially this discovery left the recipient feeling better, but I was freaking out, running while waving my arms frantically. Quite the sight, witnessed by many. But now? I'm much better with accepting my gifts of intuition and connection to the energy of other people. I am learning to own it.

Embracing My Purpose

As my husband and I develop our business in 2025, I can confidently say that I have discovered my purpose. The journey has not been easy, but it has been profoundly rewarding. I have evolved in ways I never imagined, finding strength in adversity. I have grown through pain and been transformed by hope.

My relationship with God has evolved. I no longer feel bound by rigid definitions of faith. Spirituality, for me, is about peace in the journey, not perfection in belief. I have learned that authenticity brings me closer to the divine.

I may have crystals in my pockets, sigils tattooed on my fingers, magenta hair, and piercings—but I walk with compassion, lead with light, and hold space for healing. That is the real magic.

The community of St. Louis has been a constant anchor for me and my husband. For eleven years, we have built business relationships rooted in trust, resilience, and a shared vision. I am proud to give back and to be part of a community that values healing and hope.

Lessons Learned and Moving Forward

The last five years have taught me:

- Resilience is born through adversity. The challenges we face shape us into stronger, more adaptable individuals.

- Being open to support is essential. The support and solidarity of those around us can provide the strength needed to navigate challenging times.

- Purpose is discovered, not given. It emerges from our experiences, our passions, and the values we hold.

- Faith is a living, breathing journey. It is not about having unwavering belief but about seeking understanding and peace in the midst of uncertainty.

I carry these lessons forward, knowing that purpose evolves. It grows with every challenge and every connection.

The path to discovering my purpose has been one of deep transformation. I lost my father. The world changed. And I lost parts of myself. But I found healing, hope, and an inner calling to help others rise. Through this awakening, I learned that connection with others has the power to change lives. That love—both giving and receiving—has the power to heal trauma. Authenticity became more than a value; it became a path to freedom. When I chose to live in truth and gratitude, it not only enhanced the quality of my life but also increased my capacity to thrive in business.

Today, I understand that my purpose is to guide others through their own trauma—toward a place of peace, wholeness, and possibility. A place where they can be free to step into their full potential.

"You get what you give." My father's words continue to guide me as I navigate the complexities of life. They remind me purpose is not a destination. It is a journey—one I walk with intention, love, and light.

Alexis P. Thiele is a wife and mother of two boys. They are her most rewarding gifts. She is the Co-Owner of Nexis Properties, LLC., Nick's All-Around Improvements, LLC., Nex Level Maintenance, and Legacy2, LLC. Nexis Properties specializes in property management and houses its own rental homes. Nick's All-Around Improvements specializes in the rehabbing of investor properties. Nex Level Maintenance specializes in rental property maintenance. Alexis is also a full-time investor for the selling of rehabbed homes with Legacy2. Together, these companies provide a complete service from beginning to end for investors to create revenue from their rehabbed homes. Prior to these ventures, Alexis studied Behavioral Sciences at Webster University. She worked as a flight attendant as a young adult, which sparked her love of travel. Alexis is a Reiki Master with developing Clairsentience. She is freely experiencing life, open to what presents on the journey, and believing in Magic.

Please scan the QR code to connect with this author.

Jason Meinershagen

When Down Is the Way Up

"Jason, on behalf of the Board of Directors, congratulations! They've offered you the job!"

A month after answering a phone call in early March of 2020, I stepped off the fire truck for what (I thought) would be the last time, packed up a lifetime of memories from my bunk room at the firehouse, and walked into the fire district's headquarters building as the Public Information Officer (PIO). Prior to that week, the duties of PIO for my fire district were being handled by an Assistant Chief who was multi-tasking as the Fire Marshall. I was the first to step into the role exclusively as the PIO because it was a role that didn't previously exist in this capacity.

The role was created specifically for me to do, and I was hand-picked to fill it because I had proven myself a skilled, impactful, and creative storyteller through social media in the years prior. Though I had no formal training in the other responsibilities of the role (talking with the media, standing in front of a camera, doing live interviews, writing press releases, public speaking, maintaining and updating a website, running bond campaigns and election initiatives, planning community events, and much, much, more), I was excited to take this leap into the unknown.

After nearly twenty-five years of fighting fires, I would no longer be on the front lines. I would work behind the scenes, telling the story of our firefighters and sharing with our community the work we do. A bitter-sweet departure from what I loved, entering uncharted waters and an exciting new chapter where I would have plenty of opportunities to learn and grow. I wholeheartedly placed my trust in the men who lifted me up into that role when they said, "*What we're asking you to do has never been done here before, so make it your own. The position is yours to build into what you want it to be. We got your back.*"

Recognize challenges as opportunities. Two weeks later, as the world officially came to a screeching halt with the global pandemic, our administrative offices closed and the firehouses locked down. Administrative staff started working from home. Like millions of others across the globe, the process of pivoting to a virtual world was cumbersome and choppy. It was filled with a *ton* of uncertainty and several massive communication challenges. For me, the transition from the fully immersive social life of the firehouse to an isolated and barely connected home office was discouraging and overwhelming. With the benefit of over two decades in the fire service, I found success within that pivot by embracing the challenges and taking one step forward at a time. You can't look at the finish line from the start line—it's too overwhelming. You can't even look at the finish line when your race is only halfway completed. Regardless of where you are in your race, you (have) get to focus on the step right in front of you. Read that last sentence again. Notice I intentionally changed "*have*" to "*get*". We don't *have* to face challenges. We *get* to face opportunities. One foot forward; just do the next best thing. Then the next. And the next. Rinse and repeat for as long as it takes.

Failure is not failure. It's feedback. There's a fine art to being a full-time content creator and telling engaging stories on social media. The winds of change are so fast-moving that you literally have to be ahead of the trend to catch the wave; otherwise, you're too far behind the ball to be relevant. What works to take a post viral one week is obsolete and cringe-worthy the next. The risk of being ahead of the trend—or even on top of it—in a professional and traditionally formal organization tends to put the whole team out on a limb. Sometimes those limbs aren't strong enough to hold up under the weight, and we fall. That doesn't mean you failed; it just means you received feedback. Learn from that feedback and apply that newly learned knowledge to the next attempt. Failure isn't the end; it's the fuel. Let it fan the flames and accelerate the fire within you as you rise to face the next opportunity.

You do you, and leave the few to stew. In other words, control what you can control and let the rest work itself out. Without my input or discussion, my rank and the title of my position literally changed in the first week…then the job changed again two months later when I was tasked with the added responsibility of keeping our firehouses and facilities operating—normally a job held by the Operations Chief and one hundred percent *not* what I signed up for. Although that responsibility was short-lived, the role and its responsibilities changed several more times over the next three years—from Battalion Chief, PIO to Deputy Chief, PIO. Then again to Deputy Chief of Public Information, Media Relations and Governmental Communications (WTH, I know), and finally landing at Deputy Chief of Community Relations. Until recently, I wrapped so many feelings of frustration and disappointment into what others did—or didn't do. What a recipe for disaster! The reality is, we cannot make someone do what they don't want to do; nor can we make them *not* do something they're dead set on doing anyway. Once you can let the actions of others be what they will be, you'll find a freedom like no other. I've just recently come to understand that it is only within my power to change myself. That's a freeing mindset that allows us to *respond* to experiences and other people, not *react* to them, and it clears room for us to step into our purpose—with passion.

One hundred percent of what you tell yourself will come true.
Mindset is everything. You are limited only by your internal dialogue.
When I negotiated my position, I only asked for one thing: the ability to
step back into my role as a frontline firefighter if this new position didn't
work out—for either me or the team. Looking back with the benefit of
hindsight—and tons of newfound feedback and wisdom—I can see how
that safety net imprinted a limiting belief in my mind. Unconsciously, I
knew that—within reason—it didn't matter how far I stepped out onto
that limb or how far I fell when it snapped, I would have a job. Telling
myself that—on an unconscious level, mind you—was enough to work
against me under the surface of my life. More times than not, any "trouble"
I found myself in was (in part) of my own doing— unconsciously. The
mind is a powerful thing. Way more powerful than we give it credit for.
Always remember that. What limiting beliefs are holding you back from
fully stepping into your power as the unique individual you are? Are you
self-sabotaging? If so, how?

Work is not the end. What I mean by that is, it's not everything.
It's not your identity, so don't wrap your identity up in it. What we do is
not who we are. I was in the Fire Chief's office one day when one of our
guys walked in to put in his retirement papers. He'd worked with us for
over thirty years and wept as he reminisced with us, expressing feelings
of anxiety because he felt that life as he knew it was coming to an end—
he didn't know who he would be without the routine of work and the
social life of the firehouse. It was a thirty-minute meeting with hugs, fist
bumps, high fives, and celebration. Within two minutes of him walking
out the door, the talks about who would be promoted in his place and
hired to backfill were already in full swing. The business moves on. Seats
get filled and desks get cleaned out and made ready for the next person.
The wheels of progress don't slow down for a nanosecond because that's
the job. And most jobs are transactional, not relational. It's not personal.

It just is what it is. We've all heard of the people on their deathbed and who they have surrounding them. It's not coworkers and bosses beside them! Put in perspective, a traditional forty-hour work week is not even 25% of the 168 hours we have available to us in a week. Work is the **means** to the end, and the end is what *you* make it. For me, it's family. Work is the means to provide me with the ability (money) to spend time with my family doing what really matters.

A failure to plan on your part is not an emergency on my part. Many of us have heard this—in some form or another. Yeah, I know... it's kind of an oxymoron to say that in the fire service. In my firefighting experience, when I show up on the scene of your emergency, it's **not** my emergency, it's yours. I'm there to help you resolve it, yes, but to me personally, it's not my emergency; it's my **job**. In life outside of the firehouse, the application is to know your worth. That includes the value of your time, energy, and effort. Don't let the "drama llamas" of the world pull your focus off target. Stay focused on what matters most, and don't get caught in the weeds; know your mission, vision, and purpose, and let everything (and everyone) else adjust to and align with what is most important to *you*. If they don't, cut it (or them) out and move forward.

In October 2023, three and a half years after walking into my new role as the Deputy Chief of Community Relations, I demoted myself back to a firefighter. I voluntarily walked away from the increased pay and benefits for a cut in pay, less sleep, and more physically demanding work. My time in that chapter of life didn't go like I had planned or hoped. I take full responsibility for my portion of that. I own all my contributions—the good, the bad, **and** the ugly. Because that's servant leadership. And it is perhaps the most freeing feeling ever to fully own what's yours to own. I'm blessed with the opportunities presented to me in that chapter. My time as the PIO from April 2020 to October 2023 opened doors and opportunities for personal and professional growth in ways I never could have imagined. And it was stepping out of that role to return to my love of fire-fighting that freed me to find my passion. I published my first book, *Notes from Dad*, within eight months to become a #1 International Best-Selling author. The success of that book continues to open doors and connect me with an amazing network for personal and professional growth. As I look to the future, I'll soon be hanging up the fire helmet to put on a different hat, trading my boots for freedom as I transition into the next chapter of my life. I'm preparing to launch a coaching business with the purpose of helping men—fathers specifically—heal through trauma to become the dad their child deserves; because every dad is a father, but not every father is a dad.

I have an image hanging in my studio. When I lose focus in the storm and struggle to remember what my purpose is, I look at this image to find my way back into alignment with my purpose. The image is three over-lapping circles with the words PAST, PAIN, and PASSION, each repre-senting one circle. Where the three circles overlap in the middle is the word PURPOSE. When your PAST meets your PAIN and your PASSION, they all three converge at an intersection. That overlap of the three—our past, pain, and passion—is the sweet spot. That is where you'll find your PURPOSE. For me, the *pain* (trauma) of my *past* intersects with my *passion* (fatherhood). And there is no doubt that my purpose is right there within that intersection. Will *you* do the hard work on yourself to gain clarity on your passion, examine your past, and uncover your pain? I sure hope so. Because when you do, you'll find yourself smack dab in the middle of your own unique intersection, *Discovering Your Purpose*.

A father to five beautiful children, Jason has been married to the same amazing woman for over thirty years. He and Judy have been—and continue to be—active in their community, serving and volunteering in various roles within a multitude of ministries and organizations that support and care for children and their families. As a survivor of childhood trauma and a lifetime of trauma endured as a firefighter for over three decades, Jason has come to understand what it is to endure pain and an ever-present pressure to perform.

Fueled by a burning passion for the role fathers play in our community, he has found that his past and his pain have met with his passion at a crossroads…an intersection of a life lived and a life yet to live. Jason is on a mission to fulfill his purpose and leave a legacy of strengthening family relationships, leading him to engage, encourage, and empower dads to fulfill their God-given role as the leaders of their families by equipping them to be active and engaged in the lives of their families.

Please scan the QR code to connect with this author.

Riley Dawn

Losing Everything but Me

I couldn't breathe...my hands started to tremble. My heart was racing so loudly that I could literally hear it beating out of my chest. The room fell silent, and suddenly the air felt thick. My chest started to constrict while my lungs were attempting to grasp for air. My thoughts were in complete chaos; fear, confusion, sorrow, betrayal, and heartbreak were sinking in. It wasn't just stress anymore—it was something darker. Something heavier. Grief, rage, and despair...all balled into one. How can this be possible? Why is this happening? Is this my life now?

Between 2020 and 2025, major changes altered my reality. Within that short amount of time, I'd suffer through multiple traumatic domino events. Rehabilitating from a physical injury, losing my job, breaking up with my boyfriend, fighting a custody battle that almost shattered me, and losing my mother are just a few of the things I could mention. I was physically and financially overwhelmed, but in the middle of all that mess...I discovered *my purpose*.

The Day That Changed Everything

In August 2020, my daughter was turning eleven. Like many kids, she was struggling emotionally with being home from school during the pandemic. It took away from her all that she loved: school activities, friends, parties, and her normal daily routines that gave her mental stability. I noticed her "light" fading a bit more with each passing day. It was killing me…I couldn't bear it any longer. She needed to get out of the house and get her spark back. I feared cabin fever was setting in. So…I took her to my favorite place growing up, our favorite theme park. I kept up with the new rules established for protection during the pandemic. I even checked the safety precautions at the place we were going, calling twice for emotional assurance, just to help settle my anxiety. We needed this… she needed this.

That day was meant to be a special day, filled with laughter and good memories to look back on. At least, it was supposed to be. Regretfully, less than two hours into the fun, I accidentally stepped on a jagged piece of metal in the kiddie pool. Pain immediately shot through my foot and leg, alerting my entire nervous system. I couldn't believe this was happening to me. I tried to be strong for my daughter by expressing a calm demeanor, but I knew I was in for serious trouble. My foot was now bleeding, and the children around us started to scream in horror at what they were witnessing. I looked around to make sure that my daughter was safe and that she wasn't injured, considering she was walking ahead of me. To my relief, she was fine, but her birthday was ruined. I attempted to remove the shard myself, but it broke off in my foot! "Uh oh!" I thought. I knew what was coming next.

Aftermath

The surgery came quickly. The healing didn't.

No walking for six months was the doctor's orders. I was devastated. I had always been independent, but now I was bedridden. I was also a caretaker for my mother. Anxiety started to set in. My mind started racing with thoughts…What was I going to do? What was my mother going to do? I had to prematurely move in with my boyfriend at the time, against my will, so he could help care for me. We had been dating for a few years, so I thought, why not? I trusted him. My mother's best friend, who I call my aunt, stepped up to help care for my mother. Also, my boyfriend's willingness to help made me feel assured that this could work. He even told me that this wouldn't be a burden to him, which reassured me even more. At first, I was grateful. But over time, it became clear—this relationship wasn't built for weathering storms. Emotionally, I was on my own.

Weeks later, stitches were removed, and I was finally cleared for physical therapy. Therapy was a part of my weekly schedule now, which made it hard to return to work. Sadly, I had to abandon my position to put my health first. I was consistent with my physical therapy sessions, but the pain never left. I became frustrated with my body. Constant, sharp, shooting pains were reminders that my body would possibly never be the same. The doctor said it could take years to heal—if I healed at all. Two years later, the doctor told me that the nerve damage may be permanent. I was prescribed pain meds to function without pain...pills I never wanted. I didn't recognize myself anymore. I fell into depression. Then, bitterness crept in, and anger followed. Everything around me began to fall apart.

Then Came the Call

In April 2021, another domino fell...the father of my daughter informed me that he was not going to bring her back. He was misled by the thought that I was unable to care for my daughter. The man who had once stated he wanted nothing to do with us now had the upper hand— money, lies, and manipulation. For three long years, I fought through the legal system, trying to bring my daughter home. The courtroom became my battleground. To keep myself from crying, I would sing...it became my comfort. I grew up in the church. Singing always made me feel at peace. Ever since I could remember, I loved music. I had to find something to hold onto that was full of positive energy. So, I turned to God. I started singing new worship songs and had a passion to create my own music.

Music brought a bit of calmness into the turmoil I called life. I started reading daily scriptures, and then it intrigued me further to want to read a full chapter for better context and understanding. I reached out to a therapist to process my emotions and thoughts for guidance and validation. I poured my heart out and asked God to hold what I couldn't carry anymore. Finally, 1,008 days later, I emerged victorious. My daughter came home. I'll never forget the moment I held her again. For the next two years, we worked on regaining our relationship and making up for lost time. If not for my mother encouraging me to stay strong, I doubt I would be here.

Losing My Mother

She was everything to me. We talked every day… she was my confidant. We told each other everything. She always called me her "Number one child." She was the one person who always reminded me to pray, encouraged me daily by sending scriptures, and always kept me grounded. Years of health complications had worn her down. She was experiencing symptoms of heart failure. She started retaining water in her lungs. Her breathing became labored. And then… she was gone. My mother, Beverly Ann.

The grief broke me.

Unfortunately, the aftermath only made it worse with sibling conflicts. It got so bad that my sister didn't even let me say goodbye properly before the funeral or let me see the will my mother left. She didn't even allow me to do her hair for the funeral. Even my brother tried to defame my character with lies against me. Now, probate court would bring me back to courtrooms and lawyers. My heart ached not just for my mother, but for everything that crumbled when she died.

Letting Go

My partner—my supposed support system—didn't show up for me. He didn't attend her funeral service with me. He didn't hold me. He didn't even say, "I'm sorry for your loss." I watched him play video games from the bed while I broke the news to him. "We'll talk about…" is all I got that night. Hours later…nothing. I sat alone in my grief. I felt so alone…abandoned. Days later, he saw tissues on the floor and asked if I had a cold. He was completely oblivious to the pain I was feeling.

Then, the month after her passing, my birthday came. It went completely unnoticed by him. He blamed it on work, but a birthday is not something you just forget. Him forgetting felt like salt on the wound.

That was my last straw.

Did he hate me that much? I could never do what he did to me, I thought to myself, especially not to someone I say I love and care about. It was clear this relationship was over.

After eleven years of friendship and years of dating, I walked away. For my sake, I forgave him, but I also forgave myself—for holding on too long to something that wasn't real.

The Rise

Sharing my story with others was the beginning of my healing journey. The new people entering my life were validating my experiences and relating to my story. I started to focus more on obtaining knowledge about holistic health and wellness, alongside stress management. It was interesting to learn how trauma impacts the physical body. Once you know how stress can lead to sickness and develop into a disease, you want to learn more about how to prevent it. That's how Meshdoll.com came to be.

Mesh Doll isn't just any online store. Mesh Doll is a wellness-forward ecommerce platform that specializes in stress relief education and offers curated products that help people live a more peaceful, balanced life. Mesh Doll empowers people to better understand the impacts of stress on their bodies and mentality. We offer affordable, science-backed products for the home, work, and travel lifestyle that support healing and self-care. It's a space that should be shared with others in need of stress relief and community support. It needed to be created, but it was made from both necessity and love. Initially, I created this company years ago for a different purpose, but it is being revamped in 2025 and rebranded for this purpose.

New Beginnings

I took a flight to New York in March 2025 to meet a friend. Everything started to click for me during this journey.

That casual weekend trip evolved into a business opportunity. Leaders in the hip-hop community invited me to become president of the St. Louis chapter of The Hip Hop Fraternity. The work had already started, even though the official announcement had not yet been made.

This role isn't just about music. It's about legacy…helping people who feel invisible. Assisting people in learning the fundamentals of business with proven courses, helping empower communities with social networking, and encouraging young people to make better life decisions. I understand that every failed relationship, every loss, and every instance of doubt led me to this position. It's bigger than me.

Looking Forward

I am not the woman I used to be in 2020. I've grown. I've wept. I've healed. I discovered power in locations I never believed existed before.

The grief may still linger, and it gets better day after day. I find myself keeping busy while still letting myself grieve properly. After graduating from therapy recently, I now know that these emotions are normal. I still have things that need to be resolved. Though now I begin my day with inner tranquility...with *purpose*.

Please know that you are not alone if you find yourself in this situation right now.

Keep going. The pain won't last forever. The mess holds a purpose, and the darkest night will end with light.

My book is coming. My story is still being written. My journey continues, on Instagram and Facebook for now.

Remember...you have the power to *rise*.

Riley Dawn is a St. Louis native who has shown courage, faith, and transformation in her life. Between 2020 and 2025, she experienced a series of life-altering challenges, including a traumatic injury, job loss, overcoming spousal issues, a painful custody battle, and the death of her beloved mother. In every setback, Riley found strength in her faith, healing in her voice, and purpose in her pain. She is the founder of Meshdoll.com, a wellness platform that is designed to help people manage stress, find community, and reclaim their peace. In 2025, she was invited to become the president of the St. Louis Chapter of The Hip Hop Fraternity, where she now empowers others through leadership, mentorship, and advocacy. Riley continues to share her journey on social media, encouraging others to rise above adversity and walk boldly in their truth. Follow her on Instagram and Facebook.

Please scan the QR code to connect with this author.

Cathleen Slone

Unfinished on Purpose

I had already been in the workforce for more than a decade when I began to reflect on my early career decision to enter the financial and legal services world. The fields were of interest, but where did I provide the most value? What was most rewarding to me in my work? I talked with family, friends, counselors, and acquaintances, which resulted in a lot of personal and professional reflection. I also did a lot of reflecting when I was about to select a curriculum for an advanced college degree. I wanted to be certain my educational endeavor was in alignment with my values and interests so that I could provide the best return on my investment and apply my studies to my long-term career goals.

Understanding myself and knowing that I needed input from those that I respected, I enlisted the input of my father for advice. He brought to light that I was always curious about his work duties and up for the challenge to solve the many people problems he encountered in the workforce. This was an epiphany since up until this point, I was completely focused on finance and compliance. Though, I did reflect on the fact that I always made my best effort to provide stellar service to my clients. If I do say so myself, my level of customer service was pristine. And, I enjoyed helping people very much. So, how did I define my purpose and choose my next?

A great deal of my time was spent going over scenarios with my father and reflecting on how he came to make decisions that impacted the lives of so many people that he worked with, managed, and supported. Therein opened the floodgates that I needed to discover my purpose. My father shared with me how my reactions and feedback to his employee experiences helped to influence his decisions on fairness in his workforce, including fair and equitable policies and practices, as well as disciplinary actions relating to attendance, performance, promotions, and pay equity.

Recalling that my father and I often bantered back and forth about the many facets of employee issues, I remembered the stories of the employee that complained of unfair pay, the employee that was slightly overlooked for promotion and made a grievance as such, the employee that couldn't seem to arrive to work on time and many times not at all, and even the employee that fell asleep while on duty. I was delighted to get my father's feedback that I offered him an alternative perspective to his experiences and assisted him in realizing the generational differences he encountered and how to manage and support those employee needs and the workforce changes around them.

Even today, I am honored to know that my father had come to value my input, we both enjoyed and learned from our conversations, and these interactions with him had helped me to recognize the strengths and talents that I naturally excelled at and what came easy to me. Since I understood that one's purpose often aligns with the things that one is good at and enjoys doing, I began to explore this path further.

Knowing that I wanted to make a difference for people in their work and life, I enrolled in a dual master's degree in Human Resources Management and Human Resources Development, and I loved it! Through my training and education, I began offering innovative suggestions in my workplace through my fresh Human Resources lens. I generously shared my excitement for my newfound focus and career goal with my organization. My studies taught me that I care deeply about people, the workplace culture, and the systems that support them. I discovered that my studies prepared me for contributing to something bigger and better than I imagined.

Understanding that people spend most of their waking hours at work, yet issues such as toxic cultures, burnout, lack of equity, and poor leadership are still prevalent, I became determined to help leaders become better leaders and organizations create better cultures. As a Human Resources practitioner, I can be the bridge between people and systems by creating policies and environments where employees feel seen, heard, safe and supported. I discovered that the world needs better workplaces and that I can make a difference by helping workplaces become better for employees.

My introspection helped me to realize that a world of equity and inclusion is an essential justice in the workplace and in society. As a Human Resources practitioner, I focus on policies and practices in a culture of well-being that creates emotionally healthy environments. The world also needs ethical leadership. Employees crave authenticity and integrity from leadership, and I am just the person to develop and coach leaders while advocating for leadership that inspires trust and humanity in the organizational culture.

As I stepped into my role as Human Resources practitioner, I asked myself: What problems in workplaces frustrate me the most? When do I feel most alive or fulfilled in a professional setting? Whose lives do I most want to impact or improve? What legacy do I want to leave behind in an organization? I am not a practitioner who is just filling a role in Human Resources, I am potentially transforming lives and shaping what work can be. This is a focus that aligns with my personal values and the greater needs of others. My purpose lies in helping other people discover their strengths and reach their potential. I am a champion of fairness and opportunity.

When my father became ill, I took some time to be with him. During this stressful transition, I launched a private coaching and development practice so that I could better manage my time. I started the practice with a few referrals and escalated my practice to serving thousands of people from all walks of life. I was blessed that the climate of our workforce had changed once again and created a place for me that significantly aligned with my values, work ethic, and personal needs.

I began trying many new things: volunteering in groups that supported transition and transformation, partnering with career services offices and programs, and joining professional organizations. Stepping out of my comfort zone led me to more career opportunities; engagements to develop virtual and 1:1 training programs; contractual agreements to teach business courses; the opportunity to teach adult-education classes in local trade schools, community colleges, and universities; leadership development contracts; public speaking events; and job offers!

By staying open to trying new things, I had completely stepped out of my comfort zone and created entrepreneurial opportunities in Human Resources that offered a paycheck. And, along this path, I learned what truly resonated with me. I had come full circle and landed back in roles that supported organizational transformation and creating value-driven, transparent, and empowering workplaces. I was working to build and change organizations from toxic, outdated cultures to modern, thriving, employee-friendly environments. I was fortunate to help shape mission-driven company cultures, employee engagement programs, and coaching leadership on alignment between values and behavior.

Then the pandemic knocked on our doors. The pandemic forced everyone to face the fragility of life, the instability of economies, and the profound interconnectedness of people across the globe. In the face of such widespread uncertainty, our shared need for love, care, and a sense of purpose became crystal clear, not only for me but also for people around the globe. The traditional lines between work and life blurred as people were forced into isolation or found themselves juggling multiple responsibilities, from work to caregiving to homeschooling. The disruption was universal, yet it created an opportunity for reflection and reinvention, a chance to find deeper meaning in how we work and live.

It was also the pandemic that created even greater opportunity for Human Resources practitioners to change cultures. The pandemic dramatically reshaped the workplace and brought Human Resources practitioners to the forefront as essential leaders in navigating these changes. Human Resources was no longer just about managing day-to-day operations. It was about leading organizations through an unprecedented crisis while rethinking the future of work. The pandemic helped Human Resources practitioners, such as me, find and refine their purpose. Note to self: Your purpose is ever evolving as you gain more experiences.

We faced a notable shift to workforce flexibility and remote work for organizations and people alike. Human Resources practitioners rapidly pivoted to mange remote teams, ensure business continuity, and maintain employee engagement while working from home. The shift forced Human Resources professionals to innovate new ways of collaborating, communicating, and supporting employees outside the traditional office environment. It was during this shift that I discovered my role was so much more than administrative. I became the champion of work-life balance, flexibility, and well-being in an unknown and rapidly changing environment. I had to get creative in finding ways to maintain a positive, remote organization for functions such as onboarding, virtual team building, and offerings for employee flexibility in how and where they worked.

The pandemic highlighted the importance of preserving mental and physical health and well-being in the work environment. I became an advocate for employee well-being to feel safe, supported, and valued in the work environment while working remotely. I took on the role of providing a sense of security for my employer and its employees, as well as finding new ways to conduct business. This experience changed the workforce forever.

Today's Human Resources practitioner must be agile with an ability to quickly shift priorities, including strategies for reassessing talent needs. I have become a strategic partner in helping my organization navigate a new, uncertain economic landscape. I am proactive and creative in finding solutions for workforce planning, employee retention, and supporting the financial health of my organization while remaining empathetic to employees' challenges. I hold virtual engagement meetings and provide the technology to employees to support these video conferences, continually forcing myself to become more technology savvy, enhancing the employee experience and driving innovation.

My role extends far beyond managing processes—it's about actively shaping leadership in times of uncertainty. I support managers through transparent communication, offering tools to build resilience, foster empathy, and strengthen leadership capabilities. I am deeply involved in redefining and communicating organizational culture to align with evolving values in today's workplace. As a driver of cultural transformation, I help leaders and organizations stay grounded in their values and purpose while navigating change.

The evolving landscape of work, especially with the rise of Artificial Intelligence (AI), has elevated the Human Resources function from operational to strategic and digital. My role as a Human Resources practitioner is now a vital partnership—focused on people innovation. Embracing AI allows me to become an architect of a future-ready, human-centered workforce. It's not just about adapting to change; it's about leading it, with people at the core.

In a world that is constantly shifting, especially in the workplace, the inherent need for every individual to feel valued, connected, and meaningfully contribute remains. Regardless of our professional circumstances in navigating a job transition, struggling with being overlooked for a promotion, or climbing the corporate ladder, we all share the same need for love, development, camaraderie, and understanding. Our professional journeys, whether marked by setbacks or triumphs, may change our circumstances, but they do not change the core of who we are and the fundamental needs we all share.

So, my advice to you is to stay introspective when searching for your purpose. Continue to look for patterns and recurring themes in your life. Are there particular passions that keep coming up? Recognize these patterns can provide insight into your purpose. You are discoverable again and again as you evolve as a person, a professional, a parent, a child, a sibling, a significant other, and a friend. Talk to people you admire and read about others' journeys to find purpose. We are meant to grow and evolve as we move through this life. Discovering your purpose is often a lifelong journey. Embrace the opportunities as they come, work hard when you are blessed with a new challenge, and share your experiences with others so that they grow and learn too. It is in these moments that we find the greatest satisfaction in our personal and professional lives.

Cathleen—a purpose-driven business partner, coach, author, and entrepreneur—is deeply rooted in faith, which guides her journey. Cathleen lives intentionally—believing the best way to predict the future is to create it. Her work is fueled by a desire to inspire growth, support transformation, and create spaces to thrive authentically.

Family is at the center of her life—both her biological and chosen families—and her beloved chihuahuas, whose unconditional love reminds her to embrace life's simple, joyful moments. Music is her emotional anchor, offering a soundtrack to her days and a connection to her inner self.

Travel fuels her curiosity and creativity, offering new perspectives and experiences that help shape her personal and professional growth. Each journey deepens her sense of purpose and connection to the world around her.

Through it all, Cathleen believes a life of purpose is built on faith, courage, connection, and an open heart. She remains grounded in faith, led by love, and is passionate about helping others discover their own paths.

Please scan the QR code to connect with this author.

Fielding Poe

Led to Teach

Discovering my vocational purpose has not been straightforward or easy. Some people have a clear vision for their lives early on, or at least by the time they graduate college. Then there are others like me. When I completed my undergraduate degree, I had absolutely no idea where I was headed or what line of work I ought to pursue. I always hoped and expected that the important matters of my life would naturally fall into place, and the right career would simply present itself. But it didn't work out that way.

After college I moved back into my parents' house with my diploma in hand and began searching the want ads. I bounced from interview to interview, looking desperately for anyone who would hire me. I finally landed at a high-end car dealership as a salesman. Life was looking better. I was going to wear suits to work, make good money, and drive fancy demo cars. But my car sales career lasted only a week and a half. It turns out that my convictions about honesty with customers frustrated the sales manager. I would need to alter my values or leave the dealership. I chose the latter. The new suits collected dust in the closet, and I was back to driving my old brown Honda Accord.

For the next couple years, I worked at Lowe's Home Improvement and then as a delivery driver for a heating and cooling company. This was not the life I had envisioned. I wanted a meaningful and satisfying career. I longed for a sense of vocational direction and purpose. But I was completely lost on what to do or where to turn. I recall meeting with a career counselor and reading *The Purpose Driven Life* as I sought answers. I prayed to God for help. My life seemed to be at a standstill and going nowhere, while others around me were becoming established in their careers.

A turning point came when two close friends told me, independently from one another, that I would make a good teacher. I had no idea what led them to think such a thing, but I took their words into serious consideration. This would be the beginning of my journey into the world of teaching. Sometimes other people, such as trustworthy friends, can detect qualities about us that we fail to notice in ourselves. I'm glad that I listened to my friends and explored further the possibility of teaching as a career path. After all, what would it hurt to pursue the idea? I didn't have anything else going for me career-wise.

I needed to try out teaching to determine if it could be a suitable career path for me. With the goal of testing my ability, I taught a kids' Sunday school class at my church. That experience went well enough that I decided to move toward a career in education. I enrolled in an evening program at Lindenwood University, where I earned a teaching certificate and master's degree while working as a groundskeeper during the day at a golf course. Toward the end of the degree program, I was required to student teach for a semester at one of the area high schools. During my internship, I clicked well with the students and teachers in the Language Arts department and was hired on as a full-time teacher for the following school year. When I began my first year as a high school teacher, I was twenty-six years old and felt that I had finally found my vocational purpose. The career search was over. The issue of finding my calling was settled. At least that's what I thought for my first few years in the classroom.

Sometime around year four or five of public-school teaching, I began to feel unsettled and discontent in my work. It was hard to imagine that I would be teaching high school for another twenty-five years or so. And I was constantly being nudged by the administration toward a cooperative learning approach to instruction that didn't suit my teaching style or strengths. At the same time of my discontent, I had found a new interest in studying and teaching the Bible. This newfound passion arose out of a home Bible study that I started with a group of friends with various religious backgrounds. Week after week, the attendance remained strong, and I found great satisfaction teaching Scripture, facilitating the discussions, and pointing my friends to the hope found in Jesus Christ. It seemed I had discovered a better niche for myself in teaching the Bible, as opposed to grammar and English literature. I began to think along the following lines: "If I'm going to devote my life to the vocation of teaching, then I want to study and teach the most important book in existence, the Bible."

There were other indications that my career path was being prepared for a transition. I began taking online seminary classes, and my church showed support by paying for the tuition and books. Eventually, my pastor invited me to preach on a Sunday evening. I accepted the invitation and studied hard to prepare my first sermon. Preaching that message was exhilarating, and I began to think that God might be guiding me toward a ministry of teaching and preaching. As I took steps in the direction of my newfound interest, I found support and affirmation from those closest to me. Finally, there came a point when I wanted to enter seminary full-time and devote myself completely to the study of Scripture and theology. My high school teaching job began to feel more and more like a hindrance to what I really felt compelled to do. I spoke with a couple of pastors at my church, and they supported my idea of full-time study.

While doors were opening for change, the decision to leave my high school teaching job wasn't simple or easy. There were costs and risks involved. First, I would have to give up a position as a tenured teacher in a top school district—something I might never get back. Second, I didn't really have a plan beyond graduating from seminary and then finding a career teaching the Bible. I didn't necessarily want to be a pastor, and teaching at the college or seminary level seemed like a long shot. Third, my wife would need to leave her nursing job and find a new position in a different state so we could stay together. Fourth, we would be leaving the comfort of our church and family as we set out for uncharted territory. Moving in this new direction required faith that God was guiding our steps and that he would provide for our needs moving forward.

In the summer of 2012, I resigned from my teaching position, and my wife and I set out for a new adventure in Louisville, Kentucky. I was excited to start something new and fully immerse myself in theological study. The transition to a different environment didn't prove too difficult, although it took us some time to agree on the right church as a newly married couple. After much searching, we finally landed at a congregation in Indiana, about fifteen minutes from the seminary. Being a part of this church family played a formative role in our lives. We gained close friendships, and I was given a pastoral internship, which helped to test and cultivate my call to ministry and preaching. Another milestone occurred for us in my seminary years, as my wife and I welcomed our first child.

While the time in seminary brought growth in my spiritual life and theological understanding, I felt lost regarding career direction leading up to graduation and immediately afterwards. In fact, I was entering into a phase very similar to the period following my initial college graduation. I didn't know which way to turn or what to do. I knew that I was gifted to teach and preach, but I didn't feel equipped, or necessarily called, to be a pastor with all the various tasks and administrative responsibilities involved. I would have liked to pursue a doctoral degree, but I needed to get back into full-time work, and I didn't know if I had the intellectual capability for such an endeavor. I could teach Bible at a private school, but those positions seemed rare. There was no clear path forward in my mind.

The next year and a half proved to be a confusing and difficult period, as I struggled to find vocational purpose once again. I was bitter and frustrated that I'd gone to seminary, only to feel that there was no place for me in the career world. I applied for various church ministry positions, but nothing panned out. I lacked confidence that I could succeed in such roles, and I didn't know if I even wanted those roles in the first place. I was beginning to lose hope that there was any vocational calling upon my life. But I had to work and earn some kind of living.

I opted to look for a low-stress job that would pay the bills and allow for a relatively easy life. What could possibly fit such criteria better than a mailman? Drive up to a mailbox, drop the mail in, proceed to the next mailbox, and collect a paycheck at the end of the week. But when I secured a position with the post office, I discovered that there was a bit more work involved than I anticipated. I will spare you the details, but I was miserable and lasted only six months (although it felt much longer). After that, I worked for a year at an alternative school with kids who had been suspended or were troubled in one manner or another. It was much better than the post office, but certainly couldn't be a long-term career path. One hard reality was that I now stood in a worse position careerwise than when I held my high school teaching position years earlier.

In the summer of 2016, I received a call from a church in Illinois about a youth ministry position I had applied for about a year earlier. The search committee had come back to my resume after setting it aside, and they were interested in interviewing me. One appealing factor about this church was its proximity to our home in Missouri. If things didn't work out with this position, the risk didn't seem so great since we wouldn't be moving very far away. I was also more prepared to take a job more in line with my calling to teach the Bible, even if some of the typical youth minister expectations were not the most enticing. I believe the dissatisfying jobs of my post-seminary days were useful for getting me back on track with the calling God had given me to teach His Word.

My role as a youth minister continued for four and a half years. This period served to cultivate my calling to church ministry. I was given the opportunity to teach the youth and lead various Bible studies for adults. In addition, I was granted the privilege of occasionally preaching in the Sunday services. The people of the church were mostly supportive and encouraging to me as a young minister. Overall, my experience was very positive, and I was thankful that the Lord led me to serve there for a time. However, youth ministry was not my long-term plan. I began to desire to serve the church through weekly pulpit preaching. I attended workshops on preaching and eventually entered a doctoral program focused solely on this area of ministry. I began seeking a pastoral position where I could use my gift of preaching in a full-time capacity.

An opportunity came when a small rural church contacted me for an interview during the first months of the global pandemic. After meeting with the search committee and preaching at a Sunday morning service, I was approved by the congregation to serve as their next pastor. The first few years were challenging, as I struggled to balance pastoral responsibilities with family life and doctoral studies. Additionally, it was difficult for us to find a house in the tough market that emerged during the pandemic. We lived in an apartment for three years before finally purchasing a home. Many of the initial hardships have now been resolved, as I graduated with the doctoral degree in 2023, we bought a house, and I now have a somewhat better grip on the rhythms of weekly pastoral tasks. Still, there are some unresolved issues with my vocational calling. I sense that I am unable to fulfill all the expectations of a solo pastor. I seem to excel in some areas and fall short in others. While I've made much progress in discovering my vocational purpose, I have much room for growth. And I sense that the pilgrimage is not yet complete.

As I reflect on my journey from college graduation to pastoral ministry, I can see God's guiding hand upon my life. My undergraduate degree and time in education early on served to prepare me for a calling to teach God's Word. Along the way, the Lord has placed people in my path who have helped guide and support me in the vocation of teaching and preaching. The painful times of lostness and wandering were useful for causing me to depend on God and to seek His guidance. I trust that all the details of my journey, both the pleasant and painful, have unfolded according to God's will for His glory and my ultimate good.

"He leadeth me! O blessed thought! O words with heavenly comfort fraught! Whate'er I do, where'er I be, Still tis God's hand that leadeth me."
—Joseph H. Gilmore

Fielding Poe is a Christian, a husband, and a father of three daughters. He is the pastor of First Baptist Church in Winfield, Missouri. He enjoys jumping on the trampoline with his daughters and watching them play soccer. Fielding also finds pleasure in jogging and other forms of exercise.

Please scan the QR code to connect with this author.

Elena Collins

The Ending Was Really a New Beginning

A new chapter in my life was about to begin. One of creating. Into the unknown. I had a choice with two options. One direction filled with familiarity. The other I recognized, but it was not going to be easy.

I was fighting a losing battle in my marriage with a stronghold that only God could work on. It was called the open-air prison of sin. Mentally, with sin, there is a prison door that is held open for a person to leave at any time, but they are shackled by the enticements of that sin. So, they continue to stay in that prison room until one day, the prison doors close.

God, my friends, and my family led me through the process of divorce, day by day. I knew with God, my decision would be the right one. I stayed out of my own way this time. We had already reconciled once. I was thinking that what I said would make a difference. I was hoping and praying for change. And here we were with the decision staring me straight in the face. My ex-husband and I were starting our new lives, raising our child, but separately and in different states. Thank you to my child's dad for going through the process God's way. We are all better for it.

A good friend said to me while I was in Divorce Care, "Your shattered heart will be glued together piece by piece, and while you will be able to see the crackle in the glass, it will be healed by God's love."

I knew from my experience, as a child of divorce and moving states, that life would be fulfilling, but not always easy. Those are the choices I made with the love of a mother for her child, a woman for her sanity, and respect for herself and her child. For that is the true meaning of love, and the life God truly wanted us to have in Him.

I was settling into a new state, working a new job, newly divorced, trying to make a life for my child and me, and everything in between. And in one moment, because of the pandemic, it seemed as if life just stopped. My job was over, and I had to find another new beginning. I'm so thankful that I dug in and created roots and that my child's dad kept reminding me to plug into a church once we moved. I met several wonderful groups of powerhouse ladies at church. That church was one of the best things that had happened to us. During that time, I reflected back to sitting at a table that overlooked a lake in my backyard, remembering what a wonderful friend of mine had said to me on the phone: "Day by day, moment by moment, and breath by breath." I asked God, "God, what is my purpose now?"

I was always really good at coming up with ideas and solutions for just about anything that came my way. It was a survival mode as a child trying to make our life better, and a gift as an adult. Now with literally 600+ applications and resumes submitted to companies, I went from wanting a marketing director position to chipping away at my ego and pride and in one very powerful moment, saying, "Ok, God. I'd be happy with an assistant position," which had been my first profession out of school.

I fell on my knees by my bedside and started sobbing, going through all the emotions of loss. I had been working so hard for a good life for my daughter and me, but I had no more solutions or ideas. "God, I can't do this on my own. I don't want the control. I don't have any more good ideas or things I can do. I have nothing left but to fully depend on you. It's ok if I start over again. I can't do this without you. I trust you." And then I heard... **"That, child, is where I've wanted you all along."**

With a couple of temporary positions that came my way, I was relearning what purpose meant while rediscovering myself. With each job assignment, my work taught me something specific inside. Not only that, but I now believed there were reasons why I had to learn about every department within a company.

During that time, I did not lack for anything. When I needed something, it was there. So many gifts from God through people that I can't even name them all.

When I had gotten sick during the pandemic, I was looking at myself in the mirror one day, and I noticed how my spiritual strength had grown. I also noticed that my appearance and health were not reflected in the same way. My skin was gray, and I couldn't smell. My mind and spirit were at war.

The pandemic is a mimicker, imitator and manipulator, and liar of illnesses. It's an illness you're familiar with. You'll feel you have a temperature where there is none, or it is lower than normal, and you feel cold in areas you normally wouldn't. Random and sporadic pains in different degrees. An increase of what is already ailing you. You'll feel hopelessness or a loss of feelings and thoughts. Coughing is different, almost as if trying to get rid of a foreign entity. Your muscles and skin hurt and burn. This was sickness, but it was also spiritual warfare.

During this time, what God did next is my testimony! He emptied me out, melted me, and started building me more in his image. Shortening my spans of fear and worry, teaching me His word, and building my faith until He knew I was ready for His plan. Then, He introduced me to the rest of my new life.

I have let go of so many difficulties, so many things that I thought were necessary to get through life, whether it was certain behaviors of mine, past trauma, truths that were hidden for many years, or experiences that I had gone through and had lied to myself about. He took all the guilt and shame I had carried for many years and replaced them with forgiveness and joy.

I have learned to listen to the Holy Spirit. To take promptings or nudges, not to jump on my own. I am more patient in the waiting period in times when I felt that I needed to make an immediate decision. To not take charge automatically because I've learned that there's a better way. Opening myself up for better opportunities that I could have never dreamed of, all because I waited and listened for a path and instructions on which way to go or what to do.

I have a quicker time in between a problem and trusting God for a solution, and that quickening is trusting in God instead of the control and emotions that I would go through, like panic, stress, worry, despair, and pleading. I have been given discernment to see and know that there's pain behind every interaction with someone that feels odd. I've learned not to be afraid of others and their behaviors. If they are out of control, that does not mean that I am out of control. I can choose how I respond.

I have learned by going through extreme hardships and placing my trust in God on where I should go, that He has opened many doors for me. I'm now living in answered prayers. To make sure everything is written down in a journal, because that is how I will consistently go back to Him in times of doubt and for encouragement and confirmation. I've learned to never give up when God is leading you. God never breaks His promises. When God gives you a vision, He will complete the task. It may not look like what we think it should look like, but it will be more beautiful than we ever imagined. That all things meant for your harm will be turned for your good. That God really does speak through people at a moment's notice to give you peace and guidance, and that God takes care of His children in the big and the small.

Purpose for me was focusing on my child and being the best mom I could be, just like my mom was for me. My child has witnessed the building of our faith and the struggles I've had with my mom's death, the divorce, moving from one end of the country to the other, the pandemic, not having a job, and then moving back home to Missouri, that God has been there every step, and He continues to. My child saw how the enemy operates, but she also saw how big our God is and how He makes beauty from ashes and makes us stronger because of it.

You have to let go and allow an emptying of sorts so that God can fill you just as a parent does their child.

You see, all of these things could not have happened if I had made the other choice. I know that. God was preparing me in one state to then take me back home to move forward confidently.

I went back home to Missouri for a wedding, and this time it felt different. While sitting alone outside one day, asking God what was next, He said, "Your assignment is over. It's time to go home." So again, we would go to another state, back home, except this time we had a cat, a fish, and one of my girlfriends from my church, who said I was not driving by myself. What an adventure!

After settling into Missouri and searching for a job, I was introduced to a wonderful group called Job Seekers' Garden Club (JSGC). It's a group that was created during the pandemic, consisting of job seekers, recruiters, and connectors. I met with their founder, Bob Kolf, over coffee. We exchanged stories, and purpose was mentioned. I left that meeting with a renewed spirit. I spent time thinking about purpose and what that meant for me now. After much soul searching, I know I have more than one purpose. It is to be a great mom, to share my creative gifts with the world, to encourage and uplift other people every day, to introduce and show others how to be loved by God, and to continue with my gift of empathy to help others. My journey with God and finding my new passions through myself and God has led me to many new opportunities in life. God made sure I was taken care of. I found a great job where the position quickly evolved. I'm serving as a Board Member now for JSGC. I started making updates to my home, and I'm making so much progress with my finances and what I want for our future. There is hope after heartache, devastation, and trauma. I'm living proof.

Here I am, healed, learning, evolving—watching my beautiful child grow, and awaiting the next chapter of my life to begin.

The best is yet to come...

If you've ever wondered what it's like having lived in two worlds, meet Elena Collins. She is half Cuban, and the other half is Scottish, Irish, English, German, Swedish, and French. Talk about a handful. She spent most of her childhood in Miami and most of her adult life in St. Louis.

Elena loves the arts and music and always enjoys trying something new. Writing fills her soul. She's multifaceted. She has amazing family and friends.

Elena has had many adventures along with heartaches. With each experience, she learned, healed, and continued to the next chapter. She has always been very strong in her faith; God is number one. She is back home in her new chapter, waiting for what's next.

Please scan the QR code to connect with this author.

Melissa Baldwin

Recognizing Defining Moments

The Cambridge dictionary describes "defining moments" (noun) as a very important point in time or a very important event that people will remember as having changed a situation in an important way.

In my time here on this planet amongst 340.1 million people, I continue to reflect on my individual life and how, in certain moments, if I wouldn't have made the decisions I have made, where I would be? Would I be happier? Stronger? Enjoy my life better? End up not even being here to type this story? **My story**. The truth is, these questions, to me, are what lead us to defining moments. These moments have brought me to this point in my life, despite obstacles thrown at me as if one of the pitchers from the Atlanta Braves is pitching an impeccable curveball, to continually reinvent myself.

My first defining moment, at age nine, I went with what my instinct, the Lord above, the universe, told me to do. I am sure I would not be here today, reflecting on life and how we react in these moments, if it weren't for trusting myself. That's what defining moments are about, right? Trusting yourself when something feels off. It's listening to the voice in your heart, regardless of what others want, feel, and/or need.

My life is full of these moments, and it's been spiritually related to how I perceive the world around me. Trusting myself to know what's right and what's wrong in a situation. Learning to make the best decision with the information I have, for me and my loved ones. Doesn't every decision have some type of consequence? What am I willing to accept and not accept? These are the determining factors on how we make decisions in life, and have you ever had such a strong, almost presence and/or energy come over you that's almost impossible to ignore?

Not assuming this happens to everyone in their lives, these truly defining moments have happened, for me, throughout my life. My next defining moment began in 2020, at the peak of the health crisis for the world. I was working in healthcare; I enjoyed my role more than any other role before. How much? Well, let's just say, "I was not a morning person per se back then, okay?"

Yet, this healthcare role would drive me up out of my bed eagerly at 4 a.m. Yet I was conflicted. I have my master's degree in business administration and was an experienced trainer. I knew I desired more pay, more support, more recognition, and acknowledgement of my accomplishments. I wasn't going to ask for it, though.

I should just be happy with what I have, right? I should just stay in this role and go for the promotion. So, I did, despite the cues inside of me. What I failed to recognize is you can be happy with what you have currently, while wanting and developing for more.

Having a fear of upsetting those around me and not pausing to process what was right for me became the way I operated, causing me to miss the cues. It was time to move on for me and my career. Have you ever heard the saying, "The Lord has a sense of humor?" Interestingly enough, that saying would become one of the most prolific defining moments in my life thus far and would be the catalyst for many more defining moments to follow.

Feeling secure in my role and being the only person dedicated to my business unit, when the message came that reductions in workforce would happen, I felt I didn't need to worry. I told myself amid the crisis, "I have been loyal to the organization, provided expertise, and had a positive impact on the culture. **I am safe**."

I am sure you know what comes next…my role was eliminated. It's so easy to look in the rearview mirror and see it for what it is now. In those moments, all I could see was how loyal and supportive I had been to our team and organization, and the comfort this provided to me. I ignored the internal feelings that I wasn't using the talents the Lord had gifted me, leading me to feel immediately devastated. What followed were feelings of betrayal, deep disbelief, anger, and questioning company loyalty.

The well-meant saying, "When one door closes, another one opens," was the last phrase I wanted to hear. Yet that is all I heard. There is that great sense of humor I described earlier. While I know the phrase is true, I was asking myself questions: "Can I trust myself moving forward?" "Why didn't I listen to myself when I felt like I needed more?" Being this was my first unexpected career disruption, I did not know these questions were valid. My previous experience with career disruption was by my choice. I left the workforce to focus on our youngest son after a life-altering neuro-muscular disease.

Now, this was different. The choice was made for me. I became depressed and stayed in my house. I applied for job after job, looking for something, anything, that would provide an income and help me feel better. I was focused on saying "I have a job," again. I had wrapped my identity and worth in the work I was doing. Now I had to find out "Who is Melissa?"

It was extremely uncomfortable as I navigated finding the fulfillment I felt in my job in my personal life. Having not fully processed the effects of what job elimination does to a person, I landed my next job within six months. This next role was needed for my career without me realizing it, and still, I found myself conflicted again. I learned the training process from end to end, and obtained instructional design experience and professional certifications. Like my previous role, I was the only training and development onsite resource. What was different was that the role was newly created. With no existing training materials, I assumed the responsibility of instructional design and training. I loved this!

I was so inspired by the role, and when I delivered on commitments each time with metrics that displayed the training had made a difference, it was like a rush I had never felt before! I was living out the talents and strengths I was wired to produce. Delivering on challenges and opportunities I had never been allowed to explore before felt wonderful. I was trusting myself again after the difficulty of a job loss. Now, solely relying on my talents to deliver successful commitments, I had found myself again as a professional. Bringing to life my vision vs. a team's vision was amazing.

Past grieving the loss of my previous job, I now knew what I was made of. Sounds wonderful, right? *HA!* Will I forever be quoting the sense of humor that the Lord has throughout this chapter? Why, yes, yes, I will, and I believe it to be so accurate and telling on how we receive our defining moments. We think we have it all figured out, don't we? And just when it appears that way, we are lifted straight from that story we tell in our heads, and a wrinkle in time is created, a defining moment is produced, whether we want that or not. Also, during this time, my mother was diagnosed with dementia, and I have an immunocompromised son. As the caregiver for both, I am feeling more guilty regarding the need to sporadically work from home. Additionally, a co-worker showed resentment towards my need for flexibility and exploited the difficulties in my life to show she was more committed than me.

This time, I chose to listen to the cues. After one year and six months, I chose myself and switched to a fully remote role as a program manager so that I could be closer to my mom and son. With this move, I expected to no longer have to choose between family and career, finally. What I found was that the position required long hours, and I was now faced with the struggle of balancing caregiving and career. By December 12, 2022, my mother was placed on hospice with less than three weeks to live.

It was the holiday season, and I was losing my mother. I stared out the back window of my home, while my husband and boys slept, after coming home from the hospital after twelve hours. There was fresh snow that had just arrived and was beautifully falling on the ground. In that moment, it took me back to when I was a child and my mom had come to my brother and me and said, "It's snowing outside, hurry, put on your snowsuit, snow boots, and jackets!" I could hear her voice so vividly as if she were standing next to me while recalling this memory. My brother and I looked at each other in disbelief. I was always the first to speak up in moments of uncertainty, and I found this moment to be no different when my brother looked at me to carry on that same tradition for him and me. "But Mom, they haven't called off school yet, and we may have school in the morning." I'll never forget the words she told me in that moment. Our mom said, "And if we don't enjoy it now, we may never get the opportunity to enjoy it again." My mom, brother, and I played in the snow together, the hardest I have ever played in snow as it fell for hours that evening into the night.

I'm not sure what happened to me in those moments of recalling that memory that late night. Whatever happened, I am so very grateful for it. I became a different person recalling that memory. The next morning, my husband asked me, "What are you going to do about work, due dates, and being with your mom?" Without hesitation, I said calmly, "I'm going to be present with my mom and I'll deal with work after she passes away." I wasn't going to allow this defining moment to pass without me being fully present. I was not going to miss any of the last moments. I believe my mom's words that snowy night to my brother and me were larger than living with the regret of not playing in the snow. It was reappearing as a memory to me of what's important in life. Her message was about living a larger purpose. Sometimes opportunities come our way and land in front of us, and we fail to see them. Other times, they land so hard that we are unable to shake the feeling of seeing them.

What I have found throughout my life is that we must be able to answer, "Can we live with the choices and decisions we make in those defining moments?" The regret that may follow, others do not have to carry the burden. There was another defining moment in my life where I stated earlier, was strong, that was almost impossible to ignore. As much as I wanted my career, I wanted to spend those final moments of my mom's life with her. I chose her.

I will never regret this as long as I live. When returning to work, I learned my employer did not value my choice. I had spent three weeks caring for her and three days laying her to rest. I realized my values and my employer's values did not align. Therefore, I chose to explore other opportunities. I got out of the house, volunteered with Job Seekers' Garden Club, found fulfillment in who I am as a person, not just as a daughter, wife, mom, or an employee—but as me.

What I found next in my career was something so satisfying and humanizing that I would wonder if the Lord had brought me to this point in my career purposefully or if I was imagining the way I felt. I found peace. I finally felt like no matter what was going to happen, I could trust myself enough to make the right decisions, in the right moments, for me. That those moments are sent to us to define us and make us who we are in our lives.

So, now when you are faced with career disruption, you have decisions to make that will help define you and your future, and make you who you need to be in your future opportunities that are about to come your way. Get excited and choose wisely, because you may just love who you become in your future self. Trust yourself to fall. Even the best fall down sometimes. Go volunteer, get out of your house, choose the opportunity like it has chosen you. Make the best decision you can at the time and don't live in it too long without looking around and daring to wonder if there is more. Try not to take other people's decisions too personally; they, too, have a life to live full of defining moments just like you and me.

Melissa Baldwin, MBA, PMP, is a dynamic and results-driven talent development professional with over a decade of experience in training, instructional design, and organizational development. She is known for creating impactful learning programs that improve performance, reduce turnover, and support strategic business goals. Currently serving as a training project manager, she leads complex training initiatives and evaluation strategies across Missouri operations. Previous roles include leadership development at the largest manufacturer for exterior building products in the United States and a multi-family, residential real estate company. She has built high-impact programs with an 85% Net Promoter Score and reduced first-year turnover from 41% to 25%.

Driven by her passion for developing people and improving processes, she's a trusted leader, coach, and change agent committed to organizational excellence.

In her off-time, Melissa enjoys spending time with her husband, three sons, boating, cooking, and reading.

Please scan the QR code to connect with this author.

Andrew Sippie

Pandemic-Driven Purpose

Tutoring in writing at a community college has always felt full of purpose. Tutors help students believe in themselves. They may be fresh out of high school and searching for purpose and motivation, or returning learners 20 or more years later who doubt they can learn like they used to. Students may struggle with difficult academic concepts, but the heart of tutoring is always the same: learners need to believe they can learn.

At the tutoring center, students have awed me when they openly write essays about being a survivor of a school shooting, experiencing rape, or suffering the loss of a child. One was in tears because he didn't want to work at McDonald's for the rest of his life. Another seemed to suffer from memory loss and couldn't retain information, but always left the tutoring sessions feeling more capable. For 15 years, tutoring and teaching felt meaningful to me and those I helped. Helping others learn never bored me, thoughtfully challenged me, and gave me many opportunities for personal and professional growth. Then, the pandemic happened.

In the Spring 2020 semester, thousands of students who would have visited our community college tutoring center disappeared. Campus was closed. All courses went online. We worked remotely, something I had never done before.

In the Fall 2020 semester, plexiglass barriers sat on the tutoring center tables, supported by chains that clung to the ceiling. Tutors no longer sat to the left or right of a student, we sat across. Barriers made student essays more difficult to view and trust more difficult to gain. Almost no students visited. A handful of classes, compared to hundreds, were in-person.

Every workday, I would commute twenty minutes one way to pull into a nearly empty parking lot, put on a mask, receive a temperature screening upon entering, go to my office area, and conduct online tutoring all day with a headset and webcam. In the Spring 2020 semester, we had done the exact same online tutoring at home. I saw my coworkers from a distance in their own office areas. My coworkers and I no longer talked because this was before the vaccine, and we were terrified of receiving or spreading the disease. Medical experts said you could have, and spread, the disease without symptoms.

The possibility of having permanent brain fog as a side effect horrified me. My life's purpose was not just understanding what effective college-level writing is, but to understand how someone may not understand it, may let themselves believe they cannot learn it, and to help them believe they can do it and build them up. Tutoring involves making quick observations to see what students best react to while remaining calm and encouraging. Tutoring involves considerable patience and empathy combined with sustained focus from careful reading of assignment requirements and student essays. While I love the challenge and meaningfulness of tutoring, I feared I couldn't do it with brain fog.

I also adored doing my own writing and, even more than tutoring, that requires considerable focus and thought. Slower or impaired cognition could threaten my career and my writing passion. I became more anxious. The restricted breathing that I used to have when I was younger came back. I would feel too much pain for full breaths until I calmed myself while taking shallow breaths. Late at night, as I twisted in the sheets of my bed, I wondered why we went to our offices. Sure, everyone was required to wear masks, maintain social distancing, do temperature checks, and it was understood that one should avoid in-person interaction unless completely necessary. The workplace was safe, I knew, but the worry still lingered.

My worries worsened when, within a span of 6 months in 2020, I lost my only two remaining grandparents—two grandmothers—to the pandemic. In remembering their lives, I began to sense what would lead to a broader sense of purpose. One of my grandmothers was a librarian for decades. She loved history and loved to talk outside on the porch about anything. I remember talking for hours about the Civil War. She loved to share the smaller and individual historical stories that humanized it, such as Jennie Wade. During the 3-day battle at Gettysburg, she was kneading bread in her home when a stray bullet killed her. She may have stayed inside, as many of us did during the pandemic, yet she still died.

The hundreds of thousands who died in the Civil War or the millions who died from the pandemic may not mean much because the numbers are too staggering to visualize, but take one person, one ordinary person who was trying to live life, and the tragedy is sobering. I started realizing that my life's story was perhaps too narrow. When my grandmother died, I was allowed to select any of her books to keep. They still sit on my shelf, wide ones about the Civil War and slimmer ones about ghost stories. They remind me that, somehow, life continues. Stubbornly, stupidly, bravely, miraculously, stories continue to be told. They need to be told and learned from. And my story wasn't just about tutoring, it was about telling stories creatively and writing.

My other grandmother likely was a significant inspiration for the science fiction and fantasy that I write. My grandmother loved the weird. She introduced me and my brother to the wolfman from the show *Are You Afraid of the Dark?* (1993) (who terrified me as a kid, despite her assuring me constantly that it wasn't real) and the *Langoliers* (1995) TV series. I remember my grandfather and her bickering about what to watch on TV once. She said she didn't want to see his boring wildlife and deer in the woods, and my grandpa said he didn't want to watch something where a worm burst out of someone's stomach. Her unconditional acceptance of things like interdimensional aliens eating reality meant she was always open to a conversation about anything. Yes, I was often terrified by the horror she liked, but she had such a wonder at seeing the strange and the odd. That's why I love to explore genres like magical realism.

Magical realism was one of many revelations during the Master of Fine Arts (MFA) in creative writing I took during the pandemic. Though reading *Station Eleven* (2014) for a class was difficult, a book about a pandemic that causes a post-apocalyptic world (and predicted the panic buying of toilet paper!), the experience opened my eyes even further to writing purposes beyond the academic. I was thrilled to find even more ways to express myself and that odder side of reality that my grandmother had embraced. Other classes I took felt closer to what my grandfather had loved: nature. When combined with science fiction, I learned about the emerging genre of climate fiction, which concerns how humans interact with the natural world (spoiler: it often doesn't end well for us). For a novel I wrote, I learned more about the deep ocean and the weird creatures that live down there, who communicate through glowing and can change their body shape and color to camouflage. I wrote novel after novel just for the joy of it and to know and prove to myself that I could. When I wrote, everything I had feared about brain fog at the workplace faded away. I even had a few small writings published, another personal goal to prove to myself that I could. I felt more truly connected to a purpose beyond just working in higher education or being a writing tutor.

I had also learned about how to impactfully and meaningfully write memoirs during my MFA, which would become helpful when I met with an individual who hired me as a ghost writer. As if fated, a significant childhood experience centered around a climate fiction topic, except it wasn't fiction. For years, I used many skills from writing tutoring to meet with this individual, record and interview them, meet about revisions, and discuss story changes, additions, and removals. We visited their childhood home and talked about the world and climate change and how they had lived elsewhere in the world, feeling as if they didn't quite fit in. I could relate. Together, we discussed many drafts of their childhood story they had always wanted to tell, especially because they feared they were nearing the end of their life.

Again, I thought back on my own life. When I first started tutoring as an undergraduate in the Fall 2007 semester, I had a wise and supportive supervisor who said I should consider teaching overseas because I was working with many English as a Second Language (ESL) students and was so fascinated by it. Working regularly with ESL students over my tutoring career inspires much curiosity and wonder. The more I learned about other cultures and worked with other students from around the world over the years, the more I learned about myself and the painfully narrow, specific, and set way that I live. This wide blue and green planet we all live on offers so many different human experiences. That's why I started a degree in teaching English as a Second Language in the Spring 2025 semester.

I've also been reconsidering the definition of a workplace. When working from home during part of the Spring 2020 semester, I had become more aware of the energy I feel in a quiet room at home. With multi-colored bright lights, traditional Japanese-style scroll art flowing with fog nuzzling distant mountains, and bookshelves so full of books that they are sometimes stacked, home gives me energy and purpose. Working remotely, I relearned the joy of uninterrupted focus, the flow of productivity, and the achievement that comes from within.

I especially learned the self-reliance of a remote job while training AI. What pleasantly surprised me was that I could choose whenever and wherever I wanted to work and always experienced different situations when giving the AI feedback. Also, what I knew about learning applied to helping the AI learn from human interactions. And what is weirder and more fascinating than helping something non-human learn? This side hustle showed me that if I were to work from home or anywhere, I would have the drive and determination to do so, so long as I had a passion for it.

The confinement, fear of brain fog, and loss of loved ones from the pandemic helped me to realize that I was confining myself to a specific position in a specific job in a specific place. Despite how meaningful and profound the in-person higher education tutoring experience can be, how much I enjoy it, and how well I do it, many other possibilities are just as meaningful, profound, and impactful. I realized I am so much more than a job or a place, and no matter what the future holds, if I am passionate about what I do and act on that conviction, it can and will happen.

Andrew Sippie finds his happy place writing and reading. He can often be found jogging, hiking, or walking through the woods in search of the next idea and to immerse himself in nature. He loves learning, whether personal or helping others, so he has worked in higher education for over 15 years, tutoring and teaching writing, literature, and English as a Second Language. He has also earned advanced degrees in creative and academic writing. Primarily, he does 1-on-1 tutoring, but he also teaches online and has managed a tutoring center. He has found purpose in writing's ability to help us better understand the world around us, ourselves, and to more meaningfully express how we think, how we feel, and what our story is. He writes for the sake of writing, to push personal boundaries, learn, dream, and experiment, especially with poetry, flash fiction, magical realism, and speculative fiction.Angela Russell

Please scan the QR code to connect with this author.

Noelle Robinson

The Sound of a New Beginning

"You must find a tribe. Become part of a group that can help you get the interviews. That's the best way to get the job." The professor stood in front of the classroom filled with teachers aspiring to become administrators. And for some reason, those words sparked an unsettling realization within me.

How do I find a leadership tribe when I've struggled to find a teacher tribe?

Why can't merit alone lead to promotions?

As the conversation continued into the intricacies of social politics and the competitive climb to leadership, my head began to spin. What I had always known about the unspoken rules of careers in public school education, where connections often overshadowed qualifications, was suddenly feeling more discouraging than ever. As I listened to this conversation unfold, my heart began to sink. A harsh truth was now front and center in my mind—that success in this system often depended more on connections than on skill or passion.

My inner world continued to spin as I left the classroom. I felt gut-punched. My mind raced as I reflected on my career and my future. I loved teaching so much. Through all the ups and downs, I had always felt confident that I was making a difference in the lives of my students.

But for the first time in my career…I started questioning everything I had ever felt about teaching. *Was it worth it? Was I truly making a difference?*

It was the fall of 2021. The global health crisis had done quite a number on the education system, and my heart broke daily as I watched it unfold. I had witnessed the unintentional transformation of our lives and our school buildings over the last year and a half. We went from teaching at home to teaching online, and then finally back to teaching in classrooms that now felt unrecognizable. Everything had changed. And we were left to put back the pieces. It felt like the blind leading the blind, as each person did their best to navigate this new reality.

I had finally found a school and a district that I loved. Yet, I couldn't deny that education had changed greatly since I first stepped into the classroom. Once a place of creativity, connection, and exploration, education had become a treadmill of testing, metrics, and constant demands to perform. Both students and teachers were often put under immense pressure to meet the standards that had been set by those who rarely understood the dynamics of the individual classrooms.

And throughout my career, I had changed, too. My personal journey led me to discover the importance of emotional regulation, mental health, and the power of sound and vibration for healing the nervous system. Weaving these insights into my teaching was an uphill battle. I had spent the last year turning my classroom into as much of a peaceful oasis as I could, but it still didn't feel like enough. The students I taught, their parents, and even my co-workers were facing tremendous stress and anxiety. I felt like I was standing on a bridge between two worlds: the world of education and the world of holistic health, and I was struggling to bring the two together.

As much as I wanted to help my students thrive, I began to feel like I was contributing to their stress more than alleviating it. The curriculum left little room for mental health support, and the demands of standardized testing overshadowed the deeper needs of the students' overall development. I saw students losing their spark, overwhelmed by the pressure to perform, and I felt powerless to help them in the way they truly needed.

As I reflected upon all of this after that classroom discussion, I felt forced to confront the current state of education, as well as the state of my own heart.

As the days passed, I couldn't get the thoughts out of my head. The more I ignored it, the louder the inner conflict became. Teaching had been my identity for quite some time. It was terrifying to admit that the path I had worked so hard to build no longer felt right for me. However, I also knew deep down that staying would only lead to more frustration and inner turmoil.

The inner dialogue continued to rumble in the background of my mind.

What would I do next? Where would I go? Could I find a job outside teaching? What was I even qualified to do? Did I just waste ten years of my life?

The overwhelming doubts and worries grew louder and louder. Within a few weeks, I made the decision to leave teaching. Yet, I still had no idea what I was going to do next.

It was in those moments that I leaned on my faith. I surrendered completely. For perhaps the first time in my life, I let go of control and placed my trust entirely in the unknown. I focused on two things I could control: finding my tribe and following the "breadcrumbs" that lit me up inside.

Reflecting on the idea of tribe, I realized I had been seeking belonging in spaces that weren't meant for me. This brought hard realizations that many seasons of life were filled with spaces in which I never felt belonging. I started reflecting on the places and groups of people who I felt most supported and appreciated with. There were two spaces I knew that I was loved and appreciated. One was wellness spaces, which I had been part of a few different ones. The other was Little Black Book, a women's business networking group located in Missouri and Illinois. I wasn't quite sure how I could bring those two together at first, but at least I had a good start.

I also began paying attention to the "breadcrumbs," small nudges and signs that seemed to light the path forward. These nudges lit me up inside and somewhere in my heart just felt "right." It wasn't easy to trust these signs at first, but I kept listening. I kept surrendering and trusting my intuition. Even in the moments that I felt a bit crazy, I chose to trust God and His plan for my life. I focused on doing the "next right thing," instead of trying to figure out the entire plan.

It was around this same time I noticed the growing attention I was receiving for the Paiste Symphonic Gong my husband had bought me—a powerful instrument that creates deep, flowing sounds that regulate your nervous system, and you can feel in your whole body. He had bought it as a gift, after our lives were completely transformed from attending sound immersions. A sound immersion—often called a sound bath—is a deeply restorative and meditative experience where carefully selected instruments like gongs, chimes, and singing bowls create waves of sound and vibration that gently guide the body and mind into a state of calm, clarity, and healing. Over the previous year, sound immersions had completely transformed our lives and our marriage. We were happier and healthier than we had ever felt before. After attending regular sound immersions for four months, my chronic pain and ADHD were gone. I no longer needed medication to function, and I was feeling better than I had ever imagined. The whole experience honestly felt like a miracle, as I never thought I would be able to function without medications.

After almost a lifetime of anxiety, my husband experienced a peace he couldn't truly understand, but knew he wanted more. After such huge transformations, we were committed to continuing to heal. Yet with three children, it was difficult for us to find sound immersions that fit our schedule. The sessions were often unpredictable, and they required us to pack up any blankets, pillows, or mats we would need each time. The gong was a testament to our determination to prioritize our health and wellness. I had no idea how much that gong would change my life.

At first, it was simply a tool for our own healing. But as I began learning how to play, friends started requesting I play the gong at events. Sharing the vibrational power of sound immersions lit something within me I hadn't felt in years. One evening, I played for a small group of friends, many of whom had experienced sound immersions before. The next morning, one of the women approached me in tears. For two years, she had been haunted by grief and chronic pain following the loss of her mother. That night, she experienced her first full night of sleep and woke pain-free. As we talked about her experience, she looked me in the eyes and said, "Please do this for more people. The world needs more of this." Her words echoed in my heart long after. I had only owned the gong for a few months, yet was already witnessing profound shifts in people I played for. *What would happen if I deepened my study?*

With curiosity and cautious faith, I immersed myself in books, trainings, and courses. Each one lit me up from within. My vision expanded, and I began to research other businesses that offered sound immersions. I couldn't find a model that truly reflected the experience I wanted to create. So, I began building it.

We started small, sub-leasing a fitness studio for four sessions a week. Inconveniences I'd once overlooked—like hauling blankets or struggling to find time—became opportunities to reimagine the experience entirely. Slowly, our sessions gained momentum. Clients reported sleeping through the night, releasing anxiety, and shedding chronic pain. We added memberships, and then more sessions and team members. The Sound Spa became more than a business—it became a movement

In December of 2023, our studio location officially opened in St. Peters, MO. That moment felt like the end of an era, as we closed the chapter on our temporary space and the construction project that brought our studio to life. Yet, it was truly just the beginning. The beginning of a journey that continues to challenge me and amaze me daily, one that has brought me more joy and growth than I thought possible.

Looking back, I realize that the journey to discovering my purpose wasn't a sudden leap, but a series of small, aligned actions, each one guided by faith, intuition, and the quiet nudges I chose to follow. What started as a simple effort to improve my own well-being grew into something far greater than I could have imagined.

The Sound Spa is more than a business; it's a testament to what can happen when you lean into the unknown, trust the process, and let your heart lead the way. The transformations I've witnessed—from clients reclaiming their health, to discovering inner peace—are daily reminders of the power of listening, both to the wisdom of the Universe around us and to the truth within ourselves.

Leaving teaching felt like an impossible decision, but it allowed me to step into a version of myself that I might have never done.

This journey has taught me that the road to purpose is rarely straightforward. It's filled with doubts, unexpected turns, and moments of incredible fear. But it's in those moments, the ones where you push through the fear, take the leap, and create what doesn't yet exist, that you discover not only your purpose but also your power.

Today, I stand humbled and grateful, not just for the success of The Sound Spa, but for the journey that brought me here. Every struggle, every uncertain step, and every whispered nudge led to a business making a meaningful impact in the lives the sound touches. And for that, I am truly grateful.

Noelle Robinson is a holistic wellness practitioner, sound therapy expert, and founder of The Sound Spa—a sanctuary for nervous system regulation, emotional healing, and deep restoration. With a background in education and a passion for neuroscience, Noelle bridges science and soul to help people break free from chronic stress and overwhelm. Through her signature sound immersions, transformational events, and empowering content, she guides others back to their inner peace, confidence, and vitality. Noelle believes that healing is both a personal and collective act—and she's here to help her community remember that they are worthy of rest, joy, and radiant health. Her mission is simple: create spaces where people feel safe to release, seen in their journey, and supported in their transformation. Whether online or in-person, Noelle's work inspires a return to self—one breath, one sound, one intentional moment at a time.

Please scan the QR code to connect with this author.

Julia Durant

Hope When I Had None

They gave me hope when I didn't have any.

One day while perusing LinkedIn, I came across the Job Seekers' Garden Club (JSGC). I was intrigued by the meaning behind the creation of the club and its purpose. So, I joined. It was during the pandemic, when a lot of people lost their jobs, that the founder created this wonderful club to help people with their job searches. A group of very knowledgeable and caring individuals who wanted to help.

I hadn't been a member of JSGC for very long when I was very unexpectedly let go from my job in late October 2023. I worked for an insurance brokerage, and they were going to restructure the company due to the loss of two major insurance carriers. My boss, the owner of the insurance brokerage, was very nice, but made it clear that they had to let me go. The insurance carriers had decided to close their doors. Not just pull out of Missouri, but completely close their companies because they were no longer profitable. Due to the loss of the two insurance carriers, the brokerage needed to focus on client retention and try to move thousands of clients to one of the other carriers they represented. I was a new business contributor, not a customer service representative who serviced clients, so I was no longer useful to the company.

Let go! What?! Really, after three years of hard work? I brought in over $3,000,000 of new business over those three years! I was in shock! Did I understand the situation? Yes. Did I like it? No! And just like that, my life was turned upside down, suddenly launched into turmoil, and I was overwhelmed. What was I going to do? How was I going to find a job? Not necessarily a job that I liked, but a job to survive. I have been in survival mode since I was a child, and I was weary of how much more I could endure. I became angry...how could they do this to me? I thought that I was doing a good job of bringing in new business. I thought they appreciated me and my efforts. After all, one would think that bringing in over $3,000,000 of new business to the brokerage was a significant contribution, but it didn't matter. They didn't even offer to transfer me to a different department, just goodbye. Where was the loyalty? Surprise, there was none.

I thought I had job security, but I didn't. I was in disbelief; it was like a bad dream. Like most people, I had bills to pay and wondered how I was going to make ends meet and survive. I felt betrayed by a company that I liked working for, a company that I had invested three years in, a company that I thought I would retire from.

I took a step back and some time to absorb the dreadful news. I had to do something, instead of eating unhealthy food, drinking, and crying. I need to get my rear off the sofa and try. I found it difficult to try, though, as I was in an anger-driven pity party.

I decided I would go to a JSGC meeting. There, I met the founder; he was warm, welcoming, and kind. He understood my predicament. I'm sure he had heard hundreds of stories from other job seekers. He introduced me to several people in hopes that I would make some good connections. He also encouraged me to find out how I could help connect other job seekers with someone or a job opportunity. JSGC is not just about receiving help, but also about helping others, simply because we should. The meeting was relaxed, informative, and fun. I liked talking with other job seekers and learning about their situations. I felt supported and hopeful. I had never experienced such support in my life.

However, my life never seems easy and is always a series of "everything always happens at once" regarding bad news. A big, terrible, and frightening wrench was abruptly thrown my way when my dog got sick. If anyone knows me, they know that I absolutely love animals and that animals have always been a very important part of my life. Animals are pure, supportive, loyal, and love unconditionally. I become exceptionally attached to animals and love them deeply.

My beloved rescue dog, Jesse, developed a persistent cough in November 2023. I took him to the vet and learned that his heart was so enlarged that it was pushing on his lungs and causing the cough. As I understand it, heart problems seem to be common in the Maltese breed, especially when they are older, and Jesse was sixteen. We rescued each other when he was four years old. He was such a good and loving boy. Jesse stayed by my side and supported me through some horrible times, and I loved him tremendously. I was very nervous and scared as I didn't know what was going to happen. The vet put him on medication, and in a week or two, he seemed to feel better, so we just went about our lives.

Soon afterward, Jesse became sick again. The vet told me that he had developed pneumonia! It was terrifying to have my baby so sick. I was extremely worried that I would lose him, and I couldn't bear the thought of it. Again, the vet put him on medication. The pneumonia got better, but Jesse did not. He started going downhill, but never seemed to be in pain, thank God! It was torturous to see his health decline and his light fading away. I was doing everything I could for him: carrying him so he wouldn't have to hobble around, putting him in diapers so he wouldn't have to go outside. In the back of my mind, I knew what was coming, but I wouldn't accept it. People always say that you will know when it's time to let them go. What? No! I wanted him to get better and be all right. I wanted him to live forever with me.

I thought that my deep and everlasting love for him would save him, but it didn't, it couldn't. He quickly became a shell of his former self. I believed he was just holding on for my benefit. I knew that I needed to let him go, but nooo! Then, one day, he sat down in front of me and stared at me for a bit with part of his lip turned downward, kind of like the emoji for sadness. It was "the look," the look I was dreading, the look I never wanted to see. However, I understood him. I knew it was time. I guess the old saying about knowing when it's time to let a loved one go is true. It was time for him to no longer suffer, to be happy, and to be in peace. I just wished he didn't have to go, to never leave me, and to be healthy again.

I had to put Jesse to sleep in January 2024. My baby, my friend, my boo was gone! I slid quickly and deeply into a dark and scary place.

I couldn't think clearly or really function. Several people from JSGC called to check on me and offered their help, support, and understanding. My friends and daughters were terrified that I might join Jesse. I was inconsolable, depressed, and absolutely devastated. All I wanted was to go with Jesse so we could be together forever. It took baby steps, quite some time, a lot of tears, and hard work, but eventually, and with the help of many people, including several JSGC board members, I started to feel ok. All these caring people prayed for me, and they gave me something incredible. They gave me hope when I didn't have any. I finally realized that Jesse would want me to be happy, not so depressed and, above all, to be here! It was a very long and scary process, but I survived, and I am here to succeed!

Ultimately, I came back to the realization that I seriously needed a job. I was broke, stressed out, and tired. I had climbed my way out of that deep, dark place, but not out of the bills that had piled up. I checked out the upcoming JSGC events and started attending them again.

A couple of JSGC members suggested that I apply for the JSGC scholarship worth $100-$300. That money sure would have helped me, but I was too darn proud and stubborn. Later, another member suggested that I apply, and I finally did. I was awarded a scholarship, which I am still so thankful for. It was a relief and another example of how the JSGC board and members are supportive. Sometimes I still can't believe the generosity and kindness of the board.

I was anxious, wondering how I was going to get a job, what skills I had, what websites had strong job posts, how soon I could get a job, and if anyone could help me. I thought about the people who had helped me when I was at my lowest point in life. I turned to the JSGC calendar of events and committed to attend at least two events a month. And I did. I felt good, being surrounded by helpful, caring, supportive, and well-connected members. I felt included, comfortable, and supported.

Several board members continued to support me and emphatically encouraged me to increase the number of events I attended. I participated in Zoom meetings and went to morning coffee meetings, happy hours, and events. Every time I went to the functions, I learned something new and began to feel more confident. The lectures about the importance of networking and making connections, how and where to search for a job, what job sites to use and avoid, and helping other job seekers were very beneficial. It was helpful to learn about current resume writing skills and formats, words to include and avoid, and using AI in the 21st century.

Apparently, my resume was quite outdated, maybe because I am "older" and hadn't needed to look for a job in a long time. The age of job seekers varies greatly from recent college graduates to well-experienced, mature candidates. I unexpectedly found that there is a lot of ageism in today's market, and it was a hard reality pill to swallow! I had never experienced ageism before, and it was very frustrating. Ageism is not only disturbing; it was making me lose some of the confidence that I was working to rebuild. I would show up for a scheduled interview and wait my turn to talk with the interviewer. As I was waiting, I would see a "young" candidate leave the interviewer's office, and another "young" candidate sitting next to me waiting for their turn to interview. It was surprising, and made me think, "Am I too old to apply to this job?" I began questioning my skills, worthiness, and usefulness.

Ageism is real and happens more often than we know. Recently, a pharmaceutical giant was involved in a class action lawsuit for only hiring "young" candidates. I was contacted by the lawyer who was handling the case and became involved in the lawsuit because I was one of the "older" applicants; well qualified and experienced, but never contacted. That giant was defeated in court and was required to pay a large settlement to the people affected by their discrimination. I hope the company learned that "older" candidates are experienced, knowledgeable, and, most importantly, **valuable**!

With a lot of help, hope, and support from JSGC, I got my job-seeking groove back! I decided to take a step away from my outside sales career and explore other professions. As I still didn't know what I wanted to be when I grew up, I considered this a great opportunity. This experience taught me not to limit my job search in a shortsighted manner. I needed to be open to different opportunities and to consider them before automatically dismissing them.

Along the way, I learned that my purpose is not only to be a good mom and friend, but to continue helping others as I always have, beginning with my mother and three sisters. People gave me hope when I didn't have it. Most importantly, my purpose is *TO BE HERE!*

Julia is a mother to beautiful identical twin girls whom she loves deeply. She has a cat named Piccola and a standard poodle puppy named Clementine, who is very cuddly, sweet, comforting, smart, and funny. Clementine was a surprise birthday gift from her twins and is everything she needed after Jesse went to Heaven.

Julia grew up as a dancer. One of her dancing career highlights was performing at Wayne Newton's ranch and seeing his Arabian horses! She has continued to dance throughout her life and still enjoys doing so.

Julia loves the arts, is very creative, and has a keen eye for beauty. She is experienced in dancing, painting with oils and acrylics, creating ceramics, and loves to cook. She currently teaches cooking classes part-time at St. Charles Community College.

She graduated from Lindenwood University, with a Bachelor of Arts in French, Summa Cum Laude. She loves to travel and wants to become fluent in Italian for her dream trip to Italy.

Please scan the QR code to connect with this author.

Cindy Mosher

Embracing Change

Why is change so often difficult for us? Would we lean into it more if we trusted the way change shapes our lives through discomfort? When nothing changes, nothing changes. If life teaches us anything, it is that you have to adapt to change or risk being left behind. Change hit hard in mid-March 2020—a time when everyday life came to a screeching halt, changing everything that we did and everything we thought we knew about ourselves and the world.

The pandemic was full of many changes and challenges, with so many hard and impossible moments: flattening the curve, cleaning groceries, social distancing, furloughs, quarantines, shutdowns, cancelations. But it was also filled with growth and adaptation that came from those impossible changes. We all slowed down, found more meaning in our lives, discovered new ways to do things, connected in creative ways with family and friends, improved our hygiene, and prioritized family time.

The pandemic impacted more than our health and everyday life. It affected how we worked, where we worked, and in some cases, if we were able to work at all. Without our regular routines, without the day-to-day structure of meetings, "water cooler" chats, lunches, and commutes—many of us were thrown off course. Many retreated to the safety of their couches for movies, indulged in endless bottles of wine, and took up online shopping as a new hobby. Once the reality sunk in that the work world wasn't going to be "normal" anytime soon, the world began to move forward into the new normal.

Significant changes were occurring in my industry before the pandemic hit. I had worked remotely as an editorial freelancer in academic print publishing since 2009, helping college professors bring their educational passion to life on the pages of a book. The job combined my love of reading with childhood dreams of being a teacher. The publishing industry was evolving with the onset of artificial intelligence (AI) and an emphasis on the bottom line. AI platforms emerged with the ability to edit an entire manuscript in minutes. This shift, along with the move towards digital books and cheaper editorial costs overseas, diminished the need for traditional editors.

With the onset of the pandemic, the focus quickly changed from print books to digital platforms for remote learning. This transition demanded more from schools and technology, with learning management systems and interactive programs to keep students engaged. During this time, I had been leading a publishing team on a print revision of a veterinary book. With so much change already affecting the industry, we questioned if our revision would remain relevant—and if the necessary resources would be available to continue. Once I received word that we could move forward, the book became a lifeline to keep us afloat. It gave us routine, purpose, and a reason to get out of bed when the rest of the world seemed to be falling apart. We were no longer just coworkers; we became a team. The uncertainties of the pandemic helped us to become closer and to extend each other grace and compassion as we grappled with the unknowns while trying to do our jobs. We focused less on tasks and deadlines and started getting to know the person behind the task. Day by day, chapter by chapter, we leaned on each other, supported each other, and finished building our book. A book that kept us from falling apart and brought us together, giving us the confidence and strength to handle the other unknowns in our lives.

Once the world began opening up again after the shutdown, some pandemic-related changes remained. Online ordering became a staple, with everything from toiletries to food picked up from the comfort of our cars. We adapted to working remotely, with many employees finding themselves more productive in the comfort of their own homes. Technology improved, connecting us with family, friends, and coworkers faster than ever and more reliably. But as with most advances in technology, the old world inevitably becomes less relevant. Horse-drawn carriages made way for the automobile, handmade products made way for assembly lines, and the telegraph made way for the telephone. In more current times, we saw traditional travel agents replaced with online travel websites, cashiers replaced by self-checkout stations, and for my industry, online editorial platforms encroaching on traditional editorial jobs. Was my industry the next to go? Was the technology that was so critical to connections during the pandemic now causing my job to be irrelevant?

As the shifts in my industry continued, I started questioning if my path was heading for a detour or if my path had suddenly come to an end. It's easy to be on board with the technological advancements of society until it hits a little closer to home. Suddenly, AI was everywhere, helping authors write books from only their notes, drawing illustrations, editing content—all within minutes. Traditional editors couldn't compete with work that could be done so quickly, and the shift towards digital versus print publishing became more prominent. I found myself losing projects and started to wonder if I was now the modern-day telegraph. Was there a need for editors and publishers with the new advances? My projects were few and far between, with only task-oriented ones remaining. While I was grateful for the work, I wasn't fulfilled; I wasn't making a difference. The reduced workload wasn't producing enough income, nor was it sustainable. I began the journey of looking for a job in a market still reeling from the effects of the pandemic. Very few companies were hiring, but those that were offered only in-office, low-paying positions with long commutes. After so many years working from home with flexibility, I was holding on tight to that benefit, which further limited my options. After countless job applications, rejections, and very few interviews, I was discouraged and hopeless, unsure of my purpose, uncertain of my next move.

I found myself thinking back to the heart of the pandemic and how life turned upside down. Instead of focusing on all the restrictions at that time, I had chosen to focus on doing things differently, finding the good, and looking at life from a new perspective. I created a senior car parade in 2020 when graduation was canceled, Zoom happy hours, drive-by car parades in place of birthday parties, outdoor family holidays, morning outdoor coffees with neighbors, and daily exercise for my mental and physical health. I pivoted during the pandemic, finding new ways to connect, new ways to survive the changes, new ways to embrace the changes. The one thing that stood out during that time was how the grocery stores adapted. They didn't close their doors; they didn't stop selling food and other necessities because of the unknown, the virus, or fear. They found a way to work *with* the change rather than giving up or fighting it. A pivot. They adapted and found a way to open their doors safely—masks, social distancing decals, directional arrows in every aisle, plexiglass at registers, and early shopping times devoted to more susceptible populations. I could give up and close my "editorial door," or I could shift gears and stop fighting the change, find a new perspective, look for a new way through.

I started focusing on myself physically, mentally, and socially. Instead of pouring all of my efforts into a job search that felt like looking for a needle in a haystack, I started pouring energy into myself. I learned new skills, started networking, focused on personal growth, and engaged in more self-care and self-love. And over time, things began to shift. A pivot began when I stopped focusing on what wasn't working and started opening myself up to what filled me, what I wanted, what was possible. Opportunities started to arise, interviews were offered, and solid connections were made. Hope began to resurface. New projects and assignments outside the academic editing world started popping up, and through connections and referrals, I landed a new contract to help an author develop and edit his book. These were different opportunities than I was used to, but it was pushing me outside my comfort zone. And it proved that while AI is a helpful tool, there is still the need for human connection, collaboration, creativity, and growth.

During the early months of the pandemic, I focused on my job and colleagues, adjusting to a changing world. My job helped to give me purpose and kept me centered and grounded in a time when life was so different and scary. Yet during that time, I also realized that my job wasn't the only thing to give me purpose; it wasn't the only thing to lean into when life became disrupted. Our jobs, our careers, often become our identity—how we function in the world, how we introduce ourselves to others. And if that job comes to an end or gets disrupted, our identity can also get disrupted, and we can feel lost and defeated. The pandemic showed me that my job can give me purpose, can inspire me, and give me a sense of contributing to something bigger than myself. However, I also learned that I have value and purpose *beyond* my job, and when my job becomes disrupted, I can still succeed in other areas of my life. I can find a new path even when everything appears to be falling apart. When both my personal and work purposes can come together, it's wonderful. But it's not crippling when one or both of those get disrupted. I just have to embrace the change, and pivot.

My pandemic experience was a time of change, discomfort, fear, illness, deaths of family members, and the deaths of two beloved pets. But those challenges and disruptions were also a time of growth that shaped my life to this day. Despite the discomfort, despite the fear. Most of us wouldn't voluntarily sign up for such an experience, but it's where we learn how to pivot and discover what we're really made of. For most of my career, I focused on developing authors' stories, supporting their journeys, and bringing their passions to life. The pandemic helped me realize that I need to give that same focus, that same dedication and passion, to my own life. Pivot and adapt or risk not only being left behind but also missing out on that great and amazing adventure that life is meant to be.

Cindy Mosher's passion for reading began in kindergarten, sparking dreams of becoming a teacher. Although life led her down a different path, her love of learning and working with children remained. Years later, she became a stay-at-home mom to three children, volunteering for school activities and events, as well as becoming a Girl Scout Leader and troop cookie manager for her daughters.

In 2009, her husband's layoff shifted her family's needs. An unexpected opportunity in academic publishing allowed Cindy to combine her love of reading with her passion for helping students engage more actively in their studies.

Cindy has built a fulfilling career as a freelance developmental editor, collaborating with talented authors to bring their content to life. The challenges of the pandemic inspired her to reflect on her priorities, seeking greater purpose in both her work and personal life through growth, balance, and making a positive impact.

Please scan the QR code to connect with this author.

Katie Gearin

Finding Clarity Amidst Complete Chaos

On a frigid evening in January, all peer tutors gathered at Maryville University to mark the beginning of the spring 2020 semester. While slightly cold pizza and paper-thin napkins were passed around and polite small-talk gradually diminished, the meeting began. During this time, I was a student at the college and had just become a writing tutor the previous semester. I'll admit that my mind was wandering during this meeting—as it usually does when my introverted mind deems a work meeting could have been an email—until I heard a strange word I had never heard before. Upon hearing the term, I distinctly remember snapping out of my reverie as the hair on the back of my head stood up. Slightly annoyed, I quickly turned and suspiciously squinted my eyes toward the speaker.

The speaker mentioned the possibility of expanding our in-person tutoring services to online synchronous options by using some strange and alien thing called…Zoom. *Zoom?* The first thing my mind recalled was the DC comic book Supervillain Hunter Zolomon, AKA Zoom. I quickly zeroed this reference out as helpful as a villainous metahuman speedster from another earth could sadly have no bearing on this meeting or, more importantly, our tutoring techniques. Completely puzzled and out of ideas, I turned to one of my co-workers and whispered a simple, innocent question that now strikes me as tragically prophetic: *What is Zoom?*

Little did I know then that my life would be dominated by this online platform just a little over one month later. It was probably a good thing that I didn't know. At the time, the idea of occasionally tutoring online terrified me. After all, I had just gotten over starting the position the previous semester and was still getting acclimated to tutoring in general.

Initially, entering the virtual world was daunting. Since most people were also newbies to Zoom, it was exhausting trying to decipher the enigma of sharing screens, editing online documents, and snagging a good Wi-Fi connection. However, after a few weeks of using the online platform, I discovered I was thriving. To my great astonishment, remote tutoring and inhabiting the chaotic world we call "virtual" assisted me in my journey to becoming confident and finding my purpose rather than inhibiting it. Before the global pandemic, I was a newly declared English major with a hazy sense of where I would—or could—go with my degree. After the pandemic, I found myself a wiser and more self-assured young woman equipped with new leadership skills, allowing me to decisively set my course toward a firm direction in the fields of teaching and editing.

Before I started my position as a writing tutor in 2019, I had recently become more confident in myself as a writer. When my professor called me into his office one day to say that he wanted to recommend me for a writing tutor position at the university, my emotions were mixed. I was excited by the opportunity but also terrified. Gaining confidence in one's written skills is one thing, but feeling wise enough to advise others is a whole other situation. Suffice it to say, I remained uneasy with the prospect of helping other writers. I was uncertain about my qualifications, but my professor's kind encouragement influenced me to accept the position and rise to the challenge.

Transitioning into tutoring went much smoother than I anticipated. I still felt a little awkward due to my complete newness to the role, but overall, it proved to be a pivotal experience. Helping students made me feel useful and gave me a sense of direction. Hearing back from grateful students also provided me with the validation I desperately craved. By the end of the semester, I felt empowered and ready to continue to make strides in this career.

For the first half of the spring semester, everything was going well. During the first month, news reports came rolling in about a mysterious illness that would eventually evolve into the global pandemic, but at the time, no one around me was overly concerned, so I paid it little heed. Instead, I remained focused on succeeding in my classes and my job. Little did I know that my last shift before spring break started would be my final in-person shift at the university. As I was walking through the parking lot listening to the birds singing, feeling the cool spring breeze on my skin, and observing the afternoon sunlight peeking through the trees, I could have never envisioned that in the short span of two weeks, my life would change forever.

Two days before spring break ended and classes reconvened, I received the email. Classes were to be held remotely over Zoom for the next two weeks to protect everyone from the virus. *Zoom?* Oh God, there was that word that I had just learned about in January! My work quickly emailed after and stated that, like classes, tutoring sessions would also be held on the virtual platform. I remember my heart beating rapidly as I read the emails and frantically tried to absorb the news. Having zero experience with synchronous virtual learning, I was, to put it frankly, terrified.

The next few days were a blur as I furiously watched Zoom tutorials and tried to get a sense of what on earth I would do for my first session. Not surprisingly, the first few sessions were brutal. There were so many technical blips to sort through, and students were just as unprepared and scared as I was. Not only was I stressed about learning all the features of the platform, but I was also trying to tutor successfully online when I had only been trained for in-person.

With all these virtual hiccups in place, I can easily see how the pandemic could represent an extremely bleak period in my life. I could have used all these obstacles as an excuse to halt my journey of self-discovery and sink back further into my insecurities. However, I took another path. After the first few weeks of the pandemic, when it was revealed that we would remain virtual indefinitely, I decided to take hold of the obstacles in my life and work through them. While I had strong feelings of self-doubt and anxiety, my determination to succeed overrode them.

Part of the way I turned the negative experience around was by looking at the positives of the situation. For one thing, I needed to be grateful that my job gave me the option of working from home. I reminded myself of how much worse it would be if I had a job that caused me to be in the direct line of fire with the virus daily. Secondly, I could use my workspace to my advantage. Working in my bedroom, surrounded by all my books, keepsakes that make me smile, and my loving dog by my side, could help me to relax and feel more at ease. It would certainly be more comfortable than the noisy, cramped, and hectic tutoring space at the university. Lastly, this was an opportunity—albeit an unrequested one—to learn new digital skills. At this point, I still did not know what I wanted to do in my career, but from the job searching I had conducted, I noticed all the remote possibilities. Learning virtual skills now could help me secure a job in the long run.

With this new mindset, I quickly began to succeed. Within a few weeks, I started getting more appointments than I did when I was working in-person. Likewise, several students I had helped became weekly, repeat appointments. I attribute this change to my more relaxed and confident attitude. While tutoring in person, I gave good advice, but my attitude was rather rigid and anxious. Working at home helped me relax, and I found it easier to make small talk with students. Most of the time, I took around five minutes of the session just to see how the students were holding up during the pandemic and commenting about their room or furry pet who accompanied them on the screen. In other words, I was sharpening my social skills.

I soon discovered that I had a knack for talking to students and making the writing process seem less intimidating. These chats helped the students feel more at ease with me and more willing to keep booking sessions. One student, who I worked with for an entire semester, inquired if I planned to be a teacher when I graduated because she said that I was inspirational and made writing not only easier, but fun. By the time I graduated from the university, I had earned the Tutor of the Year award for my accomplishments in working with students.

Up until becoming a tutor, I had never thought of teaching or becoming an editor since I am more introverted by nature and did not want to pursue careers that involved developing people skills. These paths demanded authority and leadership, skills I never dreamed I could learn. Tutoring, or more importantly, virtual tutoring, offered a safe place for me to start chipping away at these insecurities and form new professional goals. Instead of just settling for a career in which I could quietly remain in the background, I realized I could aim for something that truly captured my interests. I discovered that I wanted to continue to work with and help writers, both in the classroom and behind the scenes of textual production.

Today, I am in both of those fields, teaching and helping aspiring writers, and I'm further venturing into publishing my own writing. Funny enough, I'm now very comfortable with helping writers, but I'm less comfortable seeing my own words in print. I loved writing in college, where there was only one person reading my work and providing constructive feedback.. But the thought of people like family, friends, and strangers looking at, and dare I say, *judging* my words? It still occasionally feels like a violation, as though someone peeked at my diary or caught a glimpse of me undressing. Writing is one of the most beautiful ways a person can express themselves, but alas, it's also one of the most vulnerable. Nevertheless, one of the things I learned during the pandemic is to forgo letting my insecurities hold me back. Day after day of hearing stories of people losing their lives to the virus proved to me that life really is too short to not live it to the fullest. Trying and occasionally getting those rejection slips is better than never trying and remaining stagnant in life.

While the pandemic certainly will go down as a historical tragedy, I cannot help but wonder what my life would have been like without it. What would any life be like without adversity that forces you to step up and fight for your future? As Dr. Martin Luther King Jr. once said, and Kamala Harris recently reminded America, "*Only when it is dark enough can you see the stars.*" To truly experience beauty and clarity in life, we must, unfortunately, also encounter sorrow and setbacks. There are few absolute certainties in life, and adversity is one of them.

My story of finding my purpose during one of the darkest times in history is not rare. Most people gain wisdom and self-awareness only after experiencing life obstacles. The question is not whether you will encounter roadblocks on your way to discovering your purpose in life. You will. Plan on it. The question is: When you encounter those barriers, will you give up, put your head down, and turn back, or will you stand up straighter and brave the way forward, eagerly seeking the treasures of life that await you?

Katie Gearin is an Adjunct English Professor at St. Charles Community College, as well as a freelance editor, proofreader, writer, and writing coach. She frequently collaborates with Davis Creative Publishing and contributed to the anthology *Still Perfectly Imperfect*: *More Remarkable Stories of Ordinary Women Overcoming Extraordinary Circumstances* in 2024. A native of St. Charles, Missouri, she holds an associate's degree in arts and sciences from St. Charles Community College, a bachelor's in English from Maryville University, and a master's in English from St. Louis University. In her free time, Katie likes to spend time with her two dogs, Daisy and Belle, read (particularly nineteenth-century literature), watch British detective dramas, and talk to anyone who will listen about anything related to Broadway.

Please scan the QR code to connect with this author.

About Bob Kolf and Lexie Dendrinelis

In March of 2020, Bob Kolf recognized the need to connect individuals experiencing job loss to recruiters in the Greater St. Louis, Missouri Metropolitan Region. As a retired structural engineer, living in the area for thirty-five years, he had many contacts and connections. As the global pandemic continued throughout the year, so did Bob and his mission. He had the vision for something bigger, and filed for the nonprofit status of the group, recruited a board of directors, and networked all over the city and county.

It was at one of the networking meetings that he met Lexie Dendrinelis. A corporate wellness and leadership development professional, she had recently opened her own business and was networking locally often. At this meeting, Bob asked her to be a speaker at an upcoming Job Seekers' Garden Club event. She agreed, and shortly afterward, it led to her serving as the keynote speaker at the upcoming Career Conference and joining the board of directors as vice president.

Now to 2025—with Bob serving as founder and executive director and Lexie as board president—a book to celebrate the stories of hope, perseverance, career struggles, and success seemed a natural way to acknowledge the organization's five-year anniversary. With genuine excitement, both embarked on finding authors, writing personal chapters, and learning the world of book publishing. It is their honor to create a publication that hopefully will inspire you, the reader, and give you renewed hope in discovering your new purpose.

RESOURCE LISTINGS

jsgcstl.org

We foster a warm and caring community in which job seekers, recruiters, and connectors come together to nurture and support one another, and to find both career and growth opportunities through networking in order to make St. Louis a stronger and more vibrant community.

JOB SEEKERS' Garden Club™

We Do for Job Seekers What Gardeners Do for Plants—Nurture and Grow

---

DavisCreativePublishing.com

We empower aspiring non-fiction authors to publish books that engage their audience, enhance their credibility, and inspire positive change.

davis ⏀ creative PUBLISHING

GHOST PUBLISHERS OF SOLO BOOKS & ANTHOLOGIES

Georgia Ferretti – Coldwell Banker

"I am a 23-year Five Star Best in Client Satisfaction recipient who believes in serving the customer the same way I want to be served."

youtu.be/5K6H7GrH9o0

FERRETTI
- REAL ESTATE -

RESOURCE LISTINGS

enterprisebank.com

We empower privately held businesses to succeed, helping families to secure their financial futures, and invest to advance the quality of life in the communities we serve. We know that every business—and every person—is unique.

ENTERPRISE BANK & TRUST

Guiding people to a lifetime of financial success

---

alliancetech.com

Alliance Tech delivers secure, reliable IT and cybersecurity services for small businesses—keeping your data protected, systems running, and team productive.

ALLIANCE TECH

Securing Your Data. Empowering Your Team.

---

markhinson.kw.com

Helping you buy or sell with confidence through local expertise, personalized service, and results you can trust. Let's make your next move the right move!

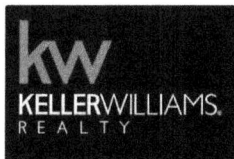

KELLER WILLIAMS REALTY

Your Home. Your Future. My Commitment.

RESOURCE LISTINGS

shelterinsurance.com/CA/agent/NGRAHAM

As your Shelter agent, I can help you make sure you get the right coverage at the right price, while providing the quality service you expect. Feel free to give me a call to discuss your insurance options today! I'm licensed in all 14 states that Shelter protects.

SHELTER INSURANCE

We're your shield, we're your shelter

---

marvinfcockrell.com

Smooth jazz pianist offering private performances, a signature annual concert, and music lessons designed to inspire creativity, confidence, and lifelong musical growth.

M.F. Cockrell
Music Focus

Marvin F. Cockrell - Master of Keys. Maker of Melodies.

---

acanetwork.org

ACA Business Club is a private network dedicated to empowering business owners and entrepreneurs with strong relationships, practical business development resources, and effective marketing strategies.

ACA
BUSINESS CLUB

Our Vision is to Help You Accomplish Your Vision.

RESOURCE LISTINGS

rockitcareers.com

RockIt Careers delivers expert career consultation to empower job seekers, strategic recruiting to connect businesses with top talent, and compassionate outplacement services to support career transitions.

ROCK T
C REERS
ROCKITCAREERS.COM

Let's Launch Your Career!

---

digitalgrowthus.com

DigitalGrowthUS delivers innovative IT software solutions, mobile apps, and digital marketing strategies to drive business growth, boost efficiency, and connect brands with their target audience.

igitalGrowthUS

You Grow, We Grow

---

seraphimconsulting.org

Experience risk-free growth: We'll run your ads for 30 days at no cost—just cover the ad spend. No fees, no risk, just results.

SERAPHIM
CONSULTING

The Answer to Your Prayers

www.ingramcontent.com/pod-product-compliance
Lightning Source LLC
Chambersburg PA
CBHW071329210326
41597CB00015B/1385